MOTHERS' IMAGES OF MOTHERHOOD

The feminist movement and the need for women in the workforce have made huge changes in women's lives, and traditional views of the ever-present, self-sacrificing mother are being widely questioned. *Mothers' images of motherhood* highlights the importance of the modern mother's need to make meaning of motherhood.

Based on qualitative, interview-based research with upper middle-class American mothers of toddlers, *Mothers' images of motherhood* explores how mothers make meaning of motherhood. Focusing on these women's images of motherhood, their desires and experiences, Meryle Mahrer Kaplan's rigorous analysis shows – in contrast with current theory – that these women want to resist reproducing the mothering they themselves received. Also, although they present an image of motherhood that is at odds with the traditional view of maternal self-sacrifice, their vision of the 'new' mother is of one who has needs but must now take care of herself as well as her child. Unfortunately, the 'new' mother continues to be located in the isolated nuclear family. These women see themselves as close to their husbands but without social supports, and lacking in the kind of close female relationships described in the feminist literature.

The book is both an exciting and a thought-provoking analysis of women as mothers today, and a test of feminist and object-relations theories. It will be of special value to feminist scholars, psychologists and other social scientists and practitioners working with women and families.

A developmental psychologist by training, **Meryle Mahrer Kaplan** is Director of Corporate Consultations at Resources for Child Care Management in New Jersey, where she studies the work and family needs of men and women at major workplaces throughout the USA.

MOTHERS' IMAGES OF MOTHERHOOD

Case studies of twelve mothers

Meryle Mahrer Kaplan

London and New York

First published 1992
by Routledge
11 New Fetter Lane, London EC4P 4EE

Simultaneously published in the USA and Canada
by Routledge
a division of Routledge, Chapman and Hall, Inc.
29 West 35th Street, New York, NY 10001

© 1992 Meryle Mahrer Kaplan

Typeset in Garamond by Michael Mepham, Frome, Somerset
Printed and bound in Great Britain by
Mackays of Chatham PLC, Chatham, Kent

British Library Cataloguing in Publication Data
A catalogue record for this book is available
from the British Library.

Library of Congress Cataloging in Publication Data
Kaplan, Meryle Mahrer, 1947–
Mothers' images of motherhood: case studies of twelve
mothers / Meryle Mahrer Kaplan.
p. cm.
Includes bibliographical references and index.
1. Motherhood—United States—Case studies.
2. Mothers—United States—Psychology—Case studies.
I. Title.
HQ759.K33 1992
306.874'3—dc20   91–42647
                                                          CIP
ISBN 0–415–06756–1
0–415–06757–X (pbk)

To Lenny and Ian

CONTENTS

TABLES

ACKNOWLEDGEMENTS

Books are fueled in many different ways. My interest in motherhood and belief in the importance of listening to mothers is rooted in my own experience as a parent, in the interesting combination of making meaning of motherhood with my husband and child, feeling that I was treated differently at work from pregnancy on, and studying developmental psychology and reading feminist and social theory during the process. I would not have turned this confluence of experiences and emotions into research and this book without a great deal of encouragement and support.

I am very grateful to those mothers willing to share their experiences with me, to those who have been my friends and family, and especially to those twelve women who agreed to participate in this study, to engage with me and my questions and to add their own questions and perspectives. This kind of exploratory qualitative research involves an intimate relationship with subjects. I have tried to tell the stories of these twelve women systematically but without losing each woman's personal concerns.

I have been fortunate to share this work with many people. John Broughton has been a wonderful mentor, friend and editor for the last twelve years and brought this work to Routledge's attention. Larry Aber invited me to participate in the design of the Parent Development Interview. Barry Farber has provided ongoing wisdom and encouragement.

Carol Gilligan's work has provided one starting point for my own. I want to thank her for her interest and enthusiasm, for the opportunity to participate in her seminar for educators at the Rutgers University Institute for Research on Women, for pushing me to make further connections, and for recommending that I use Jane Attannucci's coding scheme. Ferris Olin of the Institute has been a delightful colleague. Edie Cooper, Elon Gratch, and Bonnie Leadbeater coded data with me – with insight, dedication and good humor.

Involvement with a feminist psychology study group beginning in 1979 – especially with John Broughton, Ken Corbett, Margaret Honey, Janie Kritzman, and Bonnie Leadbeater – has made the process of thinking about and developing a research project pleasurable and has added immeasurably to my thinking. I have had the good fortune, since 1985 when I conducted these interviews, to co-teach numerous graduate courses in the Psychology of Women with Margaret Honey and, in the last few years, to be working with Margaret and Donna Bassin on an interdisciplinary anthology focusing on the topic of mother as subject. The pleasure, support, and intellectual stimulation of these endeavors have encouraged me to continue to think about mothers' images of motherhood. In addition, I have learned much from other participants in the New York Institute for Humanities' Seminar on Psychoanalysis and Sexual Difference and appreciate the opportunity the seminar coordinators – Jessica Benjamin, Murial Dimen, Ginger Gould-ner, and Adrienne Harris – provided in inviting me to present my research. Two members of the Seminar, Adria Schwartz, a long-time friend and colleague, and Ann Kaplan have been especially helpful in the book writing stage.

The people at Routledge – especially David Stonestreet and Anne Neville – have been my friends by fax across the Atlantic and a wonderful source of interest, encouragement, and much needed attention to detail.

Carolyn Heilbrun and Robert Murphy read earlier versions of the manuscript. Their own writing and their response to my efforts have been extremely helpful.

The data analysis phase of this research was partially funded by a Woodrow Wilson Research Grant in Women's Studies and by one of the first Dean's Grants awarded at Teachers College, Columbia University. I am grateful for their support and acknowledgement and for the ongoing interest of Dean Judith Brandenburg.

The later stages of this work have been made possible by a family/research-sensitive workplace. Many thanks, especially to Bob Lurie, Marlene Weinstein, Susan Brenner, and Jim Greenman, and to the rest of the crew at Resources for Child Care Management, for understanding that feminist theorizing has a place in child-care consulting and for sharing with me in the study of work/family issues. The opportunity I have had at RCCM to assess the needs of men and women at workplaces around the country has helped me put this small-scale research in larger perspective.

I would also like to thank my family. This research has made me appreciate all the more my parents' ongoing presence in my life and the value of growing up with grandparents, aunts, uncles, and cousins. Through them, I have learned the meaning of family and collective life. Thanks to my in-laws who have joined this family and to those friends with whom I have grown up and who have been so much a part of my life. To those child care people who have made this all possible, especially Edith. Most of all, to the people I live with. To Lenny, for his ongoing support and love, for making my research such a priority in his own life, and for reminding me – at crucial moments – that I was doing this because I enjoyed it. To Ian who made this work possible and impossible, who reminded me of the necessity of speaking about motherhood, and who made these years full of play and laughter as well as work.

1

THE CONCEPTUAL
FRAMEWORK

I was haunted by the stereotype of the mother whose love is 'unconditional'; and by the visual and literary images of motherhood as a single minded identity. If I knew parts of myself existed that would never cohere to those images, weren't those parts then abnormal, monstrous?

(Adrienne Rich, *Of woman born*, 1986/1976, p.23)

In the late 1980s American movie, *Baby Boom*, and the derivative television series of the same name, J. C. Wyatt, the stereotypic 1980s high-powered 'dragon lady' of management consulting deals with the problem of how to mother the infant cousin who was orphaned and delivered to her without warning. Interestingly, J. C. is haunted by the *same* image of the ever-present Mother as Rich, the feminist poet, had been over a decade before. In a fascinating episode of the short-lived TV series, two of the 'super mothers' of American cultural history, the mothers from 'Leave it to Beaver' and 'Father Knows Best' television shows, come to visit wearing aprons and carrying cookies and cleaning paraphernalia. While they look like the 'real' Mother, they tell J. C. that it was all a lie – they were *acting* as ever-present, available mothers. Really they were working mothers playing a part. They tell J. C. not to worry or be plagued by this image; it is *her* daughter that will benefit from having a 'real' role model.

In *Of woman born*, Rich also emphasizes the difference between the image, what she conceptualizes as an elaborated 'institution of motherhood,' and her 'real' experience. However, I think the image of the Mother 'haunted' Rich (to use her term) precisely because it was a vision that had come to figure both in terms of its social prominence and personal meaning. It is significant that, years later, J. C. is grappling with the same image – not one we expect to see in the 'dragon lady' career woman who has spent years 'married to her job.' Now, at the beginning of the '90s we continue to know this vision of the Mother – that selflessly giving, ever-patient, never angry, always available and loving figure. Certainly, we in the

1

United States have seen Her on mother's day cards and on television, or depicted as lovingly connected to Her child on the box of Ivory Snow soap or in advertisements for numerous products, precisely because of what seems to be Her enduring appeal.

Mothers' images of motherhood is based on a study of mothers conducted in the mid-'80s, ten years after *Of woman born* was first published, about twenty years after the publication of Betty Friedan's *The feminine mystique*. The feminist movement, affirmative action, the need for women in the workforce – to support their families and the economy – have contributed to a different landscape of privileged, white, middle- and upper middle-class women's lives. Views of women have changed. Being 'just a housewife' now provokes the question 'Is that all?' and an injunction to justify that existence. On some level, the housewife has been replaced – in the cultural imagination of the professional middle class and the media – by Superwoman, able to do and have it all.[1] The selflessly giving Mother seems outdated – or is She? This brief history seems to fall short when one considers the seemingly intransigent image of the Mother. Don't children need ever-present mothers? Can we give Her up? Isn't She what we've wished for? What could possibly replace Her?

The purpose of this book is to explore how mothers themselves make meaning of motherhood and to focus on their images of motherhood, their desires, and their experiences. Attention to the mother's experience is part of a larger feminist project. It is rooted in the idea that treating the mother as subject, as a person in her own right, is necessary to seeing all women as subjects (Bassin, Honey, and Kaplan, in press; Benjamin, 1980, 1988; Chodorow, 1979, 1989; Hirsch, 1986, 1989; Kaplan and Broughton, in press). In this exploratory study, my goal was to listen carefully to a small number of mothers. To intensify the value of this small sample research, I chose to study mothers from the same social location. There are many such groupings of mothers – of various races, classes, professions, sexual orientations, from varying locales, and so on. For this very preliminary exploration, I selected one such grouping: modern women having their first child in the mid-'80s.

The women I studied are white, older mothers (average age 36), most of whom are highly educated and had established careers before having children. While not all fit the image of 'yuppie' equally well, they are among the privileged group that Ehrenreich (1989) contends has been 'taken as a social norm' in the United States and has been the group 'against which all others are measured' (p.3).[2] The women in this study had been mothers for about two years; they were not brand new to motherhood but were dealing with children who were still dependent and, I would emphasize, not fully civilized beings. These women represent an interesting cohort. All were raised in the United States in the 1950s when visions of the ever-giving

Mother were prominent; most of their own mothers were 'full time' homemakers. These women have grown up amidst major changes in visions of femininity and women's liberation. As a population, they seem more related to those 'mothers with briefcases' (to use Rich's term from the 1986 foreword to her book) that now populate the cultural landscape than to the image of the ever-present Mother.

I wanted to explore how these women make meaning of motherhood and to examine their ideas in relation to both personal and social history. How would their images of motherhood relate to their own mothers and fathers?; to cultural notions of the Mother?; to the fact that most mothers work? How would these modern women – educated women with career aspirations and a belief in equal rights – depict a traditional woman? How would they see themselves in relation to her?; to men?; to their children?; to other mothers? To begin to explore these complex questions and the interrelationships between them, this research is based on the systematic study of twelve women and includes structured and semi-structured inter-views and some psychological tests. The research model, to be described in chapter 2, allows for the discovery and elaboration of a theory that is, as Glaser and Strauss (1967) suggest, 'grounded' in qualitative material and permits a play across 'data' and theory. The data are largely constituted by my interpretation of interview material. These interpretations are corrobor-ated, extended, and questioned by material analyzed by others: co-raters of three psychological measures and a clinician analyzing TAT material.

This book grows out of my own experience as a feminist and career woman. My life was changed and disrupted in wondrous and difficult ways by motherhood. In 1980, when my son was born, I had only one friend who was 'like me' and a mother. The notion of a lack of 'role models' fails to describe the experience. Certainly, I needed ideas of how to 'manage' each day: scheduling, child care, sharing some of the responsibility with a spouse who was (and still is) extremely supportive but not experiencing exactly the same feelings as me.

Along with these concerns were questions about how motherhood would figure in my life. What I found was that motherhood on any day was not simply a matter of a role and prescription – what should I be doing? – but of desire, a profound pull toward motherhood and toward my child that I had not fully anticipated.

In a sense, motherhood has become my occupation. I relish what I have come to call the 'otherness' of it; it is unlike any other experience. From my graduate studies, to developing parenting groups, to working as a child care consultant, I continue to face the issue of how to make meaning of motherhood. This is not just my issue. Even in corporate board rooms, where I now spend a considerable amount of time, in the midst of well researched discussions of the feasibility of child care centers and flextime,

3

Donna Reed rears her head. Working mothers speak of the image of the family portrayed by Donna Reed, star of the 1950s TV show: doctor's wife and key figure in the family. Working fathers speak of the pain of not being able to be the breadwinner and of having wives that have to work. As these fathers and mothers see it, men in positions of power still have wives at home. Child care by someone other than the mother is foreign to these decision makers' lives as well as to employees' visions of the family. In some sense, then, the Mother continues to be a more familiar and powerful figure than the real women – who are either sitting in the board room or working in other positions throughout the workplace.

WOMEN AND MOTHERHOOD AS DISTINCT

From the vantage point of the 1980s, there is a distinction between women as people and motherhood. Titling his 200-year history of women and the family in America 'At Odds,' Carl Degler (1980) comments on how, 'after two hundred years of development, both the future of the family and the fulfillment of women as persons are at odds as never before' (p.473). Stated in even more extreme form, Degler says, 'many women today find the realization of themselves as persons impossible to achieve within a family situation' (p.472). Degler is not speaking simply of the juggling of multiple roles but instead is posing a personal, political, and philosophical conflict between individualism and the concern for others.

This vision of self-actualization as necessary to being a fulfilled person is central to Friedan's (1963) argument in *The feminine mystique* and a theme in her more recent book, *The second stage* (1981). In her highly influential earlier work, Friedan named home a concentration camp and a source of severe deprivation for women. She argued against domestic responsibilities defining women's lives and set the stage for women's move into the workforce. Yet, even today, it is important to consider how dilemmas of personhood are expressed by women in relation to child rearing. In particular, do mothers' own images of motherhood revolve around the selflessly giving mother or do they include some sense of the mother's own needs and subjectivity? Do they present images of an isolated mother/child dyad or do fathers, child care people, and schools figure within this relationship?

Child rearing manuals provide one valuable indication of cultural responses to these issues.[3] In a very interesting analysis of the twentieth-century American government child rearing manual, *Infant care*, Nancy Pottishman Weiss (1978) documents the continued presence of 'the prevailing cultural ideal of the existence of an exclusive, dyadic relationship between mother and child, the two forming between themselves a homeostatic and self-sustaining unit' (p.29). Notably, Weiss finds that earlier in the century there was considerable attention to treating child rearing practices

4

in terms of their benefit to the mother who had a range of responsibilities. However, this 'sympathetic orchestration of rights and responsibilities' of both mother and child changed dramatically (p.39). The mother actually *lost* rights in the home just as she gained influence and responsibility for the child's emotional life and character.

> The dissonant note in the literature is a reinterpretation and expansion of maternal obligations and a *winnowing of the mutuality of interest* between mother and child. In the first edition of *Infant care*, what was good for the mother was good for the child. By World War II, what benefited the child was not necessarily in the mother's best interests.
>
> (Weiss, 1978; emphasis added)

The post World War II period is significant in this and other histories of motherhood. Mitchell (1974) and Riley (1983) argue that women's post war move back into the home and their immersion in child care were supported and encouraged by the highly influential psychological theories of Bowlby and Winnicott. These theories present an image of the mother who is properly submerged in the mother/child dyad and 'loves to let herself be the baby's whole world' (Winnicott, 1973, p.88). The notion of such a primary maternal preoccupation has prompted one psychoanalyst to suggest that,

> For Winnicott, the work demanded of women required then a veritable sickness; a forgetting of their personality, a total and exclusive abandonment to the child . . . the schema of the 'maternal' which Winnicott describes for us is a form of madness that only a woman can have, *the woman defining herself by her capacity for the abandonment of self*.
>
> (Plaza, 1982, p.83; emphasis added)

The call for an exclusive bond between mother and child that becomes the mother's primary occupation and source of satisfaction supports a society in which women (white middle and upper middle class women) are expected to be full time mothers. As Plaza defines her, 'The mama is a person who is defined by the services she gives to a child; her existence has no meaning except in relation to a child whom she must carry, bring up, attend to, serve, calm down' (*ibid.*, p.79). This is the image of the selfless, ever-giving Mother so prominent in American society in the 1950s, the time when my research subjects were growing up.

While in the '50s there was a prescription for motherhood and many women, on the surface, seemed to be living it, as Friedan argued (1963), this mothering was not easy or always beneficial to women or their children. Bader and Philipson (1980) consider the effects on the middle class of the post war move to the suburbs and the increasingly isolated mothering in which the 'child tended to replace the increasingly absent husband, mother, and friends in a woman's unconscious life' (p.321) and mothers had particular difficulties in accepting their children's separation from them. In her major sociological exploration, *The future of motherhood*, Jessie Bernard (1974) makes the cogent argument that full time mothering in the solitary nuclear family is the wrong way to organize the complex, demanding task of child rearing and socialization.

Mothers of six cultures (Minturn and Lambert, 1964) also documents the difficulty of mothering in the isolated nuclear family. This study is part of a larger project examining socialization practices in New England and in five other cultures (Whiting and Child, 1953; Whiting and Whiting, 1975). The anthropologists found that, because of overload, the pressure of American individualism to do it yourself, and the lack of respect for nurturant activity, the New England mothers were inconsistent in the expression of warmth and not always psychologically available to their children. In the light of this cross-cultural study, the image of the ever-patient, tirelessly available American mother begins to sound like a wished for rather than 'real' mother, with it's insistence on care and connection being virtually impossible for isolated, devalued mothers, lacking social supports to fulfil. This relationship between image and wish is central to the present study.

THE INSTITUTION OF MOTHERHOOD

Bernard (1974) also explores in detail the tensions between the image of the giving mother and the lives of women. She defines this still familiar image as a Victorian invention in which the mother maintained the home as a sanctuary against the demands of industrialization and urbanization. The Mother's position was 'increasingly idealized – by definition loving, gentle, tender, self-sacrificing, devoted, limited in interests to creating a haven for her family' (p.12). For Bernard, this Victorian notion has never represented the experience of mothers and has been a 'parody' deemed unsuitable by women for decades.

By the turn of the century, it was already becoming apparent that there was something wrong about the 19th century model for the role of the mother. Women were finding it increasingly difficult to perform it. Invoking the idealized model did no good. 'Putting on a Madonna-like pedestal the often impatient, irritable mother who feels chained to her duties may suffice for the aims of idealism and wishful thinking, but makes life easier neither for mothers nor for children. True, it saved society the feeling that it should change itself.' But aggrieved women were not to let 'society' spare itself the comfort of standing pat. If they were poor, they were protesting against having too many children; if they were affluent, they were protesting against the confinement of the doll's house. They wanted out.

> (Bernard, 1974, p.14; the quotation
> is from Mitscherlich, 1963, p.57)

According to Bernard, this rebellion has increased as women speak out, 'daring to say that although they love children, they hate motherhood' (*ibid.*).

The idea of a socially supported and defined 'myth' or 'institution' of motherhood is shared by many feminist writers (Comer, 1974; Gordon, 1977; Heilbrun, 1979; Kaplan, 1983; Kristeva, 1981a, 1981b; Rich, 1986/1976; Ruddick, 1980, 1989). These writers agree on the importance of dismantling the myth but have differed in the extent to which they treat these 'social' notions as deeply rooted within women or see the ordinary mother, singly or joined with other mothers, as capable of experiencing a disjunction between her own experience and the social institution. Bernard, like many other authors in the 1970s, seemed to discount the tenacity of the image and the means of socialization and control used to enforce it. She also did not consider the extent to which what she sees as a social myth relates to early experience and deep psychological wishes. Other, more psychologically oriented writers have focused on the relationship between these social myths and early experience and consider a more deeply held maternal imago.

CULTURAL AND PERSONAL CONSTRUCTIONS OF MOTHERHOOD

The relation between cultural and personal representations is worthy of further exploration. In 'The fantasy of the perfect mother,' Chodorow and Contratto (1982) focus directly on representations of motherhood. They argue that the individual's visions of the mother have infantile roots that actually merge with culture. Because of their primitive origins, such images have an 'unprocessed quality;' they have not benefited from reflection or a more mature vantage point. The Mother in this image is less a person than an all-powerful figure who, in isolation with her child, can make or break that child.

> For the infant, the mother is not someone with her own life, wants, needs, history, other social relationships, work. She is known only in her capacity as mother. Growing up means learning that she, like other people in one's life, has and wants a life of her own, and that loving her means recognizing her subjectivity and appreciating her separateness. But people have trouble doing this and continue, condoned and supported by the ideology about mother they subsequently learn, to experience mothers solely as people who did or did

7

not live up to their child's expectations. This creates the quality of rage we find in 'blame-the-mother' literature and the unrealistic expectation that perfection would result if only a mother would devote her life completely to her child and all impediments to doing so were removed. Psyche and culture merge here and reflexively create one another.

(Chodorow and Contratto, 1982, p.65)

This is an interesting formulation of the particular and unique power of images of motherhood. Yet, in presenting a monolithic merger of culture and psyche, Chodorow and Contratto do not explore fully enough the ways in which different people may connect with culture differently and the ways in which people may even feel at odds with it. While they make the important point that collective political action is needed to move beyond these primitive images, they do not consider directly the question of this book: how does the mother herself relate to images of motherhood?

The possibility of varied connections between culture and personal history has been systematically studied in the seminal work of Adorno *et al.* (1982/1950) on the authoritarian personality. These authors see culture as composed of a variety of ideological trends. While suggesting that the trend that appeals to a particular person and his/her underlying needs forms an 'organized whole,' they speak to a range of possible connections.

The same ideological trends may in different individuals have different sources, and the same personal needs may express themselves in different ideological trends ... Ideologies have an existence independent of any single individual; and those which exist at a particular time are results both of historical processes and of contemporary social events. These ideologies have, for different individuals, different degrees of appeal, a matter that depends upon the individual's needs and the degree to which these needs are being satisfied or frustrated.

(Adorno *et al.*, 1982/1950, p.2)

While stating that individuals ease into 'patterns that are more or less uniquely their own,' they expect that 'common patterns will be discovered' (*ibid.*). Among these patterns are different ways of both appropriating or rejecting traditional values.

The rejection of traditional values is central to much feminist work. Some, like Rich in *Of woman born*, focus on the particular gap between women's experience and the naming and prescribing of that experience by culture. In this work, because culture is seen to have its roots in patriarchy, culture 'speaks for' men and in service of their needs; it leaves women's experience and concerns largely unspoken. When women speak of their own experience, they can expose culture's male bias and provide an alternate, and more meaningful, representation.

8

Other theorists see the presence of a pervasive gap between culture and the person as a central characteristic of the human condition. Robert Murphy (1971), following the German sociologist, Georg Simmel (1950, 1968), argues that culture has been 'made' by a collective of other people and, having been developed in the past, cannot fit any individual's experience well. At the same time, Simmel and Murphy view culture as essential to human development as a source of coherence and representation.

> There is reality, but there are also representations of reality, which are very real to those who live with them. The two are not the same. Thanks to life in society, however, the images of the mind are not completely individual fantasies, for people tend to share the representations of reality and thus to legitimize and reinforce one another's interpretation of it. This gives rise to collective fantasies (and, therefore, no longer fantastic), which we anthropologists call 'culture.'
>
> (Murphy, 1971, pp.90–1)

As Murphy goes on to suggest, collectives of people are selective; cultural meanings are found in only one aspect of reality. People 'falsify the world, at the very least, by omission' (p.239). Although culture 'perpetuates an illusion,' Murphy argues that we can look for 'opposedness' and seek to focus on that which is excluded by culture from representation.

The highly influential work of Lacan and those who value his work (e.g. Jameson, 1977; Kovel, 1981; Lemaire, 1977; Rose, 1982) also deals with the issue of a gap between culture (the 'symbolic order') and experience. This work considers how culture serves historically to locate and channel our deepest strivings and experience. This naming of desire necessarily involves a gap between individual experience and culture and becomes constitutive of our subjectivity. Because the child's early relationship with his/her mother involves satisfaction and its loss, representations of the Mother are necessarily implicated in desire. Following this approach, it is important to consider the naming of desire in images of motherhood.

AMERICAN PSYCHOLOGICAL FEMINISM: MAKING THE CONNECTION BETWEEN WOMEN AND MOTHERHOOD[4]

Interestingly, the dominant trend in recent American work in the psychology of women does include a particular vision of motherhood. The Mother as nurturant and relational is evident in the influential theories of Nancy Chodorow, Carol Gilligan, and others. She is characterized by close connections to others. She is available and selfless, perhaps overly so. She is relatively undifferentiated, especially from the female children in whom these characteristics of availability and selflessness will be reproduced.

This vision is striking, in part because it is quite different from that of the necessarily frustrating, horrifically powerful mother of the unconscious, the mother who 'eludes total capture by the child's desire' (Wood, 1983, p.18) that numerous psychoanalytic thinkers (e.g. Adams, 1983; Chasseguet-Smirgel, 1964, in press; Dinnerstein, 1976; Klein, 1964/1937) see as an essential concomitant of early experience. This vision is also different from Simone de Beauvoir's (1952) treatment of motherhood as central to female devaluation and from the notion of women as actually 'unmothered' precisely because their own mothers were stressed and devalued (Flax, 1978; Rich, 1986/1976).

The reproduction of mothering: Nancy Chodorow's theory

Because of its influence and its distinct and intriguingly positive view of the Mother, I am using American feminist psychology as a focus for this study. Nancy Chodorow's work (1971, 1974, 1978, 1979, 1981, 1989) provides the most detailed and influential exposition of the place of motherhood in women's development. Chodorow is explicitly feminist in orientation, arguing against asymmetrical gender arrangements and for shared parenting. At the same time, she dignifies the difference between men and women by celebrating the very female tradition of care and connection that, from other vantage points, is seen to present problems – especially for liberated women.

Chodorow makes a brilliant, well-argued contribution to the growing body of feminist work. Yet, if we focus directly on her vision of women's close connections to their own mothers and to the reproduction of tradition and of motherhood, Chodorow seems to be depicting a world in which women are – and want to be – like their mothers. In at least some ways, this vision of reproduction seems at odds with the experience of women who are committed to living their lives differently from their mothers and, in a broader sense, to being different kinds of people than their mothers. I will go on to describe Chodorow's theory in detail and, in this study, will be exploring where its 'truth' and appeal lie.

Chodorow's theoretical approach is a combination of object relations theory (see Greenberg and Mitchell, 1983, for an introduction to this theory) and Mahler's separation/individuation theory (Mahler, 1968; Mahler *et al.*, 1970, 1975). In the context of the present study, her work can be seen as resting on the assumption that the child's own mother is an essentially good, competent, and identification-worthy object. Because of the mother's essential goodness, the child does not need to construct an alternate, a better and wished for, maternal object. It should be noted that other object relations theorists present a different picture. For example, Fairbairn (1952) posits the construction of alternate and more positive maternal objects and Klein (1964/1937) focuses on the child's struggle with the experience of both good and bad maternal objects.

Table 1 Summary of Chodorow's model of female object relations

MOTHER

Early mother–child unity is blissful. Mother is good, caring, responsive, and seen as without needs of her own. Child aims to be loved and satisfied without being under any obligation to give anything in return.

Ongoing object of identification for the daughter who experiences herself as continuous with her same-sex mother.

Mother treats her daughter as an extension of herself and is unable to distinguish between her own needs and those of her child. Daughter feels 'empty of herself' and in her emptiness is likely to depend on her own children.

As girl tries to differentiate, mother represents dependence, regression and passivity. Girl responds to her with fear and hostility.

In 'normal outcome,' girl accepts her femininity and her connection with her mother. Mother is object of personal identification. She is seen as good and effective and girl learns what it is to be a woman from her.

FATHER

Seen under the sway of the reality principle – not object of merger or frustration like mother – but less known than mother.

As girl tries to differentiate, father represents freedom from her mother. Through splitting, he becomes an all-good, idealized object.

Treats his daughter as special, as sexualized object. Daughter will deny his limitations and depend on feeling loved by him.

Not a strong enough object to break primary tie to mother. He is an erotically primary but emotionally secondary addition to a relational triangle.

HUSBAND

Looks to wife for undemanding primary love. He can have a sense of reactivated fusion with his mother through his relationship with his wife.

Since husband is psychologically constructed as a separate male, he cannot be similarly responsive to his wife's needs. In addition, since he lacks a female body, he cannot provide his wife a sense of refusion with her own mother.

CHILD

Given men's difficulties with love and lack of opportunity for close relationships with other women, women come to want and need primary relationships to children.

Recreates the desired mother–child exclusive relationship and completes the relational triangle. Woman responds to the child with primary identification and empathy.

Mother may depend on the child to fulfill emotional needs and erotic desires that should be met by adults.

Sons – seen as husband-substitutes, treated as opposite sexed, male other.

Daughters – seen as mother-substitutes, treated as extension of self.

Table 1 summarizes Chodorow's model of female object relations. In Chodorow's account, boy and girl infants are similar and share an early and positive experience of feeling merged with the mother, projecting frustrations outside the parent–child unit. For both, the mother becomes the object of egoistic 'primary love,' and is viewed as she who satisfies the child without needs of her own. The ongoing attempt of adult life is to reactivate this essentially positive experience.

Because girls are mothered by a person of their sex, they form a continuous identification with her and 'experience themselves as continuous with others' (Chodorow 1978, p.169). The mother contributes to this experience, treats the same-sex child as an extension of herself, and is unable to distinguish between her own needs and those of her child.

The developing girl struggles to differentiate herself from her mother and turns to her father as a symbol of freedom. However, because he has not been part of the girl's earliest experience, he is not an object with sufficient strength to break the prior, deeper maternal connection. Instead, the girl adds her father to her previously dyadic world of primary objects and defines herself in a 'relational triangle,' a concept borrowed from Deutsch (1944). For Chodorow (1978, p.167), 'men tend to remain *emotionally* secondary', despite women's heterosexual involvement with them.

The boy's situation is different. Because his mother is of the opposite sex to him, he has a consistently heterosexual love object. However, he has the difficult task of shifting from identification with a woman to identification with his same-sex but relatively absent father. Grappling with feelings of connection to his mother, the boy has to repress his early feminine identification and engage in emphatic individuation and a defensive firming of ego boundaries. Consequently, 'the basic masculine sense of self is separate' (*ibid.*, p.169). The mother impacts on this separateness. She experiences her boy child as 'a definite other' who, in the absence of adult males, becomes the object of her often seductive fantasies.

In Chodorow's view, female mothering produces male separateness and female connection. It also is deeply entwined with views of mothers and of women. For Chodorow, these views are gender-linked because of family organization and not because of any inherent characteristics. As Chodorow emphasizes even further in more recent work (1989), because of the mother's singular role in infancy, she is objectified and seen in terms of her capacity to serve the needs of others. For the child moving toward differentiation, the connection with the mother raises the possibility of engulfment. The mother becomes the dreaded representative of 'dependence, regression, passivity, and the lack of adaptation to reality' (1978, p.82).

The father occupies a different position in the child's emotional experience. Because of his work outside the home and his masculine, more bounded ego, he is neither the object of merger nor the source of immediate frustrations. Instead, the emotional relationship to the father begins later and is less primitive – less fraught with ambivalence and more under the sway of the reality principle. In order to ease the child's difficult shift from mother to father, both boys and girls use the primitive defense mechanism of splitting, and preserve the father as an all-good object who incorporates the split-off good parts of the mother as well as his own goodness.

According to Chodorow, the boy's contempt for the mother 'serves to free him not only from his mother but also from the femininity within himself. It therefore becomes entangled with the issue of masculinity, is generalized to all women' (*ibid.*, p.182), and becomes part of what Chodorow sees as a male-based cultural heritage.

As Chodorow emphasizes in *The reproduction of mothering* (1978) and, more recently, in the 'Gender, Relation and Difference' essay in her collected volume (1989), female core gender identity is *not* deeply affected by this devaluation of women. The 'primary sense of gendered self that emerges in earliest development constantly challenges men, and gives a certain potential psychological security, even liberation to women' (1989, p.112); it is 'defined positively, as that which is female, or like the mother' (*ibid.*, p.111).

Chodorow does recognize that girls have difficulty with mothers who are overly available and who are unable to make a distinction between themselves and their daughters. However, Chodorow sees the girl's dread and ambivalence as limited because of an essentially positive early experience and because of an opportunity for identification with her available and competent mother.

> A girl's devaluation of or hostility toward her mother may be a part of the process [of separation], but its 'normal' outcome, by contrast, entails acceptance of her own femininity and identification with her mother. Whatever the individual resolution of the feminine oedipus complex, however, it does not become institutionalized the same way.
>
> (Chodorow, 1978, p.182)

> Because she is also female and presumably does not feel herself dreadful or fearsome but rather the reverse, it is likely that a girl will not generalize her dread to all females.
>
> (Chodorow, 1978, p.183)

The move to the maternal place

According to Chodorow, women are prepared to mother through the construction of the female, related self and through identification with their mothers. Although erotically heterosexual, Chodorow's women are 'encouraged both by men's difficulties with love and by their own relational history with their mothers to look elsewhere for love and emotional gratification' (1978, p.200).

In their search for connection in a world that Chodorow sees as foreclosing options for close relationships with other women, 'women come to want and need primary relationships to children' (*ibid.*, p.203). Motherhood is valuable for women because the relationship with the child recreates the early mother–child relationship and also allows a dual identification – with both the mother and the child simultaneously.

On the level of psychic structure, then, a child completes the relational triangle for a woman. Having a child, and experiencing her relation to a man in this context, enables her to reimpose intrapsychic relational structure on the social world, while at the same time resolving the generational component of her Oedipus complex as she takes a new place in the triangle – a maternal place in relation to her own child.

(Chodorow, 1978, p.201)

In her emphasis on gender reproduction, Chodorow implies that the woman's move to the 'maternal place' in the relational triangle does not involve significant psychological change. Motherhood is a matter of women's early formed being; the doing of it fulfills, but does not transform that being. Chodorow does state that 'mothering is invested with a mother's often conflictual, ambivalent, yet powerful need for her own mother' (*ibid.*, p.212). However, instead of focusing on the experience of being, rather than having, the good mother, Chodorow feeds the woman's need for mothering back into her model, suggesting that daughters who were treated as an extension of their own needy mothers will feel 'empty of themselves,' develop insufficiently individuated senses of self, and become dependent on their own children. Although her more recent work includes attention to the creativity and change involved in adult life, Chodorow's primary emphasis is on the reproduction of connection and mothering.

The mother as magical and terrifying: Dorothy Dinnerstein's theory

Dinnerstein (1976) sees the maternal place in a radically different way than Chodorow. Rooting her analysis in the theory of Klein(1964/1937) rather than Mahler (Mahler, 1968, Mahler *et al.*, 1970, 1975), she emphasizes the absolute, terrifying, and magical power of the mother who controls all resources and necessarily frustrates her child. 'The inner world that [the girl] must come to embrace belongs, on an inarticulate level of awareness, to the magically powerful goddess mother of infancy' (p.85). Because of this, Dinnerstein stresses the difficulty of becoming a woman who is necessarily unable to fit her early-formed notion of femininity and is still terrified of the mother's power. While Chodorow emphasizes the way that the girl's continuous identification with her available and known mother prepares her for becoming a mother herself, Dinnerstein's argument suggests the importance of examining the meaning of the maternal place for women.

Need for mother as subject: Jessica Benjamin's theory

Jessica Benjamin (1978, 1980, 1987, 1988, in press) begins her analysis from a somewhat different point. She argues that children not only want their mothers to act in service of their needs and provide them with total satisfaction, but also need their mothers to be independent subjects. For Benjamin, recognition is the key to relationships:

> Recognition is that response from another which makes meaningful the feelings, intentions, and actions of the self. It allows the self to realize its agency and authorship in a tangible way. But such recognition can only come from another whom we, in turn, recognize as a person in his or her own right.
>
> (Benjamin, 1988, p.12)

In Benjamin's neo-Hegelian presentation, true selfhood depends on 'mutual recognition' and develops as one affects and is recognized by another with an 'independent center.' Since sense of self and sense of the other develop simultaneously, unless the child can see its mother as a person, the child's own selfhood will be damaged. Self-sacrifice, the hallmark of the ideal Mother, is damaging to the child. Instead, the child must know that its mother cannot be sacrificed or obliterated and that she will survive as a person, regardless of aggression, conflict, and imperfection. Although Benjamin is clear that the 'possibility of balancing the recognition of the child's needs with the assertion of [the mother's] own has scarcely been put forward as an ideal' (1988, p.82), it is precisely this balance that she argues is essential.

In Benjamin's presentation, recognition is inherently problematic because of the paradox of depending on another person, outside of an individual's control, to recognize his or her independence. Because this paradox is 'difficult to endure,' the impulse to split takes over. Already polarized males and females then introduce children into a world in which males are recognized for their independence and women are the recognizers.

In this process, women become objects, instruments of the needs of others who cannot act as givers. The nurturance so clearly associated with this giving woman is devalued in western culture and banished to the home. This privatization of nurturance deprives women of needed recognition and increases the likelihood that they will depend on their children for self-esteem.

While Benjamin reiterates Chodorow's picture of the reproduction of existing social arrangements, she also suggests that men and women continue to look for the side lost to them. Benjamin suggests that the struggle for recognition is ongoing and relationships that achieve or fail to achieve mutuality continue to affect our humanness. Benjamin's work, then, can be understood to raise the possibility that the mother's subjectivity might be affected by the child's interest in her and capacity – albeit infantile – to recognize her.[5]

Relationality as female, not maternal: Carol Gilligan's theory

Carol Gilligan (1982) shares with Chodorow and Benjamin a vision of male–female difference and an emphasis on relationality – responsive, caring, and empathic connection to others – as the hallmark of femininity. Among these theories, Gilligan's work represents something of an extreme because she shifts attention away from motherhood and particular relationships with specific 'objects' toward a more generalized sense of female connectedness. Instead of focusing on the roots of female relationality and male separateness, much of Gilligan's work has developed in response to Kohlberg (1969; Kohlberg and Kramer, 1969) and involves the articulation of levels of female identity formation and moral development. In her highly influential book, *In a different voice*, Gilligan (1982) outlines three stages. At Stage I, the Pre-Conventional Level, women are concerned about their own survival. At Stage II, the Conventional Level, goodness is equated with caring for others; caring directly for oneself or asking for care from others is considered selfish. Despite its roots in traditional sociocultural arrangements, Gilligan stresses that this stage is psychologically inadequate and unstable. The move to Stage III, the Post-Conventional Level, involves including the self in the equation of care; self-sacrifice becomes immoral as the ethic of care is extended to the self as well as to others.

Gilligan's more recent work (1986, 1988, 1990) focuses on the extent to which women can 'disbelieve' the dominant perspective and acknowledge and voice their own experience. Here, Gilligan has paid particular attention to adolescence and has considered the girl's sense of the disparity between her engagement in relationships and the cultural tradition emphasizing independence. Gilligan and her students (Attanucci, 1984, 1988; Willard, 1983, 1988) have examined 'in whose terms' women see relationships.

Both Attanucci and Willard study mothers and the 1990 anthology which Gilligan co-edited, *Making connections*, includes a chapter on how the mother–child relationship is perceived by the daughter (Rich, 1990). However, Gilligan herself has not focused directly on the mother's experience. While emphasizing that the 'attributes desirable for women presume an other' (Gilligan, 1982, p.79), Gilligan has not fully considered what it means when this other is a child rather than an adult. Although speaking of the fetus in the context of her work on abortion decisions (Gilligan and Belenky, 1980; Gilligan, 1982), she does not consider the extent to which the child speaks 'in a different voice' to that of an adult. The young child's dependency, its need for care in order to survive, and its babbling, crying, and laughter may well present the grown woman with a unique kind of other and a new perspective from which to consider care of and connection to adults.

While it is striking that Gilligan has not yet focused detailed attention on the mother–child relationship, her interest in self–other relationships and her concern with the extent to which women can voice their own experiences and see things in their own terms as well as the child's are important to a consideration of motherhood.

THE SOCIAL CONSTRUCTION OF THE CHILD

It is interesting that much of the feminist literature that places the mother in social context does not consider the fact that views of the child are also historically influenced. Despite the apparent attraction of the idea of a child unmarked by history, we can better comprehend images of motherhood if we understand that images of the child are also socially constructed. In terms of the present study, there are interesting questions about the way in which privileged, educated, New York women see their children. Do they, for example, emphasize high-powered intelligence? Do they see boys and girls differently?

There is a substantial historical literature that discusses childhood (Ariès, 1962; de Mause, 1974; Hunt, 1970; Shorter, 1975). I am going to focus on these aspects of the literature that are particularly relevant to two-year-old children. Martha Wolfenstein (1955), in her classic paper on the 'fun morality,' draws attention to the ways in which children represent our impulses, our treatment of children being an indication of our relationship to those impulses. Through her historical analysis of child rearing documents from colonial times through the 1950s, Wolfenstein chronicles a qualitative transformation of our orientation to impulse, revealed in a trend away from the puritanical view of children as dangerous, and toward a view of children as benignly exploratory. Yet, she suggests that there has developed a mandate that child rearing be 'fun' and, as she sees it, this fun is itself a puritanical defense against far more intense and disruptive pleasure.

Through an examination of the last two decades of developmental psychology, Harris (1987) has extended Wolfenstein's analysis by arguing that a view of the infant as 'increasingly rational, planned, goal-directed and intentional' (p.35) and suited to life in a bureaucratic society has superseded a sense of the child as 'conflict-filled, fluid, and inchoate' (p.46). As

17

Wolfenstein suggests, the notion of the rational, competent child may also help parents defend themselves against the potential disruptions that their children present.

Recent work on the mother/child dyad (Greenspan and Lourie, 1981; Sander, 1962; Sroufe, 1979) shows us the appropriate companion to Harris's 'competent child.' Instead of being measured against the ideal of complete identification with the child, as in the post war era (Riley, 1983), the mother is now supposed to be the objective reader of the child's needs and patterns who can mediate between the child's organization and that of the world.

Certainly, interest in the mother as objective reader is in many important ways different from the image of the mother identifying fully with her child. Yet, both visions seem to call for the mother to accommodate herself fully to her child. In addition to ignoring the mother's individuality and subjectivity, these views also do not reflect the possibility of conceiving of the child as radically and disruptively different from an adult.

Kristeva's paradigm (1980b), probably unique among modern feminist psychologies, recognizes that at least part of the mother's experience involves dealing with the child's otherness. Her approach, for example, contrasts with that of American theorists like Chodorow and Benjamin who have focused on male–female difference and emphasized the child's identificatory competence and the way the child becomes molded to and complements the parent's very being. Kristeva, a French psychoanalytic feminist, focuses on how the relationship with the infant is a relationship with a being not yet itself marked by language or socialization. The child can present the adult with 'what within the speaker is not yet spoken' (1980b, p.272), and can refer that adult to the largely unconscious, 'semiotic' place in which the speaker's own language, sexuality, and laughter remain infantile and never totally rationalized. In this sense, the child provides 'access (an excess) toward the Other,' an opportunity for rediscovery of the inchoate experience that has been inadequately supported in development. Kristeva does caution that the mother may feel overly empowered or captivated by the child. However, while introducing the factor of otherness, she underestimates the extent to which the mother may feel intensely uncomfortable with her child's impulsivity.

THE EFFECT OF BEING A MOTHER ON THE CONSTRUCTION OF MOTHERHOOD

Clearly, the experience of motherhood is highly significant; it can have a powerful effect on women. As already described, Adrienne Rich's landmark work, *Of woman born*, provides a striking example of how the experience of motherhood can provide a basis for questioning society. Sara Ruddick (1980, 1989) continues in this tradition. She suggests that a kind of thinking, 'maternal thinking,' is rooted in the practice of mothering. She argues that this thought has universal characteristics based on the demand to foster the life of the child in such a way that s/he might grow and fit within the social milieu. While this thought can be at odds with dominant values, Ruddick also emphasizes that the particulars of a society will have considerable effect on how mothers act and see their function. Thus, in American society, while maternal praxis might lead to unconventional thinking about supporting all life rather than individualistic and competitive concern for one's own child, pacifism rather than violence, openness to change rather than investment in control, Ruddick expects that dominant values and the mother's subordinate social position are likely to direct her attention in conventional ways.

Two psychoanalytic theorists, Therese Benedek (1959, 1970a, 1970b) and Melanie Klein (1964/1937), have developed views of parenthood as a source of considerable personality change. In Benedek's important formulation, identification with the child and introjection of the child as a new object into the parent's 'self-system' lead to substantial personality reorganization. Benedek sees the relationship between mother and child as an interpersonal process with effects on both parties. The mother's behavior and feelings affect the child; the child's satisfaction/dissatisfaction defines the mother – her sense of competence, her self, and her sense of what might constitute good and bad mothering. The mother's representations of her child and her self then are intertwined in a 'spiral of interpersonal processes' that create intrapsychic changes in both mother and child.

Further, as Benedek and Klein would suggest, now in the position of mother, the woman may be able to empathize with and come to terms with her own mother, repair her vision of mother and motherhood, and become more comfortable being a parent. Klein suggests there is considerable value for adults when they 'play the part of a good parent'.

> By reversing a situation, namely in acting towards another person as a good parent, in phantasy we re-create and enjoy the wished-for love and goodness of our parent. But to act as good parents towards other people may also be a way of dealing with the frustrations and sufferings of the past. Our grievances against our parents for having frustrated us, together with the feelings of hate and revenge to which these have given rise in us, and again, the feelings of guilt and despair arising out of this hate and revenge because we have injured the parents whom at the same time we loved – all these, in phantasy we may undo in retrospect (taking away some of the grounds for hatred) by playing at the same time the parts of loving parents and loving children.
>
> (Klein, 1964/1937, p.312)

Kristeva's work (1980b) is also important in this context. Kristeva em-

19

phasizes numerous changes that may occur as a consequence of mother-hood. The woman may rediscover her early attachment to her own mother, experience *jouissance* (the ineffable pleasure that escapes the social contract), and value the maternal in a way that is at odds with social devaluation. By attending to their experience, women as mothers might distance themselves from existing images that do not give voice to that experience, create new images of motherhood, and, in the process, transform the symbolic order of culture. In this way, motherhood can be considered creation rather than reproduction.

All of these perspectives suggest that the mother herself has an experience as a parent that is significant. Her experience is worthy of meaning-making. Its meaning relates to culture as well as to her own personal family history. This meaning-making is complex because mother-hood is so entwined with early experience, resonates with shared images of the Mother, and involves the complicated, deeply stirring, and unique connection with her child. Because the lives of middle and upper middle class American women have undergone so much change in the last decades and because the way we in America make sense of children and of the family continue to be in flux, questions of how the mother makes meaning of motherhood may be particularly salient at present. This study of twelve first-time mothers provides one opportunity to explore mothers' images of motherhood.

The review of the literature leads to a number of questions that will be addressed in this research:

1 Do the women in this rather homogeneous group share an image of motherhood? How do their images relate to their own mothers? to traditional notions of the Mother? to notions of the mother as subject?
2 How do these women depict their mothers, fathers, husbands, children? Do their object relations fit Chodorow's model and exemplify the reproduction of mothering and the kinds of relationships Chodorow describes?
3 Do these women characterize themselves as caring and closely connected to others? Are the men in their lives characterized by separateness?
4 How do these women depict a female tradition? Do they feel connected to that tradition? How do they see themselves in relation to other mothers?

2

RESEARCH FRAMEWORK AND METHOD

The research presented in this book is intended as a theory-building, exploratory study of the thoughts, feelings, and desires of the mother herself. The focus of the study is an analysis of how a small number of mothers represent their mothers, fathers, husbands, and children, how they speak about their relationships, and how they make meaning of motherhood, appropriating and resisting traditional cultural notions. Based on a review of the literature and on an initial pilot study of four mothers (Kaplan, 1987), three conceptualizations – object relations, relationality, and traditionality – were selected to provide a framework for the organization of the analysis. Because of the importance of exploring complex intrapsychic relationships among these three conceptualizations, the research uses the case study method and is based on the systematic interpretation of interview material. As such, the study provides a qualitative research model that relates findings to theory and also leads to topics for further, larger scale research.

THE CASE STUDY METHOD

Each of the twelve mothers who participated in this study is treated as a 'case,' as an individual worthy of detailed study. As in other research concerned with both intimate experience and social processes, 'we can see reflected in cases cultural contradictions, discontinuities, and deficiencies as well as certain positive cultural values' (Rapoport and Rapoport, 1976, p.29). In small scale research like this, the shared characteristics of the subjects contribute to the possibility of examining the relationship between the intimate and the social. At the same time, the study is clearly limited by its attention to a small and relatively homogeneous group of women.

My aim in using the case study approach is to add empirical work to theory and to introduce a more detailed dimension to the empirical research conducted in the psychology of women. Much current theoretical work in the psychology of women, like that of Chodorow, combines psychoanalytic and social theory with clinical case material; it makes generalizations about women without detailed empirical research. Often, empirical research in the field has used interviews to move on to more generalized discussions of categories of thinking, experience, or femaleness (Attanucci, 1984, 1988; Belenky et al., 1986; Gilligan, 1982; Leifer, 1980). Much life history research has been geared to identifying shared themes (Levinson, 1978; Gould, 1978; Vaillant, 1977) but has been criticized for its emphasis on normative development and for ignoring sources of conflict between the individual and social life (Broughton, 1986; Corbett, 1984; Jacoby, 1975; Kovel, 1974; Lasch, 1976) and for using particular cohorts or classes to make generalizations about men or women with little or no attention to the particularity of the research subjects (Rossi, 1980).

Within this exploratory research, I try to pay considerable attention to similarities and differences among cases, to the relationship of cases to theory, and to generating questions for further research so that as little as possible of the complexity of the cases is sacrificed.

THE RESEARCH POPULATION

While strategic selection of cases can allow for research focused on subjects who exemplify a specific population (Keniston, 1960; Piotrkowski, 1978; Rapoport and Rapoport, 1976), the cases presented in this study were not selected because they represented some 'ideal type.' For example, I did not search for the perfect 'yuppies' and would not label these women by that term. Instead, this research relies on criteria that define a subject population and, within those criteria, on Robert White's (1952) notion that each individual is worthy of study.

The twelve middle and upper middle class women who participated in this study contrast with the 'average,' younger and less educated women who are usually selected for studies of motherhood, as in the work of Boulton (1983), Leifer (1980), Oakley (1980). As already indicated, they represent a socially significant population. The present research sample is also unusual because these women are mothers of toddlers. Interestingly, despite the theoretical contributions suggesting that parenthood can involve ongoing change, most research on motherhood has focused on the transition to parenthood from pregnancy through the early post-partum months (Bibring et al., 1961; Liefer, 1980; Oakley, 1980; Rossi, 1968; Shereshevsky and Yarrow, 1973). Despite this, the toddler period is significant for parents. Although no longer new to parenthood, the mothers in this study continue to grapple with issues of how motherhood fits into their lives. They also deal with children who are not fully socialized beings. The cultural notion of the 'terrible twos' suggests that toddlerhood is seen as a unique and difficult age. Psychological literature suggests that children's impulsivity (Oliner, 1984), negativity and anger (Slade and Aber, 1986),

22

separation–individuation (Coleman *et al.*, 1953; Mahler, 1968), gender development (Benjamin, 1987, 1988; Chodorow, 1978), and language acquisition (Urwin, 1984) may be particularly salient for parents of toddlers.

Subject selection

Criteria for subject selection

Criteria were established in order to define the potential subject population and place a boundary around the universe of possible subjects. All subjects were to be married, middle- or upper middle-class, college-educated, Caucasian women who were brought up in the United States, and, at the time of the study, lived in the New York metropolitan area. To stipulate an extent of parental experience, all were to be first-time mothers with a child between the ages of fifteen and thirty-six months and were not be pregnant with a second child at the outset of the study. Six were to be mothers of girls and six mothers of boys. The study also was designed to articulate with research projects at a local university Center for Children ('Children's Center') and to include subjects who were mothers of children enrolled at the center's two-morning-a-week program for toddlers. Because of the program's small size, the research was designed to include six center mothers and six mothers matched for similar social circumstances.

Building the subject population

In small scale research like this, each subject has an impact on the study. Her generosity, her concerns and interests, and her willingness to participate and to engage with me and my questions are central to the very interpersonal research process.

Seven Children's Center mothers met the research criteria. I contacted these women by telephone and invited them to participate in a study that would involve analysis of information from their intake interview as well as a second, and more open-ended, two-hour interview with the opportunity to discuss topics relating to motherhood and some psychological testing. I also told them that their identities would be masked, that our discussion would not be shared with Children's Center teachers, and that I did not know and would not be studying their children. After discussion, during which each woman could raise questions about the study, five mothers agreed to participate.

The sample of twelve mothers was completed by seven women who were referred to me by friends of friends. These women met the research criteria but were not women with whom I was personally involved. I contacted these women by telephone, told them that I was conducting a study of mother's experiences of parenthood and of key relationships in their lives, and that the study would involve two interviews and some psychological testing. After discussion, during which each woman could raise questions, the seven women consented to participate.

In addition to the criteria for selection, shared characteristics of four of the five Children's Center mothers led to further definition of the research group and influenced both the selection of other participants and the nature of the study. These four were upper middle class women in their thirties and forties who had earned post-baccalaureate degrees and established careers before having children, and had husbands whose educational level and career achievement either matched or exceeded their own.

While all subjects met the research criteria, they were not all equally privileged or high achieving. For example, 'Karen,' the fifth Children's Center mother, met the general research criteria but was in her twenties, studying design, working in an office, and living in a fifth floor walk-up apartment with her husband, a graduate student.

Of the seven non-Children's Center mothers, six matched the core of the Children's Center group. The seventh, 'Anna,' and her husband were decidedly less career-oriented and more 'hippie' than the rest of the population. In addition, she was breastfeeding her thirty-six-month-old daughter and advocated at-home education. Anna was included in the study because she met the research criteria and because she provided the opportunity to study a woman with what can be described as a symbiotic relationship with her daughter.

'Sharon,' a Children's Center mother, raised another question about inclusion. She was two months pregnant at the time of the second interview. Probing during the second meeting suggested that Sharon was not preoccupied with the new baby, a finding supported by theory and research indicating that the fetus typically does not become a psychologically meaningful internal object until after quickening (Bibring, 1959; Bibring et al., 1961; Leifer, 1980; Zayas, 1988).

Additional differences between the mothers underscore the extent to which this is a study of twelve individuals who were not perfectly matched. For example, mothers varied in family background and ethnicity. Six of the subjects were Jewish and three of these women were the children of immigrants. Three subjects had mothers who worked. The women also varied in terms of current work status. At the time of the interviews, four were working full time in careers they had established prior to childbirth, four began working part time and in somewhat different jobs after their children were born, and four have been full time mothers since childbirth.

Table 2.1 summarizes the characteristics of the mothers and displays the average ages of mothers and chidren in Center versus non-Center samples and in mothers of girls versus mothers of boys.

Table 2.1 Characteristics of the twelve subjects

	Mother's age	Child's age		Work status	Children's center
Mothers of girls					
Susan	32	23/27	mo	f/t	no
Myra	35	22/28	mo	p/t	no
Anna	36	30/36	mo	no	no
Sharon	32	23/28	mo	p/t	yes
Linda	42	28/34	mo	f/t	yes
Lauren	35	17/23	mo	no	yes
Mothers of boys					
Julia	44	21/27	mo	no	no
Denise	42	17/23	mo	p/t	no
Harriet	34	24/29	mo	no	no
Kathryn	33	24/29	mo	f/t	no
Karen	25	24/29	mo	p/t	yes
Ellen	42	25/31	mo	f/t	yes

Average ages of mothers and children by subgroups

	Mother's age	Child's age at first interview
Girls' mothers	35 years	23 months
Boys' mothers	37 years	23 months
Center mothers	35 years	23 months
Other mothers	37 years	23 months
All mothers	36 years	23 months

INTERVIEW METHODOLOGY

The interview method is particularly valuable in this type of research which focuses on subjects as makers of meaning. It allows for treatment of the mother as subject, preserves what Frenkel-Brunswick (1982/1950) calls her 'uniqueness and flavor,' and provides material that is rich, textured, and suited to exploratory research. As subjects speak, they consciously and unconsciously make associations that are personally meaningful and provide a good foundation for testing and building theory.

Before describing the interview process, it is worth considering the limitations of the interview approach. The interview method does not allow examination of how people actually behave, nor can we consider that the subject's representations of other people are 'objective' or unchanging views of these 'real people.' Urist (1984) emphasizes this point in a discussion about researching object relations:

Assessing object relations refers, then, to an evaluation of intrapsychic functioning, not to social behaviors per se. In such an assessment, we are interested in observing the ways in which feelings and conscious and unconscious ideas about the self, about other people, and about the relations between self and others are organized in an individual's mind.

(Urist, 1984, pp.821–2)

The particular value of interviews is also apparent in a consideration of the use of parents as 'informants.' In a review of the literature, Maccoby and Martin (1983) discuss the limitations of interviewing parents: parents may not be fully aware of their behavior, the meaning of descriptive terms may vary among subjects, and retrospective reports are unreliable indicators of past events. The authors indicate that 'in the worst case our findings might then represent little more than documentation of common parental theories of socialization' (p.17). This 'worst case' is central to the purposes of the current research on mothers' ideas and feelings about motherhood. In addition, Maccoby and Martin find that interviewing is valuable in identifying parental attitudes and their experiences of their children especially when, instead of parents being asked for generalizations, they are asked to provide detailed descriptions of events and people that the researcher can then systematically analyze.

The view that parental reports are inadequate as retrospective data requires further comment. Within the present study, it is assumed that subjects are speaking at a particular point in time. The study explores how they currently make meaning of parenthood and of experiences and relationships in their lives. Their retrospective accounts are not seen to reflect permanent and unchanging memories. Instead, as Pipp *et al.* (1985) suggest in their study of adolescents, these 'reconstructions are part of adaptation in the present, not necessarily an accurate representation of the past' (p.992). Certainly, for parents, the present involves the powerful impact on them of dealing with their offspring. In addition, the interview process itself can affect the making of meaning. For the women who chose to participate, this study provided one context in which to focus on motherhood and numerous relationships. The analysis explores the meanings created by women within this particular interview context.

Motherhood interview

In order to compare and contrast subjects, the present research includes a structured and an open-ended interview as well as a number of standardized measures that allow subjects to respond verbally and uniquely to a set of questions, stories, and pictures. The interview has two parts, each of which took approximately two hours and was audiotaped and transcribed. All interviews were scheduled at the convenience of the subjects and carried out in complete privacy, at times when the subject had no other responsibilities and I would not encounter other family members. The second interview session was conducted four to six months after the first. The time gap allowed for transcription and preliminary analysis of the first interview and provided the opportunity to explore indications of change from one session to the other.

Part I: Structured interview

The structured 'Parent Development Interview' (PDI) (Aber, et al., 1984) was developed at the Barnard College Center for Toddler Development and has been part of the intake process for all enrolled families. It includes four basic areas of questioning: view of the child, view of the parent–child relationship, view of the self as parent, and view of changes experienced since parenthood. Questions about the subject's parents, her spouse, and her images of good and bad mothers are also included to develop a context for the subject's experience of parenthood. (See Appendix A, Standardized measures and guide to the second interview, for copies of interview and testing materials.)

Part II: Standardized measures and semi-structured interview

About 75 per cent of the second session was devoted to an individualized interview that followed up on the first meeting and was open-ended enough to follow the structure of the particular subject's thought and experience. An interview guide was developed in order to outline a number of questions related to the research perspectives that would be addressed at some point in each interview, including probe questions about family members, traditionality, the embodiment of motherhood, and experience of relationships with friends.

The second meeting began by inviting subjects to reflect on the first interview and express any feelings about the study process. The stand-ardized measures were administered before the major portion of the open-ended interview in order to minimize the effect of individualized interview content on those measures.

Gilligan dilemma (1982). In order to have a standardized measure of relationality, each subject was asked Gilligan's interview question: 'Have you ever been in a situation where you didn't know what was the right thing to do?' and standard probes. This dilemma was administered first because it focused on the subject's own experience and allowed her to shape the content of the discussion.

Newberger working mother dilemma (1977). This dilemma was selected from Newberger's interview materials designed to assess levels of aware-ness of the parent–child relationship. In this hypothetical dilemma, a well-to-do mother decides to work because it will make her happy but she is faced with an unhappy child. Subjects were asked standard questions about the mother and child. While the Newberger dilemma was originally written about an eleven-year-old daughter, for the purpose of the present study the child's age was changed to four years old – old enough to talk but nearer in age to the subjects' children – and the child's sex was adjusted to match that of the subject's child. This dilemma was administered second because it asked the subject to respond to a hypothetical situation and to issues presented as part of the research situation.

Thematic Apperception Test (TAT). Four TAT cards were administered in order to tap unconscious material about object relationships, quality of relations, and impulsivity, and to examine the 'emotional counterparts of cultural communalities' (Henry, 1951, p.234) and the 'feeling assumptions' people make about basic social interactions. The TAT cards were administered third when the subject might be more comfortable in the research setting and most able to accommodate the shift to a projective measure. The following four cards were administered:

Picture 1   A young boy is contemplating a violin that rests on a table in front of him. This card tends to elicit material about the subject's relationship with parental figures, and conflicts between autonomy and compliance with authority.

Picture 2   Country scene: in the foreground is a young woman with books in her hand; in the background a man is working in the fields and an older woman is looking on. This card tends to elicit material about family relations, autonomy from and compliance with traditionality, and gender differentiation. In addition, since the older woman can be seen as being pregnant, the subject may respond by discussing feelings about pregnancy and motherhood.

Picture 5   A middle-aged woman is standing on the threshold of a half-opened door looking into a room. This card tends to elicit material about impulsivity and control, especially in relation to a maternal figure.

Picture 7GF   An older woman is sitting on a sofa close beside a girl, speaking or reading to her. The girl, who holds a doll on her lap, is looking away. This card tends to elicit material about the mother–daughter relationship and expectations of motherhood.

ANALYSIS

The analysis of data focused on the development of a case study of each subject and the development of an individual profile including: a case summary of interview material; use of the Assessment of Qualitative and Structural Dimensions of Object Representations (AQSDOR) (Blatt *et al.*, 1981) to score interview material and three other reference measures to analyze responses to standardized indexes; and a within-subject comparison of measures.

In order for the analysis of interview material to be as independent from the reference measures as possible, the case study did not include analysis of material elicited in response to the measures and each case was developed prior to the coding of interview material by the AQSDOR or other reference measures for that subject.

In order to analyze data systematically and organize it in a fashion that facilitated cross-case comparison, a uniform format of analysis and presentation of material was developed. This systematic approach is crucial to the kind of qualitative research presented here. It should be noted that, at the same time that this approach enables a researcher to engage with and interpret extremely rich, qualitative material, it also limits this endeavor. This study, then, provides an example of a particular kind of qualitative analysis. I shall describe the mode of analysis in detail before proceeding to a presentation of the cases themselves.

Analysis of interview data

First, an overall assessment of the interview was made with attention to tone and relationship with the interviewer and the interview process.

Second, a condensed summary of the subject's background, work and parenting arrangements was made to provide some context for the case material.

Third, interview material was sorted in terms of object relations, relationality, traditionality, and more specific themes through the 'constant comparative method for qualitative data' (Glaser and Strauss, 1967). This method is especially suited to the building of theory from qualitative material. Theory is located within the data rather than in more abstract and generalized notions.

To analyze material systematically, interview statements were categorized according to as many themes as possible. Themes such as 'connectedness,' 'self-sacrifice,' and 'own mother as object' came from existing theory. Themes like 'image of a good mother,' 'loneliness,' 'inability to connect with child,' and 'sense of children having either positive or negative power' were introduced through the review of interview material.

In order to consider the less conscious, less intentional aspects of subjects' discussions, analysis focused not only on what subjects said but on how and when they said it. Attention was paid to whether the subject or interviewer introduced a topic. In addition, as Gilligan (1986) suggests, attention was paid to whether there were variations in the tone of the interview and distinctive patterns of speech – pauses, stutters, repetitive phraseology – associated with particular themes. Based on Main's (Main and Goldwyn, 1984; Slade and Aber, 1986) analysis of adult attachment interviews, degree of coherence, use of examples to flesh out descriptions, and presence of contradictions and conflicts were also considered.

In order to analyze the interviews of a particular subject, all interview material related to a theme was noted and studied to illuminate patterns. Differences in content and tone between the two interviews were considered. Themes identified through one case were then considered in the analysis of material from other subjects. In this way, analysis accommodated the emergence of new themes as well as the consistent exploration of already established areas of study. The twelve case profiles reflect this process of attention to all themes.

While the individual case analysis focused on the subject's own words and feelings, in order to compare and contrast subjects, names of themes were identified – often using subjects' shared language. Subjects were categorized according to those themes in tables. This move toward categorization is an important methodological step that facilitates cross-case comparison and is useful in identifying groupings of subjects (Miles and Huberman, 1984).

Clearly, the identification of themes within complex and multi-faceted interview material relies heavily on that which strikes the particular reader. The themes I consider important relate to my personal and theoretical interests but also reflect themes that were surprising to me. The diversity of the twelve mothers' thoughts, feelings, and modes of expression give this research its richness and complexity. In addition, second raters of reference measures and colleagues who read interviews and case studies extended my attempts to make meaning out of the interviews.

Organization of case summary

In order to allow for comparison of subjects, each case description is organized around a standard format that grows out of the research and defines the location of various themes. It must be noted that, by adhering to a system of presentation, these case studies are less literary and less lively than they would be if topics were introduced in a fashion suited to each individual subject. However, this standardization contributes to the ability to make interconnections among subjects. The standard format is as follows.

1 *Introduction.* Brief statements of: family of origin, marital and work history, transition to parenthood, child rearing arrangements, and tone of interview.

2 *Object relations*. Analysis of material concerning the subject's ideas and feelings about: mother, father, good mother, husband, child.

3 *Relationality*. Analysis of material concerning the subject's experiences of connectedness, separation, independence, giving and getting care and recognition, neediness.

4 *Traditionality*. Analysis of material concerning how the subject described a traditional woman and experienced herself in relation to that tradition. Included here were the subject's view of social history, current lifestyles, presence and absence of social supports, and maternal values. Also included here was material relating to the image of the self-sacrificing, caring, full time mother[1] that has been prominent in American culture and has been shared by many women. This image of the mother often includes absence of impulsivity. Material related to impulsivity was included in this section because the mother in this image was not supposed to be angry or aggressive (Rapoport *et al.*, 1980; Rich, 1986/1976), wildly playful or sexual (Weisskopf, 1980).

Finally, numerous socio-historical analyses (Bernstein, 1975; Lasch, 1979; Shorter, 1975) suggest that the public–private distinction made by Chodorow and others reflects a traditional arrangement that has been superseded by a more modern breaking down of distinctions between work and home, men and women, and adults and children. In order to explore traditionality, material related to such distinctions was included in this domain.

Analysis of reference measures

Object relations: Assessment of Qualitative and Structural Dimensions of Object Representations (AQSDOR)

This scale was used to code interview material and to explore areas of similarity and difference among a subject's representations of her mother, father, husband, and child. The scale was designed to assess the qualitative and structural dimensions of object representations in spontaneous, written descriptions of parents and, according to its authors, is useful in coding lengthier interview descriptions of spouses and children (Blatt *et al.*, 1981).

Representations of mother, father, husband, and child were coded on a seven-point scale in terms of the subject's view of the object on thirteen dimensions. Scores of 1, 2, 3 indicate little presence of the quality or presence of its opposite. Scores of 5, 6, 7 indicate substantial presence of the quality. Based on the 1981 scoring system, a score of 4 indicates that the dimension was uncodable owing to lack of material. Following Blatt *et al.* (1981) the dimensions are organized according to two factors: nurturance and striving.

31

Factor I – Nurturance
  Nurturant: giving care with no strings attached
  Positive ideal: object of admiration or respect
  Benevolent: benevolent intent or effect on others
  Warm: ability to make others feel loved
  Constructive involvement: responsive to the subject's own interests
  Affectionate: physical expression of affection
  Strong: stability, ability to endure or resist
  Successful: subject sees individual as happy and successful

Factor II – Striving
  Judgmental: judgmental and critical
  Ambitious: driving of self and/or others
  Punitive: inflicts pain or loss as retribution
  Intellectual: rational, intellectual
  Successful: subject sees individual as happy and successful
  Strong: stability, ability to endure or resist

The AQSDOR scale includes two additional codings:
  Degree of ambivalence. A score of 1 indicates no mixed feelings about the person; 2 indicates moderate mixed feelings; 3 indicates very mixed feelings.
  Conceptual level. The extent of differentiation and integration of behavior and feelings within the representation. Levels are as follows:[2]

1 *Sensorimotor-preoperational*: little sense that the person is a separate entity; emphasis is on value of person for the subject;
3 *Concrete-perceptual*: person is defined as a separate entity but primarily in terms of satisfying the subject's needs;
5 *External iconic*: person is defined as a separate entity but primarily in terms of behaviors;
7 *Internal iconic*: person is defined as a separate entity but primarily in terms of thoughts and feelings;
9 *Conceptual representational*: person is defined as separate entity in a way that integrates his/her thoughts, feelings, and behaviors.

Interview material was coded by me and independently by a second rater who was blind to all characteristics of the subjects and blind to the purposes of the study. We trained on two of the twelve interviews and on pilot interview material. Following Blatt *et al.*, degree of reliability was assessed for each dimension across ten of the twelve cases and expressed as degree of agreement for each classification, calculated by the Pearson product moment correlation. After reliability assessment, we resolved our differences.

Blatt *et al.* present interrater reliability coefficients ranging from 0.45 to

0.92. The intercorrelations in the present study showed a comparable range, from 0.47 to 0.96. Table 2.2 displays intercorrelations from both studies.

Table 2.2 Assessment of Qualitative and Structural Dimensions of Object Representations: intercorrelation of judges' ratings

Item	Present study	Blatt et al. expert and trained rater
Affectionate	0.86	0.45
Ambitious	0.75	0.72
Benevolent	0.83	0.77
Cold–warm	0.71	0.92
Constructive involvement	0.83	0.57
Intellectual	0.88	0.81
Judgmental	0.91	0.82
Negative–positive ideal	0.96	0.87
Nurturant	0.77	0.80
Punitive	0.65	0.60
Successful	0.75	0.90
Weak–strong	0.78	0.79
Ambivalence	0.47	0.41
Conceptual level	0.86	0.88

Relationality: Attanucci coding of Gilligan dilemma

Carol Gilligan reviewed some interview material and suggested that responses to the Gilligan dilemma be coded by a scheme developed by Jane Attanucci (1984, 1988) in her study of mothers' perspectives on self and role. The scheme involves four categories.

Category I: self instrumental to others, others instrumental to the self. Women use the reciprocal language of roles to describe themselves and their relationships. People are not differentiated from roles and roles are understood to be in balance.

Category II: self instrumental to others, woman sees others in their own terms. As in Gilligan's Conventional Stage II, the woman 'respond[s] to the other in the other's terms, subordinating [her]self to the needs and demands of others' (Attanucci, 1984, p.102). In her attempts to be helpful to another, she may be uncertain about how to proceed.

Category III: self in self's terms, other instrumental to the self. The woman looks for self-fulfillment regardless of her effect on others; she often seeks to dominate and sounds uncompromising and self-assured.

Category IV: self in self's terms, other in their own terms. An 'authentic'

relationship between self and other, involving dialogue and consideration of each other's terms.

In Attanucci's analysis, Category IV indicates connectedness to others. Categories II and III reflect positions of inadequate connection, of inability to reconcile or acknowledge the terms of both self and other. Subjects may vacillate between the two positions, unable to be responsive to the other and to the self simultaneously. Category I indicates an inadequate connection that is based on roles rather than interpersonal relationships.

The validity of Attanucci's coding system receives support by the extent to which her codings agree with assessments of separateness and connectedness on the Scheme for Coding Considerations of Response (relationality) and Rights (separateness) developed by Gilligan *et al.* (1982) ($\chi = 11.52$, df = 2, $p \leq 0.003$). Attanucci reports an intercoder reliability proportion of exact agreement on ten cases ranging between 75 per cent and 90 per cent, depending on the other to whom self was related. Using Cohen's Kappa statistic to report the proportion of agreement after chance agreement has been removed from consideration, Attanucci reports probability levels ranging between 0.001 and 0.008.

Following Attanucci's method, each case was read and units of evidence identified that included a statement that referred to both self and other and any surrounding material. A second rater blind to all other information about these subjects reviewed this material. Units of evidence were agreed upon before coding began, were independently scored, and labelled in terms of self and particular other. After training on four cases, reliability assessment was based on the remaining eight cases. Percentage of exact agreement between raters on the fifty scorable units was 86 per cent. Percentage of exact agreement by types of self-description are displayed below.

Types of self description	Number of units	Percentage agreement
Self in relation to child	35	80
Self in relation to experts	6	100
Self in relation to others	11	90

After reliability assessment, differences were resolved.

Traditionality: Newberger dilemma

Newberger's (1977) coding scheme elaborates on particular aspects of conventional and non-conventional thinking. There is a progression as parent–child relationships become emotionally complex, interpersonal exchanges. The levels can be summarized as follows.

Level 1: egoistic conceptions. Child and parent are known by their actions with the child's intentions inferred as 'projections of parent's experience.' The parent–child relationship is conceived in terms of 'what each does for the other' with conflict resolved with the needs of either parent or child predominating.

Level 2: conventional conceptions. The parent's understanding of the child comes from cultural definitions of children's feelings; the individual child is not distinguished. The relationship is understood as a 'two way exchange of roles' with emphasis on fairness and satisfying terms of 'externally defined responsibility.'

Level 3: subjective–individualistic conceptions. Each child is seen as unique and having a 'psychological layer underlying action.' The parent–child relationship is seen as a unique emotional exchange in which feelings are shared and addressed.

Level 4: analytic conceptions. The child is understood to have deep psychological layers with sometimes conflicting forces and processes which cannot always be controlled or resolved. The parent–child relationship is seen as 'mutual' but one in which both parent and child grow.

According to Newberger, responses to the Newberger working mother dilemma usually focus on two issues – resolving conflict and meeting needs – but may also include attention to other issues. The dilemma was coded according to Newberger's scale. A second rater who was blind to all characteristics of the subjects and blind to the purposes of the study also coded the material. After training on the first six cases, reliability assessment was based on the remaining six cases and expressed as the degree of agreement for each scoring within each case, calculated by the Pearson product moment correlation. After the reliability assessment was completed, differences were resolved. Newberger indicates an interrater reliability coefficient of 0.96. The interrater reliability coefficient in the present study was 0.87.

Thematic Apperception Test

Transcribed stories were given to a clinical psychologist, skilled in TAT analysis, who knew subjects were adult women but was blind to characteristics of the subjects and to the purposes of the study. Subjects' stories were analyzed individually and then an overall assessment of each subject was made. The clinical analyses are quoted in the case summaries and are organized into the following categories.

Import. The precise rendition of the statement made by the story, presumed to reflect the outlook of the subject generalized to other such relationships.

Conflicts. Story content was used to analyze: (1) overt statements of conflict; (2) ineffective solutions to the story which suggested a compromise between conflicting positions; (3) use of two characters who were interpreted as two facets of the same person. When the form of a story indicated some deterioration around an issue, that issue was seen to present anxiety.

Internal representations. Representations were based on generalization from particular characters to the category of character and included subjects' descriptive adjectives and inferences based on the way characters behaved.

Quality of relations. Attention was given to whether the subject showed empathy with characters and whether characters engaged in dialogue, expressed affection, were physically close to each other, or showed insights into the motivations and behaviors of other characters. In addition, analysis considered whether the interaction was neurotic: did characters have a neurotic mode that restricted the quality of relations?

Overall impressions. Included conflicts mentioned in more than one story and style of defense reflected in what happened when an issue arose. Impulse control was examined by looking at whether there was impulsive acting out in stories, what defenses were used, and whether they were effective in modulating impulsivity. Impressions were listed in order of their certainty. Those mentioned first were particularly clear; those mentioned later relied on clinical judgment and inference.

Within-subject comparison of measures

This final section of the case summary considers what can be learned about the subject from examining both the case study and measures. Particular emphasis was given to what new material the reference measures added to the case study analysis. Where discrepancies existed between measures or between measures and the case study, these differences were explored. The purpose here was to make sense of the subject, and to reconcile these elements of the analysis without assuming that the person under study had to be consistent and without conflicts. In fact, discrepancies often highlighted conflicts and led to some final comments modifying the case study analysis.

CROSS-CASE ANALYSIS

The cross-case analysis moves from individual subjects to a comparison of subjects. Object relations, relationality, and traditionality were reviewed across subjects in order better to understand individuals and identify groupings of subjects, as well as to analyze theories and suggest areas for further study. Before grouping together Children's Center and non-Children's Center mothers, or mothers of boys and mothers of girls, an analysis of any prominent subgroup differences was carried out.

3

INDIVIDUAL PROFILES OF SUBJECTS

The individual profiles of the twelve subjects are presented in this chapter. In order to protect the identities of the subjects, all names have been changed and occupations modified slightly. Background information concerning family, work, and marital history and age has been unchanged. Individual profiles of mothers of girls are presented first, followed by individual profiles of mothers of boys. The main points of each case are presented in Table 3.1, Individual profile summaries: mothers of girls, and Table 3.2, Individual profile summaries: mothers of boys.

Table 3.1 Individual profile summaries: mothers of girls, part 1 (Susan, Myra, Sharon)

	SUSAN	MYRA	SHARON
MOTHER	• Supportive, caring, involved; a playmate. • Guider and rewarder; holds back her anger. • Needs to be good, wants Susan to be strong and approving.	• Symbiotic, intrusive, judgmental, controlling, perfectionist. • Depressed, inadequate homemaker, a dependent child. • Fearful, histrionic.	• Nurturant, wise model. • An opening ear; non-judgmental in her love. • Expressed anger easily. • Fearful; life is one dangerous thing after another.
FATHER	• Calm and giving but secondary, breadwinner. • Proud, approving.	• Reasonable, understanding. • Depressed, unable to impose his will, little boy in man's world. • Histrionic, fearful.	• Rarely mentioned. • Something of a nurturer, more loving with Greta, but over-protective, picky. • Undependable, played out anger, invested in Sharon's career. • Dependable for serious problems.

	SUSAN	MYRA	SHARON
GOOD MOTHER	• Spends time, talks, listens. • Own mother – but feels under pressure to act like her. • Bad mother – bothered, does not guide or uphold traditions.	• Adequate homemaker who brings life into home; law for her children. • Gets child to leave so she can care for herself and not humiliate unsatisfying child.	• Her own mother. • Available, especially for problems, questions. • Rolls with the punches not bothered by unavoidable. • Bad mother – abusive, not bad person.
HUSBAND	• Liberated, involved. • Interchangeable, but Susan more important parent; Jake man of the house. • Jealousy, dyads denied.	• Like Myra, comes from difficult family; both got lives together in marriage. • Needed a child more, gives over to child, focuses more on her than on wife. • Needs an authority figure.	• Different from Sharon. More physical play, teaching. • Less nurturant, relational. • Supportive of Sharon's career issues, not helpful enough with Greta. • Like father, solver of ultimate problems.
DAUGHTER	• So like Susan that she is re-living self and mother. • Good, sweet, nurturant, including, pleasing. • Devious and sly. Not demanding, confronting.	• Stranger to Myra, matched to husband, source of female competition. • Optimistic, easy to love, source of visceral pleasure. • Unbearably demanding, Myra must leave, but admires her power.	• Like Sharon loves attention, togetherness, also fearful. Has father's way with people, play. • Loving, bright, purposive, busy. Subsophisticated, demanding, and provocative.
RELATIONALITY	• Giving, loving, accepting. • Positive feelings – can't be weak, demanding, angry. • Lacks real engagement. • Separation, difference, and conflicts problematic, strangers dangerous.	• Focused on family, needs recognition of her adulthood. • Speaks of own needs and child's as a battle not mutuality, puts self aside, feels obliterated. • Satisfaction depends on power to demand compliance.	• Nurturant without depletion. Feels supported by women. • Conflict is avoided and detracts from relationships. • Independence but not separation; seeks familiar objects in world filled with dangerous spaces.

	SUSAN	MYRA	SHARON
TRADITIONALITY	• Gradual generational progress and connection. • Likes work and parenting, shifts from serious to playful, childlike. • Denies anger, aggression.	• Values traditional woman's competence, power. • Adequacy depends on same skills inside and outside the home. • Multiple mothering good. • Imposer of standards, not playful, values sexuality.	• 1980s – have conflicting choices but possibility of balance between work and family. • Women seen as relational, both sexes as masterful, powerful. • Not authoritarian, explains rules. • Enjoys Greta's provocations, does not see her as aggressive. • Love affair with daughter, not husband.

Table 3.1 Individual profile summaries: mothers of girls, part 2 (Linda, Lauren, Anna)

	LINDA	LAUREN	ANNA
MOTHER	• Role model for intimate relationships. • Judgmental, unaccepting, misreading woman, could not establish her own values and could only respond to achievements.	• Not encouraging, supportive, or accepting. • Invested in propriety, opinionated, can't hear other's wants and needs. • Had something to do with Lauren turning out so well.	• Wants to see mother as good, loving, accepting, relaxed. • Suffocating and isolated. • Frustrated as a wife but could not express anger.
FATHER	• Compassionate, generous, delighted in his children. • Inarticulate. • Not a model for Linda now (deceased).	• Lauren's real father; same looks and temperament. • Wonderful, smart, can step back, be fair and responsive. • Wanted Lauren to be happy. • Not tender.	• Not good at opening up or being close to people. • Angry one who used conventions to control against disruption. • Encouraged physical daring.

	LINDA	LAUREN	ANNA
GOOD MOTHER	• Accepts, enjoys, but not overly invested in child. • Breastfeeding – circle that makes mother feel good. • Bad mother depends on and directs child to do things that fulfill the mother.	• Loving, caring, disciplining; able to step back calmly. • Teaches autonomy. • Selflessly spends time on teaching child. • Bad mother is impatient, not calm.	• All-giving looks good to Anna; becomes irritating to child. • Nursing – model of generous mother caring for all children. • Bad mother is suffocating or ignoring; says one thing to control kids, does another.
HUSBAND	• Nurturant, supportive, establishes good values; better mother than her own. • Child detracts from marriage, extends sense of husband as good, playful, responsible.	• Makes Lauren feel loved, happy, secure. Fulfills fantasy. • Aggressive, independent, strong-willed, athletic. • Wanted Lauren not to work. • Less responsible and more playful parent.	• Shares Anna's values; insightful, but not motherly boy. • Sees Anna as devious, manipulative. • Burdened by being breadwinner, feels uncared for.
DAUGHTER	• Separate, beautiful, demanding; must be shunted off at times. • Bright, humorous conversor, someone to be silly with. • Totally accepting of Linda.	• Responsive, caring, rounds Lauren. • Takes from, makes Lauren less a person. • Bright, independent, wilful, active rather than easy. • A friend. • Lauren wants her more confident than self, to nurture her.	• Confident, strong, in charge but dependent, needs nursing. • Attuned to parents' wants; emotions between mother and daughter matched as are female bodies. • Verbal, enjoys being out, and treated like a grown-up.
RELATIONALITY	• Not invested in nurturing but happy closeness, sharing. • Men caring, wise companions. Colleagues kindred spirits. • Uses separation to keep angry and needy feelings to herself to protect others.	• Values getting more than giving. • Values selflessness but needs demanding child to go away. • Values independence from what others think. • Has close friends, but feels unclose.	• Relationships as either close or far away. Hold daughter close. • Likes being by herself. • Says she is giving but speaks of taking in, receiving care from other women.

	LINDA	*LAUREN*	*ANNA*
	• Separates from traditional. Values career, competence, life all of a piece. • Interested in physicality, silliness, no clinging. • Likes levelling when angry, but her rage can become violent.	• Former career woman now unlike working mothers, who don't know their kids, and traditional wives, who take care of husbands and houses. • Values achievement, glamour. • Acts tough, but avoids confrontations and anger.	• Communal values, feels stodgy, out of sync. • Values freedom, home, must plan time, outings. • Wants smooth relationships – controls, manipulates. • Takes pleasure in symbiotic relationships.

Table 3.2 Individual profile summaries: mothers of boys, art 1 (Julia, Denise, Harriet)

	JULIA	*DENISE*	*HARRIET*
MOTHER	• Attentive, question answerer with valuable aggressive stance. • Self-centered. • Invested in propriety, but her control could be subverted. • Fearful and threatening.	• Goodness unclear, hard to reproduce. • Tenacious, disapproving. • Unhappy, task oriented, unable to enjoy her kids.	• Loving and supportive, but overbearing, needed to be there, help with everything. • Took charge at home.
FATHER	• Loving, gentle, tolerant, fence mender. • Interested in people's own interests. • Overly protective, not assertive or ambitious.	• Delights in young children, then abandons them, becomes judgmental. • Socially lacking, guarded, with little self-esteem.	• Loving, liked being with his family. • Stubborn, holds things in, lets them build up. Harriet feels she is like him.
GOOD MOTHER	• As in all relationships, honesty crucial; mother must be truthful about her needs. But child can obliterate mother's needs. • Bad mother gets child to comply with her projections.	• Paradigmatic relationship, with mother accepting but needing separate existence and not overly connected to child. • Bad mother suspicious, cannot delight in child.	• There for child without being overbearing. • Can put a smile on a child's face. • Bad mother never around, ships children off.

	JULIA	DENISE	HARRIET
HUSBAND	• Patriarch, deeply loving; shares wife's values but is demanding, non-nurturant. • Unhappy, deeply needy.	• Romantic, with infantile desire for closeness, feels displaced by child. • Not presented as father. • Honorable, powerful, rigid, struggling with difficult history.	• So like Harriet that it's scary, both even keeled, family-oriented. • Understanding, supportive, dependable.
SON	• Uniquely loving, knows and responds to Julia. • Gives as good as he gets. • Bright, insistent, powerful, quick-tempered child who cannot be bribed and can shut his mother out.	• Bright, determined, empathic like father and mother; more like Denise. • Adored source of unqualified love and proof of Denise's goodness. • Not all good: overly separate and aggressive.	• Like Harriet and husband; fit in well; not different. • Lovable, cute guy, funny, easy-going personality. • Gives Harriet positive feedback. • Overly apprehensive, bothersome, and frustrated.
RELATIONALITY	• Invested in caring for difficult people. • Shuts others out for calm sensuous, connection to Max. • Separation associated with rejection, with lack of connection. • Self-involved, self-caring.	• Responsive, caring, empathic, wants closeness with women feels lonely and judged. • Men – sexualized, ambivalent. • Feels bad seed, damages people by being authentic – critical and unentertaining.	• Enjoys togetherness; flat lack of engagement. Needs others to feel better. • Not sure she is available or effective with child. • Separation a relief from feeling tied down.
TRADITIONALITY	• Devoted to child and husband but sees the traditional woman as dull hag. • Mired down in norms, demands. • Associates impulsivity and outcome; is serious. • Sensuousness intense, pregenital quality.	• Emphasizes maternal pleasure, beauty; criticizes social but unable to reject society; wants to be *Cosmopolitan* woman. • Child's companion, not teacher, limit-setter. Unsure whether likes routine or adventure.	• Identifies with full time mothers, but motherhood diminishes self; feels old, overburdened. • Cannot leave son; damages will show up later. • Anger is dangerous; she is humorous and somewhat playful.

Table 3.2 Individual profile summaries: mothers of boys, part 2 (Karen, Ellen, Kathryn)

	KAREN	ELLEN	KATHRYN
MOTHER	• Superficial, didn't recognize deep emotional or physical needs, or talents. • Loving, affectionate, • Task-oriented, sometimes did too much for family, never played.	• No intimate conversation, arguments or questioning. • Reinforced Ellen's being nice, constricted girl. • Admirable, hardworking, still learning, discovered feminism, became independent.	• Empathic, excited, genius with small children. • Associated with regression, insecurity, demand, lack of understanding, babbling.
FATHER	• Patient, treated his children as special; nurtured their interests. • Liberal, non-disciplinarian with conservative ideas about women's place in home.	• Accepted all people including disenfranchised. • Never forgot where he came from. • Had drinking problem and difficulties accepting his own advancement.	• Understands Kathryn and her life, shares similar career. • Emotionally remote.
GOOD MOTHER	• Selfless. Child comes first, but mother has own interests. • Her own parents' standard. • Bad mother is not interested in children.	• Can work but must adjust her life to be with her child. • Encourages children to say what they are feeling.	• God-like, able to anticipate and respond to child's needs without being needy herself.
HUSBAND	• Older, wise, leadership figure; advocate of in-depth relationships. • Involved in caretaking but lesser parent. Impatient and inexperienced; child's loving pal.	• Supportive, helpful, involved. • More strong-willed, secure, and interested in ideas. Less in questioning values. • Think and act the same as parents. • Triadic togetherness; but less time for marital closeness.	• Best friend, a companion who shares career, interests, and parenting. • Not presented as giving or needing support or in terms of sexuality.

	KAREN	ELLEN	KATHRYN
SON	• Mama's boy. Shy, easily frustrated, warm, humorous, like Karen. • Makes her cuddly, confident, wild, and bountiful home base. • Provocative, chipper, there are power struggles but cooperative.	• Wants him to be unlike her, to be exploring, expressive, unconstricted. • Is strong-willed, secure, independent. Otherwise, Ellen tentative about him.	• Resembles parents, goes beyond them in giftedness. Bright, charming, verbal. • Powerful guide and negotiator. • Both playful child and adult.
RELATIONALITY	• Likes caring, responsible connection; feels awkward, superficial, unresponsive. • Wants child to be responsive. Cuts him off when demanding. • Separation implies rejection. • Maturity equals responsibility for others.	• Closeness, mutuality, togetherness, sharing. Relationships require work. • Nurturant to colleagues but cannot give endlessly, unsure what she gives son. • Feels too insecure to take a stand.	• Connections with admired men; likes cheerful relationships; sees danger in own needs, anger. Negotiation helps connection. • Likes sameness or defined, organizational differences. • Separation is a problem.
TRADITIONALITY	• Equal rights and special maternal position. • Freedom of expression for her son, Alex, but must contain self. Anger equals loss of control. • Enjoys play, being a wild woman, but not good at it.	• Feminist, but more the full time parent than her husband. • Tradition equals over-niceness. • Wants child to have freedom but subjected to his power and to expert opinion. • Avoids disagreement, rage, speaking of pleasure.	• No bond with traditional woman; prefers to think of present. • Likes male–female similarity, but sees women as more realistic. • Likes combining work, motherhood; uses similar skills in both. • Makes adult–child distinction.

INDIVIDUAL PROFILE: SUSAN

Case summary

Susan is a thirty-two-year-old Jewish woman who grew up in Brooklyn with her eastern European immigrant parents and her younger brother. Susan describes her family as quite poor; her father was a salesman and her mother began part time office work when Susan was in junior high school. Susan has an M.A. degree in finance and is the business manager of a college. She met her husband, 'Jake,' in college; he has an M.B.A. and works for a city agency. Susan and Jake looked forward to having children. Pregnancy and birth were described as wonderful experiences. Susan took a three-month maternity leave.

'Ronda' was twenty-three months old at the time of the first interview, twenty-seven months at the time of the second. Susan and Jake take Ronda to a weekly evening gym program. The family has a live-in housekeeper.

Susan comes to each interview on her way home from work, wearing sexy, flattering business suits. She seems to welcome the opportunity to get together. She is interested in participating in this study and arrives promptly with coffee cake in hand and ready to focus on the interviews. I get the sense that she has shared her story before but is intent on having her situation – career woman deeply invested in motherhood – heard. Susan presents herself as a very warm, energetic, and gutsy woman. It is my sense that this is a familiar stance for Susan. Not only does she want me to like her – which I do – but I feel Susan needs to be strong rather than conflicted or uncomfortable.

Object relations

MOTHER Susan's presentation is characterized by a balanced but extremely positive sense of her mother. She made domestic activities into 'sharing situations,' played with Susan, and was actively involved in her extracurricular activities. She recognized Susan's talent as a swimmer and even swam laps with her.

Susan feels she was 'brought up to be good', but presents her mother as appropriately supportive rather than judgmental.

And if there was something. I would tell her the truth and she wouldn't yell if it was something bad. She'd try to, she'd hold back. And we'd discuss things. And she didn't make me as scared of things as she was.

Susan never expresses concern about this 'holding back' or indicates that she got negative messages from her mother. When Susan was doing something she shouldn't be doing, she would get 'the look' from her mother and then would correct herself. 'Right after, I would get the smile afterwards. So I got the reward. I got the warning and I got the reward.'

Susan describes her mother as fearful, concerned about losing the approval of others, and 'resenting' her own 'compelling need to be good.' Goodness here is defined in terms of femininity and typified by acting as a nurturant hostess and advisor. Resenting the need to be good and regretting not being better, as a child Susan's mother was called 'holy Leona' by the parents who sought her advice. Her mother now seeks Susan's advice and depends on her to be the calmer, more confident, wiser partner in this dyad. Susan wants to be nurturant without repeating her mother's regrets, resentments, and anxieties. The struggle in this mother–daughter relationship is openly discussed in the interview and palpable in comments like, 'You know what it's like to be holy Leona, don't put the burden on me.'

FATHER Although Susan speaks of her mother, husband, and friends often, she rarely speaks of her father, never describes his feelings or conversations with him, and never presents him as involved in struggles with her mother. Although he is described warmly, as the 'calm one' and as a giving person, Susan never relates her own calmness to his. He is distinguished as the 'breadwinner' who had little time or money to share with his family. Susan emphasizes that he was an officer in the local 'Y' and was proud of his children. He would come over to Susan while she was a lifeguard.

> It got to the point where it got embarrassing at times. But very, very proud. But as much as it was embarrassing, it was nice. You knew you did really good. And I want to instill that in my daughter and everybody. That they are really doing good.

GOOD MOTHER Susan characterizes the good mother as one who 'spends a lot of time with her children, who can talk to their children, who can most importantly *listen* to her children.' Susan goes on to say, 'I think I had a good mother' and indicates that her friends convinced her that her mother was special. The lack of conviction about her mother's goodness is interesting and seems to relate to a feeling that her mother was too dependent and anxious to act fully as the Mother. Overall, Susan emphasizes her mother's presence as a model but also, inadvertently, indicates the unrelenting demands of goodness. 'I think I had a good teacher. So I will sit there. And I will listen. And I will talk. And I will spend time. And I think, therefore, because I had a good example, I will be a good mother.'

The bad mother she describes is the mother of a childhood friend who sounds both unconventional and depressed. She drank, did not want to be 'bothered' by her daughter and her friends, did not guide their behavior, and was not actively involved in her child's life.

HUSBAND Susan mentions Jake often, presents their relationship as fun-filled and comforting, but focuses on his nurturant behavior rather than on his feelings. Jake is a 'liberated husband' who is 'willing to do his share and he's willing to support me in my career.'

> He's also a friend, a protector [to Ronda]. Um, maybe she doesn't. She comes to me to ask for things a little bit more than him. But if I'm not around she goes and asks the other one. So pretty much the same. But certain things that come from me are a little bit more important. But uh, do what I, you know. We're interchangeable.

Susan distinguishes herself from Jake at the same time that she stresses their similarity. Although she is the more important parent, Jake is a very

46

important person. Friends come to visit 'Jake's house;' he is the man of the house purchased with combined incomes.

Parenthood has 'improved the marriage.' While the shared pleasures of parenthood are clear throughout this interview, Susan also raises but denies feelings of exclusion as the two parent–child dyads impact on the threesome. 'Um, I don't think there's any jealousy that Ronda's with Jake and I'm left out. Or Ronda's with me and Jake feels left out. There's none of that that I read about. We don't feel any of that. We're a threesome.'

DAUGHTER Ronda is described as a good, sweet, and nurturant figure who looks and acts so much like Susan did that Susan says 'I feel I am re-liv[ing] myself in her' and also 're-living what my mother did.' Sometimes shocked at now being the mother, Susan experiences first-time behaviors as a repetition of what her own mother did. She runs to get the camera – just like her mother did – when Ronda is pulling all her clothes out of the drawer – just like Susan did as a child. Ronda adds to the maternal connection: 'Ronda makes me do something that makes me feel really like a mother.'

Throughout the interview, Ronda is presented as the all-inclusive caregiver: she feeds her dolls and her parents so that 'no one should be excluded' and makes believe she is putting Susan to bed. Susan associates this nurturance with acting 'grown up' and being good. 'She is a good child. She, she means, she's constantly, she's sharing things. Um, somebody lies down. Mommy too has to lie down. Everybody's gotta do this too.'

Susan never describes Ronda as demanding or bossy. Instead, she is presented as a child who 'loves to please you. And if she knows it makes you happy, then she's thrilled that she's doing it.' Susan never considers that pleasing others might be a source of pressure for her daughter, an unfortunate reproduction of a family pattern. Instead, pleasing adds to Susan's enjoyment of Ronda and relieves her of the burden of disciplining her child. Susan also describes Ronda as 'devious and sly' but seems pleased that the child is indirect rather than confrontational. Susan 'loves the way Ronda reacts trying to be Miss Independence and then, every once in a while, "uh oh, I need mommy."' She never voices concern that as Ronda gets older she might reject Susan's help or resist taking care of her.

Relationality

Susan presents herself as a giving, tolerant, strong, loving person involved in close relationships with family and with the friends who are 'like another family' to her and Jake. Throughout, Susan describes relationships rather than persons and tends to re-enact conversations, especially with women. Interactions are tangible but feelings of closeness, joy, and interdependency seem to overshadow person to person engagement.

In speaking about a best friend, Susan feels that they can 'talk to each other about anything.'

You don't have to be. Uh, you know, 'Will they like me? Won't they like me?' Hey, we've gone through it all together. You really, it's really let your hair down. Don't. You don't have to watch what you say. You can tease each other. Make fun of each other like this and no one gets hurt.

Susan's valuing of close relationships must be seen in the context of her sense of people as potentially hurtful, a concern which parallels her mother's sense of people as disapproving. Susan emphasizes that she was 'afraid' to go to a college where she did not know anyone, a fear still meaningful over a decade later.

While valuing caring, Susan maintains that she is not a martyr like her own mother. She emphasizes – perhaps trying to convince herself – that as a working parent with a good marriage, 'I, I traded, I didn't give up,' 'I can still have what I wanted and not really give up anything.'Speaking of a dramatic change now that she has 'an extra person to love,' Susan allows that worrying about this 'helpless little thing' is a 'big burden.' She immediately continues, 'it doesn't have to be a burden in the bad sense.'

When asked what she gets from her child, Susan's response indicates that asking for care is a loaded issue. Her solution is to see Ronda as giving by nature, not by maternal demand.

She doesn't have to give me anything. I just have this wonderful sense of being able to raise this child and to give her anything that I can. I don't need anything in return. Because just the pride in seeing her develop, seeing her grow into what I think right now, so far, being a loving child. She doesn't *have* to give me anything.

Traditionality

Susan believes that the movement toward combining work and parenthood has involved gradual and progressive changes in women's and men's lives. Men who parent are 'becoming more like a mother. I think they're getting a better understanding, getting more of a closeness.' Women from different generations support and learn from each other. In her view, conflicts exist intergenerationally among women who must 'defend themselves' against each other's lifestyles. The range of options is 'given' by society and, often, mediated by men who define their wives' positions and may resist change. When there is no choice, 'you accept life because that's the way it is.'

Susan is not sure whether or not she is a 'traditional woman of the eighties.' 'Our generation is, you know, pioneer women. And I don't feel like I'm a pioneer. But I am.' Instead of feeling disruption or stress, Susan likes being able to combine work and parenthood. After satisfying but 'mental' discussions about the *Wall Street Journal*, 'I'm ready to talk baby talk in the evening. I want to be a child in the evenings.' For her, 'being with a child you're just having fun. It's physical. Your mind is at ease and you just play.' Susan indicates that she can shift from serious adult interactions to less worrisome and more pleasurable childishness. In only one instance, when she has to send Ronda to bed, does Susan describe herself as an 'older mother' and speak of the position of the mother as involving control and prohibition.

While emphasizing the mother–daughter play so important to her enjoyment of her own mother, Susan never speaks of playing with her husband or with her father. Except for one euphemistic comment about 'sowing your own wild oats' before having chidren, there is no mention of male–female sexuality in this interview.

In addition, there is a denial of aggression and anger and a sense that negative feelings can be 'held back' and unacknowledged. Asked if she has ever been angry as a parent, Susan says, 'I've never ever regretted being a parent, never been angry at all.' While Susan proudly describes herself as 'even keeled' and able to handle most situations, the absence of intense but seemingly unwholesome feelings is striking.

Reference measures

I Object relations: Assessment of Qualitative and Structural Dimensions of Object Representations (AQSDOR)

	Mother	Father	Husband	Daughter
Factor I – Nurturance				
Nurturant	6	6	7	6
Positive ideal	5	5	6	6
Benevolent	6	6	7	7
Cold–Warm	6	5	4*	7
Degree of constructive involvement	3	5	7	6
Affectionate	4	4	4	7
Weak–Strong	2	4	5	5
Successful	2	4	4	4
Factor II – Striving				
Judgmental	2	1	2	4
Ambitious	6	5	4	5
Punitive	4	4	4	4
Intellectual	4	4	4	4
Degree of ambivalence **	2	2	1	1
Successful	2	4	4	4
Weak–Strong	2	4	5	5
Conceptual level ***	9	3	3	5

* 4 = uncodable, inadequate material
** Three-point scale
*** Scored on scale of 1, 3, 5, 7, 9

Despite differences in the quality of the presentations, all four objects are presented as nurturant, benevolent, admirable figures; none is described in terms of punitive or intellectual characteristics. Susan speaks with somewhat more ambivalence when describing her parents than when describing her husband and her daughter. Notably, Susan presents her mother at the highest conceptual level, as a particularly distinct person with her own thoughts and feelings. Ronda is presented as somewhat distinct but with attention to her behaviors rather than to her feelings. In contrast, male figures are less differentiated and presented in terms of how they make Susan feel.

Susan presents her husband and daughter as more nurturant and more able to respond constructively than her parents. Jake is a particularly accepting, nurturant, and responsive figure although she does not mention loving or affectionate characteristics. In contrast, Ronda is presented as extremely warm and affectionate and striving to please and care for Susan. Although Susan's mother is nurturant, accepting, and able to respond constructively, she is weak, unhappy with herself, and so dependent on Susan that she pushes rather than responds to her daughter's needs. Susan does not speak of her father in terms of strength or self-satisfaction but presents him as moderately able to respond constructively.

II Relationality: Attanucci coding of Gilligan dilemma

Types of self-description	Number of responses by level			
	I	II	III	IV
Self in relation to husband	0	1	0	0
Self in relation to daughter	0	2	0	1

Susan describes an incident a few weeks prior to the interview when Ronda had a fever and Susan felt that, instead of acting like a 'nervous mother,' she and Jake should take care of her without a doctor. However, they followed Jake's opinion and took the child to the doctor for an antibiotic (Level II). Susan says that her 'initial reaction was wrong' but quickly adds, 'I never look at myself and say, "you made a right decision or a wrong decision." There are various choices and you just take what's best for you at the time.' Susan also emphasizes her need to protect Ronda from her mother's fears. For 'Ronda to be free, to do her own thing,' Susan feels she must 'worry about her in the privacy of my own mind, in my own room, without her seeing me worry.' This material is scored at Level II because of Susan's presentation of herself as instrumental to the child's needs. She moves to a Level IV response when she focuses on the history of her own fear of doctors and its impact on her response to Ronda. Only at the end of the dilemma does Susan indicate that Ronda had become sick on the night of a much anticipated, romantic anniversary celebration. Instead of discussing her need to be with her husband, Susan speaks only of the importance of responding to Ronda (Level II).

III Traditionality: Newberger dilemma

Issue	Final score
Resolving conflict	3
Subjectivity	3
	3: Global level

Susan's response to the working mother dilemma begins at Level 2, with a call for balance between the needs of the mother and the needs of her child. She quickly moves to a Level 3 concern for identifying and communicating feelings because feelings affect relationships. Susan stresses that the mother will 'resent' the child if she gives up her job, especially because the child will soon be involved in after school activities rather than being at home with her mother. Susan sees the mother's need to work as unambivalent; she has 'mixed feelings' only after her daughter protests. In contrast, Susan's presentation of the daughter's feelings is considerably more complex. While she may at times be 'glad' that her mother is away because 'she's having a good time with her sitter,' the child may also feel 'that she did something wrong that's taking mommy away.' Susan says the mother must respond to this feeling and also explain how the child will benefit from her mother's income. Throughout, Susan relates parts of conversations and emphasizes that mother and daughter both have 'gotta learn to sit down and talk it out and understand that both their happiness is important.'

IV Thematic Apperception Test

Story I, Card 1

The boy is practicing the violin, perhaps because his 'parents want him to.' He is 'not doing a good job,' is 'dreading' going to see his instructor. He is 'frustrated and so he puts it down and that's the end of it.'

Clinical assessment

Import: when you are not good at something, you feel frustrated and quit.

Conflicts: conflicts about performing and meeting standards. The boy feels frustrated and angry over his lack of competence and is fearful of going to his instructor.

Internal representations: boy seen as compliant, angry, frustrated, fearful.

Quality of relations: cannot be inferred directly. There's a suggestion of fear of authority.

Story II, Card 2

A girl is so 'absorbed in her school work' that she is 'oblivious to everything around her.' The other characters may be family members or farm hands; they enjoy their work and 'probably don't understand her world any more than she understands theirs.' The other woman has no interest in schooling.

Clinical assessment

Import: when you don't belong, you don't.

Conflicts: there is a strong sense of alienation and denial of need for others.

Internal representations: young woman seen as oblivious and self-absorbed; other woman seen as oblivious and narrow-minded; man is ignored.

Story III, Card 5

Mother hears children making noise, wants to get the situation 'under control,' avoid complaints from neighbors, and make sure children are 'not destroying the house.' Children are temporarily quiet and then go back to what they were doing and mother has to make another 'appearance.' Story is told in a humorous tone.

Clinical assessment

Import: a mother cannot control her children.

Conflicts: obedience–defiance. There is a power struggle between mother and children. She is unable to put an end to their disruptive behavior, or they ignore her statements and continue after she leaves.

Internal representations: mother seen as ineffectual; children seen as defiant.

Quality of relations: there is a lack of relatedness and a sense that the children are only a burden for the mother.

Story IV, Card 7GF

A woman who is probably a mother is reading to her daughter. The daughter is playing that her doll is her baby and daydreaming about when she will be a 'real mother.' Time spent together reading suggests there is 'warmth' and 'love' between mother and daughter.

Clinical assessment

Import: time spent with one's daughter is a sign of love.

Conflicts: cannot be inferred.

Internal representations: mother seen as loving and warm *in her actions*, not in words or personality; daughter seen as in a 'dream-like state.'

Quality of relations: There is mutual warmth and proof of love. But the time is structured (story reading) and the daughter is in her own fantasy world. Thus, there is no real capacity for closeness and no sign of empathy.

Overall clinical impression

This subject is quite guarded in her responses. Her view of people is superficial and global. The characters in her stories are alienated, distant, self-absorbed, and ineffectual.

The subject may have a great deal of self-doubt and low self-esteem, especially in response to the first and third cards. She may also be quite anxious, since there is plenty of laughter. Her stories either reflect her guardedness or constriction or a deep sense of alienation, lack of empathy or insight, and emotional withdrawal.

There are indications of aggressive impulses as in her reference to children destroying the house but no suggestion of poor impulse control.

Within-subject comparison of measures

The Thematic Apperception Test analysis suggests that Susan is characterized by an unempathic and superficial view of people as well as by alienation, self-doubt, and self-absorption. This analysis is in marked contrast with the case study presentation of Susan as a caring and responsive person and the Newberger scoring which suggests a rather elaborated view of a mother and child relationship in response to the working mother dilemma. The scoring of the Gilligan dilemma indicates that Susan gives evidence of authentic connection at a moment when she is considering feelings that she and her daughter share but, more often, presents herself as instrumental to the needs and opinions of others. Because of the absence of her own terms and of engagement between self and other, scoring suggests that she is caring but not really connected to others.

Interestingly, the TAT stories that give indication of the least amount of interpersonal engagement are those cards suggesting to Susan differences rather than similarities among characters. In the farm scene and the scene showing the woman at the door, Susan does not look for engagement and underlying conflict. After the testing Susan refers to the third card and indicates that her own mother would have been playing with the children rather than acting as the different and more intrusive figure. In the fourth card, mother and daughter are presented as similar; it is here that Susan sees warmth and some sharing of destiny.

Although Susan is invested in close relationships with similar and caring others, as the TAT analysis suggests, these relationships may lack some sense of engagement. Similarity between the figures in the scoring of the Assessment of Qualitative and Structural Dimensions of Object Representations may provide further indication of a somewhat constricted, homogenized sense of relationships.

Susan's desire for safety in connection does not seem to accommodate conflict or difference very well. Within the interview, conflict is only allowed in the closest of relationships, that with her mother, and only when Susan feels most burdened. Although when she does engage in conflict the process is valuable, the indication in the TAT analysis of self-doubt and concern about exclusion suggests that Susan may be likely to abandon rather than fail in efforts to assert herself.

Susan presents herself as a gutsy, caring, and achieving woman and uses modern images of the liberated woman to support the value of this persona. However, the pressure to be good and strong seems to require that Susan 'hold back' feelings of being ineffectual, needy, and aggressive. Susan's response to the Gilligan dilemma is interesting in this regard. Not only do her own needs remain unclear and consistently under the surface, but Susan speaks of having to remain calm and to worry in private. This particular means of coping is also reflected in her desire to be outgoing to cover up her own shyness and in the way she seems pleased that her mother 'holds back' negative feelings. Susan seems to desire that underlying negative feelings will not affect relationships and that relationships can be based on the sharing of positive feelings and responses.

INDIVIDUAL PROFILE: MYRA

Case summary

Myra is a thirty-five-year-old Jewish woman. She is an only child and grew up in the New York metropolitan area. Her father is a salesman and her mother a full time homemaker. Myra has been married to 'Bruce,' a forty-year-old cardiologist, for fifteen years. Myra began doctoral work in educational psychology and left precipitously because of faculty shifts coincident with her pregnancy. At the time of the first interview, she was working in a hospital-based program for retarded adults. She had applied to re-enter a doctoral program in organizational development. At the time of the second interview, she had been rejected from one program, felt very depressed, and was trying to decide whether to shift to work in industry.

Having a child is described as Bruce's idea. Myra does not speak about her pregnancy or childbirth. 'Rissy Anne' was breastfed for three months and was twenty-two months old at the time of the first interview, twenty-eight months at the time of the second. The family has a babysitter four days a week who also takes Rissy to a local toddler program.

Myra came to the first interview in a dress more suited in style to a young girl. In terms of appearance and style – with tone and vocal quality shifting dramatically within and between responses – she seemed both childlike and mature. Myra seemed to approach the interview from at least two vantage points. On the one hand, some questions seemed to be treated as though they were part of the therapy sessions familiar to her and included a good deal of free association. On the other hand, as a student of psychology who would have been working on her own dissertation during our interview period had her own graduate study not been interrupted, Myra valued being a competent interviewee and colleague. She shared information and tried to discern what I was doing and how, or if, she fitted into the research population. Her answers were lengthy, serious, and full. In the interview process, her generosity and her personal struggle to move toward a more satisfying adult position were palpable.

Object relations

MOTHER Myra presents her mother as a 'symbiotic lady' from whom she had trouble separating. Her presentation suggests a highly aggressive relationship rather than one of peaceful merger or positive identification. Myra speaks of her mother as 'depressed,' an 'inadequate homemaker,' a 'child' requiring care rather than a suitable object for identification. Although personally weak, this mother is described as both pushing her daughter and holding her back, as an 'intrusive,' 'judgmental' woman who pressured Myra to meet 'perfectionist' standards but 'injected fear into situations of mastery,' and tried to plan Myra's life and control her impulses.

My mother would treat me like a child. (Mmhmm.) She wasn't *connected* with the person who was maturing inside. (Mmhmm.) Um, you know, 'Children are like this' is what she's like. 'Adolescents are like that.' And I found it terribly insulting to be an adolescent and my mother's you know, 'teenagers are like this and like that' and therefore that's why you have [to be home by midnight]. There was no connection to who I was. And uh, if she left me alone I'd be here by twelve or I'd be there by one. But I wouldn't you know, I was not going to become, you know a mainline drug user. My mother was always, you know, planning my life. As if I was going to be taken over by the devil.

FATHER In contrast, Myra says, her father 'didn't treat me like a child. He had more of a sense of what was going on inside.' Although sympathetic and reasonable, her father is seen by Myra as weak and as 'disappearing completely' rather than intervening when Myra and her mother were engaged in struggles during her adolescence.

Though he has graduate education and he's this, that, and the other, he's still like a little boy in an adult world. He feels very much like an out of, you know, he couldn't control things and things sort of happen. He couldn't seem to be able to control what was happening to him. He was powerless in a sense.

Myra presents her father as powerless rather than dependable. She seems to protect him rather than direct aggression toward him.

GOOD MOTHER The desire to create a more adequate maternal object comes through clearly in Myra's lengthy presentation of the good mother. This Mother is a 'competent homemaker' who can be 'an adult in the adult world' but has the unique female power to 'bring life into the home' and be the 'glue between generations and between members of the family.' She is not particularly child-oriented but benefits the entire family and has needs of her own that can take priority.

When asked to speak more about this Mother, Myra shifts from describing a powerful to a needy mother who, like Myra, is trying to make progress in her career. Myra's good mother is a divorced woman she knows who sends her son to live with his father while she goes to medical school.

If you're truthful with your kids, they understand and they give you, they can give you their sympathy. And you can rely on them for you, you know for your help. You can actually get that from your own kid.

In Myra's discussion, the Mother is not satisfied by the child who understands Her needs and who goes away to help Her and to spare himself the 'humiliation' of being unable to make Her happy.

HUSBAND Myra describes a mutually supportive, long-term marital relationship through which she and Bruce were able to 'get it together as individuals.' In her presentation, this closeness was disrupted by parenthood. Bruce 'needed a child more,' and insisted that Myra become pregnant when his residency was finished even though her doctoral work was far from complete. As Myra sees it, Bruce has a child who 'fits him hand in glove,' 'fits right into his narcissistic image of what a daughter would be like.' He 'gives himself over' to being a child, to what sounds like some kind of primary oneness with his daughter. He is so much the 'playmate' that

Myra feels she has to 'remind him to become the parent again' and, although this is unspoken, to become the husband again.

> I'll have to say at that point, 'Take her into bed. This is it. She needs to go to bed *now*'. Well, he, I actually see him as a father like starting to roam around in the wilderness between the kitchen and the dining room because he [laugh] he doesn't know what to do. He needs to have an authority figure to say it's bedtime.

Here, Myra willingly becomes the authority figure but also feels the loss of the marital dyad and feels exclusion from the father–daughter relationship. DAUGHTER Myra introduces her daughter by saying she is a 'stranger.' For a year she felt that she was 'raising someone else's child' and expected the child's real parents to pick her up. Myra at first saw no resemblance between herself and Rissy other than their shared athleticism. Then, Rissy drew Myra into a relationship. 'She was a stranger to me, but I was drawn to her because she had a nice temperament [pause] she was, she didn't cry and cry and cry, she had a sweet cry. And, and I was curious.' In contrast to Myra's depressed parents and the 'gloom and doom' she expected to reproduce, the 'sparkly bright' Rissy is a surprise. She is a 'confident,' 'basically optimistic person' who 'adds so much enjoyment' and has 'taken me even further away from my childhood.'

While Myra looks to Rissy for 'thrills' and 'excitement' and emphasizes the 'real discontinuity' between her present household and her family of origin, she also speaks of Rissy as 'intrusive and demanding,' characteristics reminiscent of her mother. The child wanting attention is experienced as 'pulling and tearing' at Myra. In addition, while Myra likes Rissy feeling 'good and powerful' when Myra 'gives' her the power to define their play, the two-year-old Rissy also takes control of situations 'when it is not her time.' Speaking of hair combing and food incidents, Myra says 'Damn it, she feels very much in control. She doesn't feel as if she's begging me for anything.'

Myra speaks of needing to get away fom Rissy in aggressive and desperate terms: 'If I had to be with her all the time, I'd be crazy out of my mind.' At times, Myra feels that she is 'dying,' that she 'just cannot be the kid's mother right now' and must 'hand her off' or get away to protect the child and herself. While having a child has brought Myra the possibility of becoming the adequate mother her own mother never was, Rissy is a demanding competitor, a threat to Myra's existence as an adult. She gives Rissy to another woman whom she considers an able substitute for herself, thereby preserving the child and the good maternal presence.

Interestingly, while shared language and patterns of speech increase Myra's connection to her daughter, shared femaleness problematizes their relationship. Although Myra enjoys being imitated, in the second interview she sees Rissy as a source of competition, as 'modeling me sexually' and

57

wanting to 'take her side of the marital dyad.' She feels that whether the child will be treated as a sexual object by her already devoted father is out of her control.

Relationality

Myra often brings family members, experts, and Rissy Anne's babysitter into the interview with her but she never mentions friends. It is as if Myra has no peers. While the lack of discussion of friendships may reflect a rather old-world attention to family, it is also an indication of Myra's ongoing concentration on issues of connectedness, power, and adulthood. These issues are rooted in family relationships and continue to be played out in that domain.

When asked what aspects of non-family relationships make her happy, Myra speaks of the 'core' of aunts and uncles who are 'witness to my life' and who now treat her as an adult rather than a child. 'It's a tremendous compliment to be related to just as another person. I used to be a child.' While Myra values autonomy and mastery and has struggled to get away from her mother, separation continues to be problematic. Myra says she could not leave Rissy until the child had 'the understanding that I existed, even when I was not there. Then I knew she would make it without feeling that abandonment, that terrifying abandonment.' Here it seems that the terror is rooted in the fear of obliteration and the lack of recognition. Myra needs to leave to save herself; yet in her absence she fears her daughter will not know she exists.

Myra speaks of her own needs as well as those of the child. However, instead of articulating a sense of mutuality, Myra's discussion suggests an aggressive, intrusive battle of needs. As she speaks about the parent–child relationship and about her image of the good mother, the fluidity of movement from parent as caretaker to child as caretaker reflects Myra's ongoing neediness and uncertainty about who is the adult, who is the child. Interestingly, while her image of motherhood concerns the child's willingness to leave the Mother who calmly voices her own needs, Myra's family relationships are considerably more aggressive; satisfaction depends on the the power to intrude and demand compliance.

Traditionality

Myra indicates that she has tremendous admiration for what she sees as the traditional woman and, by trying to break down public–private and male–female distinctions, also points to what can be considered a more modern perspective. Throughout, Myra's emphasis is on the homemaker as a powerful, competent, self-respecting adult who makes a major 'contribution' to her home and community. Interestingly, it is Bruce who first articulated the family's need for a homemaker. Both husband and wife believe that Bruce is the chief breadwinner, agree that he does not have time to be at home, and believe that homemaking and work are not mutually exclusive. For Myra, 'parenting is the embodiment of what an adult *is*. And part of being an adult is negotiating in an adult world.' Adequacy, which both her parents lacked, is a bridge between the old, full time mother, and the 'great social change' of women in the workplace.

Because adequacy depends on the same skills at home and at work, it is also the connection between public and private life. It is relevant here that Myra speaks of her desire to 'grow into adulthood wanting to break down the barrier between inside the family and outside the family.' This same barrier is broken by 'multiple mothering.' She speaks of 'sharing child rearing' with Rissy's babysitter and has a great deal of respect for this woman.

Despite her interest in breaking down barriers, Myra speaks of family relations as hierarchical and wants to be in the position of power. Although Myra wishes to be 'tolerant' of Rissy's individuality, she sees childhood as difficult, she 'cannot spare the pain of growing up,' and must impose adult standards – which make her own life easier – on her daughter.

In other ways, Myra tries to encourage the child to experience considerable mastery. In her presentation, mastery is directly associated with impulsivity.

> When she runs up to something and it's not [pause] socially acceptable, like, um, she's about to squeeze all the toothpaste out of the tube, I first tell her it's great, it's wonderful and then when it gets too far I say, 'But look, let's not do it all the way.' But I don't stop her before she gets going.

Myra enjoys her daughter's impulsivity. She also speaks with pride of how, with the help of her therapist and her husband, she has moved beyond her inhibited background and can now easily touch her husband and child and speak about sexuality. Myra has more difficulty initiating play and trying to 'empathize' with and explain things at the child's level. Here, she feels 'cognitively taxed.' Anger is also difficult for Myra. While Myra does not present herself as sweet, even-tempered, or non-aggressive, it is rage that is particularly troubling and unacceptable.

Reference measures

This display of scores indicates that Myra presents her parents at a low conceptual level, concentrating on the way they gratify and frustrate her. Both parents are seen as weak, depressed figures with whom Myra does not wish to identify. In striking contrast, Myra represents her husband and daughter at the highest conceptual level, in terms of integrated repre-

I Object relations: Assessment of Qualitative and Structural Dimensions of Object Representations (AQSDOR)

	Mother	Father	Husband	Daughter
Factor I – Nurturance				
Nurturant	3	5	5	1
Positive ideal	2	3	5	5
Benevolent	2	6	5	5
Cold–Warm	6	5	5	5
Degree of constructive involvement	1	6	3	3
Affectionate	4*	4	6	6
Weak–Strong	1	2	3	7
Successful	4	4	4	6
Factor II – Striving				
Judgmental	7	5	4	4
Ambitious	5	4	6	6
Punitive	4	4	4	5
Intellectual	4	5	6	6
Degree of ambivalence**	1	1	3	3
Successful	4	4	4	6
Weak–Strong	1	2	3	7
Conceptual level***	3	3	9	9

* 4 = uncodable, inadequate material
** Three-point scale
*** Scored on scale of 1, 3, 5, 7, 9

sentations of their own feelings and behaviors as well as of their impact on Myra. While Myra is very ambivalent about both, she also admires them to some extent.

Myra presents her mother as a malevolent, needy woman who is unable to respond to her daughter constructively as a separate, unique individual. She is a depressed, inadequate and yet highly judgmental woman who drives Myra to meet her perfectionist standards. Myra presents her father as similarly weak and depressed but as more rational and more able to care for and respond to Myra. While he is more benevolent, she does not admire him because of his depression and lack of power.

Myra sees her husband in quite positive terms, as an affectionate, fairly nurturant, and admirable figure who has had a rather positive influence on her life. However, like her mother, Bruce has been unable to respond constructively to Myra's own needs. The higher scores on intelligence and ambition reflect qualities that relate to Bruce's career success; Myra appreciates and benefits from this success although these qualities are not directed toward her.

Myra presents her daughter as extremely demanding and unable to recognize Myra's needs. Unlike Myra's parents and husband, the child is presented as having a lot of striving characteristics; she is ambitious, bright, powerful and the only person Myra depicts in successful and punitive terms. Although in some ways admirable, her demands are more stringent.

II Relationality: Attanucci coding of Gilligan dilemma

Types of self-description	Number of responses by level			
	I	II	III	IV
Self in relation to daughter	0	2	6	0
Self in relation to husband	0	2	0	0
Self in relation to others	0	1	0	0

The dilemma Myra presents concerns the issue of when she can 'safely require things' of her daughter, specifically when can she 'force' the child to sit still at dinner. Myra speaks both in terms of social norms, specifically the importance of 'civilizing' the child, and in terms of her own need finally to have a quiet dinner (Level III). Myra describes a particular incident when she forced Rissy to 'comply,' Rissy got 'all full of tantrum,' and her husband and the babysitter were 'mortified and hurt by watching Rissy suffering.' When speaking in relation to these adults, Myra speaks in their terms (Level II), focuses on their attention to the child and how they are being 'killed' by Myra's demands. While Myra is concerned that Rissy looks at her with fear (Level II), she continues to reiterate her interest in the child complying with her own needs (Level III).

> What I need. (Yeah.) That's the problem of being a parent. You have to be, you have to be an adult even when you don't want to be an adult. [sigh] And yeah, that's the loss of my freedom. To be childish when I want. Or demanding when I want to be demanding.

While she shifts her perspective to consider the child's needs and says 'I must put myself aside in her presence' (Level II), the organization of Myra's dilemma suggests that attention to the child takes away from Myra's needs. Although responsive to the opinions of other adults, she experiences conflict with her daughter (Level III).

III Traditionality: Newberger dilemma

Issue	Final score
Resolving conflict	2
Meeting needs	3(2)
Subjectivity	3
	3(2): Global level

Myra's response to the working mother dilemma includes responses at the

61

second and third levels of parental awareness, with the majority of her scores at the more advanced level. Responses at the conventional Level 2 revolve around a generalized view of the child – 'any kid wants to have their mother at home' – and a similarly generalized but less elaborated view of the mother's mixed feelings as 'natural.' Myra resolves the conflict by speaking of the importance of 'compromise' and elaborates a view consistent with Newberger's sense that at the conventional level parents try to redistribute emotional supplies in order that they be perceived as equally shared.

Myra moves to the more advanced subjective–individualistic level by frequently referring to the communication between mother and child. The hypothetical Mrs Stewart (the mother in the Newberger dilemma quoted in the Appendix) can meet her child's needs by speaking about how much she loves and cares for her daughter and how much she is available even if she is not always physically present. Also at Level 3, Myra presents the child as having mixed feelings, including both pride for her mother and feeling that she may be getting second best at times. Myra resolves the dilemma by speaking of the value of 'multiple mothering,' suggesting that the child may miss her mother but 'get things for her personality from her various babysitters that she would never get from her mother.'

IV Thematic Apperception Test

Story I, Card 1

The child is being 'forced' to practice the violin by parents who are 'molding him into something he ought to be.' The son is 'obstreperous' and 'doesn't comply.'

Clinical assessment

Import: when parents overwhelm their son with their own needs, he gets back at them.

Conflicts: obedience–defiance; success–failure.

Internal representations: parents seen as demanding, critical, narcissistic. Son seen as defiant.

Story II, Card 2

The girl is 'misplaced' in the rural setting, feels she belongs in school, and is trying to leave. The other woman may be her mother or sister, is 'aloof and distant,' stays on the farm, but may feel resentment toward the one who is different and who leaves. The man is busy working and is well placed.

Clinical assessment

Import: a woman should actualize her ambitions.

Conflicts: belonging–alienation; mind–body; autonomy; identity.

Internal representations: woman is seen as distant, aloof or conflicted. Men seen as down-to-earth, constricted, content.

Story III, Card 5

'Matronly' but somewhat sensuous, 'invasive' woman 'intrudes' in room without knocking, delivers a message, and gets 'compliance.' No indication is given of what is going on in room or whether it is 'a child perhaps or another adult.'

Clinical assessment

Import: a woman can control others.

Conflicts: control–ineffectuality.

Internal representations: mother seen as intrusive, critical, demanding, controlling, self-entitled, angry.

Story IV, Card 7GF

Mother or housekeeper is reading to daughter. Although child is relaxed and seems close to the mother, she also seems 'distant.' While meeting is not 'forced,' child would rather be playing with her doll; mother is 'leaning in' to the child and trying to keep her attention on what may be a scheduled religion lesson and not a children's story.

Clinical assessment

Import: when a mother is not attuned to her daughter's needs she loses her.

Conflicts: obedience–defiance; separation.

Internal representations: mother seen as rigid, coercive, demanding. Daughter seen as passive–aggressive.

Overall clinical impression

As represented by these stories, the subject appears to be concerned primarily with conflicts over obedience to authority figures. Should she act in overt defiance or resort to passive–aggressive maneuvers? These concerns seem to involve internal representations of a critical, demanding, intrusive and controlling, narcissistic maternal figure.

The subject may feel that her needs are not seen by others. She may have concerns about separation and identity.

Impulses appear to be adequately contained by higher level defense organization.

Within subject comparison of measures

Scores on the Assessment of Qualitative and Structural Dimensions of Object Representations support and extend the case study analysis. The scale highlights the similarity in Myra's representations of her mother and her father. Her father's ability to pay attention to her as a growing individual is central to her considerably more positive sense of him. Her mother's judgmental stance and inability to see her as a separate and developing person are central to Myra's negative representation. The more ambivalent but more positive presentations of her husband and daughter indicate the 'discontinuity' she feels between her family of origin and her present household. However, problematic characteristics of her parents are repeated in the husband who is only marginally able to respond to her as an individual and the daughter who is demanding. Rissy's unique power and success suggest that she has characteristics Myra desires but that Myra feels she uses them to make unbearable demands.

While Myra's response to the hypothetical Newberger dilemma articulates the wished-for, loving mother who can separate from and understand her daughter, Myra's TAT stories reflect the issues of intrusion, control, and separation that are central to the case study and object relations coding. Interestingly, while the Newberger response indicates a consistent focus on the child's feelings and the case study and Gilligan dilemma reflect Myra's attention to her own needs, the TAT stories indicate some shift of focus. While primarily identifying with the child, Myra does consider the parent's feelings of resentment and desire to remain close.

The independent TAT analysis highlights the importance of conflicts over obedience to authority. As in the case study, these authority figures are demanding, critical, intrusive, and unresponsive to the child's needs. The TAT analysis lends support to the idea that Myra has difficulty with anger and raises the possibility of an obstreperous but passive–aggressive response to authority figures. In addition, the analysis highlights the salience of issues of identity and success for Myra, issues recognized but less central to the case study which was focused on motherhood.

The reference measures and case study suggest that Myra is engaged in close relationships with others but, particularly where women are concerned, sees those relationships in terms of a battle of needs. This struggle is reflected in the scoring of the Gilligan dilemma. Attanucci suggests that a mix of scores at Levels II and III indicates a difficulty in connection, a vacillating between the needs of self and others, without, or prior to, being able to integrate these needs at a more advanced level. Myra's distribution of scores suggests a somewhat different picture, one in which a person's position of authority affects the focus of attention. Myra attends to the terms of other adults. However, in conflicts with her daughter, she responds in her own terms. Although the Newberger dilemma indicates the possibility of a satisfied child, the case study, TAT analysis, and AQSDOR scores all suggest the extent to which Myra takes the position of the needy child and feels that Rissy resembles her own intrusive, unresponsive mother. Connection here is both dangerous and necessary for satisfaction.

Scores on the Newberger dilemma indicate Myra's ability to think at the post-conventional, subjective–individualistic level. As in the case study, Myra focuses on the value of women working and sees children as benefiting from multiple mothering. However, while Myra is able to envisage this modern arrangement, she is troubled by conflicts over her own identity. As the case study indicates, she appropriates the modern notion of woman as a competent adult inside and outside the home and also speaks of the strength and value of the traditional woman. However, she cannot move beyond her own history of family relations as hierarchical battlegrounds of needs. Women have the capacity for benign power and for unique contributions as homemakers. However, as mothers and daughters they are horribly demanding.

INDIVIDUAL PROFILE: SHARON

Case summary

Sharon is a thirty-two-year-old Jewish woman who grew up in the New York metropolitan area and is the oldest of three children. Her husband 'Jay' is thirty-eight and a physician involved with public health policy. As planned, 'Greta' was born immediately after Sharon finished law school. A self-described 'hard driven career type,' Sharon expected to take three months off to be with the child before beginning work as an attorney. Sharon cancelled her job plans immediately after Greta was born in order to spend more time with the child. She says she was 'shocked at how much she loved motherhood,' although she describes months of feeling depressed and inadequate before feeling 'in my element' as a mother. After a year, she began part time administrative work for a large charity organization.

Greta was twenty-three months old at the time of the first interview, twenty-eight months at the time of the second. She was enrolled in the university Center for Children two mornings a week and the family has a half time babysitter. Sharon was two months pregnant at the time of the second interview and was included in this study because she was not preoccupied by her relationship to the fetus at this early stage.

I did not interview Sharon the first time. She seemed unwilling to participate in this research project until learning my opinion of her work decision. Although generous about sharing her viewpoint with what she deemed a receptive audience, Sharon placed severe limitations on interview time. She spoke quickly, almost as if she was trying to say all she could in the abbreviated time period. My sense was of a woman who is quite rational, strikingly 'together,' and in control of her emotions. Her answers suggested an absence of struggle, an absence of probing of the contradictions and conflicts she willingly expressed, perhaps because she had shared these thoughts and feelings before. Being interviewed did not seem a meaningful experience for her. She treated me as a temporary listener. I feel she trusted me enough to speak but, except for her time limits, did not ask much of me in return.

Object relations

MOTHER Sharon speaks of an increasingly close relationship with her nurturant mother. Although her mother was a full time homemaker, Sharon feels she is able to provide good advice about being a working mother. Sharon emphasizes her mother's availability and support.

> I mean she was always an opening ear. If I came home from a date at 1 a.m. and I was unhappy, you know, my mother would talk to me. And we'd talk, conference sometimes until three o'clock in the morning. And you know, there was never a time that I tried to communicate that my mother wasn't receptive, and listening and caring.

Sharon sees her mother as 'judgmental in telling us we were doing crazy things' but as 'non-judgmental in her love.' She was able to 'roll with the punches' and deal with anger: 'If she got angry at you, she'd yell and it was over.' 'And I want to be that way with Greta. I want her to know that she can, you know, that I'm always there to listen. And always there to talk. No matter what it is. And that I love her no matter what.'

When asked how she would like to be unlike her mother, Sharon describes her mother as 'phobic.' 'Life for her is one dangerous thing after another. And she made me like that a lot.' Sharon speaks as if her mother's particular fears are foolish and do not detract from her wisdom, nurturance, or dependability. Sharon herself sees the 'world as familiar objects with dangerous spaces in between' rather than as a 'welcoming meadow.' She feels this characteristic is central to her personality. It is also emblematic of Sharon's enduring connection to her mother.

FATHER Sharon rarely mentions her father and speaks about visiting 'my mother's house' as if her father is not there. While Sharon says her father has 'always been something of a nurturer' and says she sees an 'openly loving,' patient, and never angry side of him with Greta, she continues to see him as 'over-protective,' picky, and undependable. In childhood, Sharon says she and her siblings 'were always worried about how daddy would react,' especially because he 'tended to internalize anger and play out a little more.' His lack of support for Sharon is most evident when she speaks bitterly of the way her father was overly invested in her career and 'wrote me off' when she became pregnant.

Despite his inadequacies, Sharon speaks of turning to her father for particularly serious problems, thereby suggesting her father's ability to rise to the occasion when most necessary and, perhaps, when her mother was too fearful to respond.

GOOD MOTHER Sharon's own mother is her model for the good mother. Although her presentation relies on her experience as a child, Sharon puts herself fully in the position of the Mother. She believes that the good mother is there for problems more than fun and argues that 'quality [time] is in quantity' because the child's hurts and questions do not carry over until the weekend. To be dependable, the Mother must 'roll with the punches' and not be bothered by things like children throwing up all over her clothes at a wedding.

> A good mother, I think, doesn't, doesn't let those kinds of things that
> you can't avoid get to her. It's not even that you hide your feelings.
> It's that you don't even, it doesn't even bother you 'cause it's like a,
> you know, like a drop in the bucket compared to the other things.

Sharon does not seem interested in defining the bad mother or criticizing women who organize their lives differently. She is more concerned with making a distinction between Mother and person; a bad, abusive mother is not a bad person.

HUSBAND Sharon mentions her husband often but seems conflicted about whether to present him as a supportive figure or as a secondary, inadequately nurturant male. Although they share numerous hobbies, Jay is decribed as a 'completely different' person and parent. Interestingly, her presentation suggests that he responds in a similar manner to his wife and daughter. He teaches both about the world and is physically playful, 'dragging' Sharon to engage in sports and games and providing a valuable outlet for Greta's playfulness. Although 'less nurturant [than Sharon] in the overall sense,' like Sharon's father Jay is able to solve ultimate problems. As Sharon speaks of how comforting this sense of 'my daddy will do it' is for Greta, she also seems to be speaking about her own feelings. Mother and daughter here are indistinguishable.

Jay is presented as 'completely supportive' of Sharon's need to resolve her own work and parenthood issues and as less surprised than most people when she left her job. 'He knew me better and always saw me as, sort of like being the very nurturing one in our relationship and stuff.' However, Sharon would like Jay to be more involved in child care. 'Rationally or irrationally, I thought that I, I should have more support from my husband.' Sharon devalues her own neediness rather than arguing for co-parenting: 'My husband could probably give me twenty-four hours a day and I wouldn't think I was getting enough.'

DAUGHTER Sharon speaks of Greta as a very loving, verbal, bright, purposive, busy, demanding, and fearful child. All of these characteristics seem to support Sharon's connection with her daughter. Sharon seems comfortable with Greta's resemblance to Jay: she 'has his way with people' and is reserved and a great player like he is.

Most prominently, Sharon presents Greta as sharing her own love of attention and enjoyment of having 'all the people that she loves right around her.' Sharon 'always wanted a hug' and sees her daughter as 'just that way.' She does not find Greta's 'insistence on attention' to be demanding. Instead, Sharon enjoys being put in the caring position.

Sharon has felt most comfortable when Greta could speak and say what she wanted. Sharon could then be the opening ear able to respond to her own daughter. Perhaps because Sharon gets ongoing support from her own mother, she does not seem to look to Greta for care.

Relationality

Sharon presents herself as a nurturant person who is invested in close relationships with others. At the same time, however, she was concerned about becoming a mother, felt that she wouldn't be 'nurturant enough,' suffered from post-partum feelings of tremendous inadequacy, and says that 'Greta brought out more of the nurturance in me.' She says she is not a 'great altruist' but finds motherhood particularly rewarding. This is 'totally irrational in a way. That you want this *demanding*, kind of *clinging* um, sub um subsophisticated [laugh] grimy, sticky person hanging on you all the time and that's your idea of, you know, heaven!'

While recognizing the distinctiveness of the maternal position, Sharon says,

> I'm the same with my daughter as I am with anyone else around me.
> It's the kind of nurturing aspect really of it. Um, with my friends, it's
> the way we can exchange problems in a way. I'll give you yours, you,
> I'll give you mine and you'll give me yours kind of thing. And the way
> in which we can rely on each other for a kind of emotional succor.

While Sharon speaks of what she later calls an 'emotional exchange,' the principle of exchange inadequately represents the confusion about who is giving and naming whose problems. All of Sharon's close relationships are with other women, especially with other mothers. 'Mothers understand, can make you feel a million times better about something.' Sharon emphasizes the 'emotional catharsis' involved in relationships with friends. She can say she wants to 'wring [family members'] necks' to a friend who is not the target of those feelings. These friendships help Sharon avoid direct engagement in conflict and allow her to ventilate and accept frustrating situations. Sharon does not look to relationships to bring her in touch with frustrated desires. Instead, she believes her wants are 'out of the question' and feels that, like other adults, she has lost the sense of 'direct linkage between your needs and gratifications.'

Sharon does not value or enjoy situations of physical separation from loved ones but she does value independence. In one of two references to the new baby, Sharon says that if Greta can do things for herself, she will be less bothered by the sense of 'Who will take care of me?' when the baby is born.

Sharon enjoys seeing Greta as a 'whole separate person, that she's just completely herself,' doing things that she and Jay would never do, and as involved in an unknown children's culture. Sharon never speaks of ways her daughter might conflict with her, of ways in which difference might be threatening rather than interesting.

Traditionality

Sharon locates herself in historical context and says she has been influenced by the full time mother of the fifties and the seventies 'superwoman', who was able to have both a high-powered, non-stop career and a family. Sharon sees the 1980s in terms of a struggle for a more adequate 'balance' between work and family but laments that 'It's not clear at all what the straight and narrow is.' She struggles with the 'cross-pressures' she feels that 'different parts of society have on you at different times.' Sharon does not engage in social critique but focuses on her own need for acceptance and respect. Making choices about work and parenthood breaks connections – with her father and between herself and her women friends.

Sharon believes that women are 'better at relating' than men and more interested in 'expressing emotions.' In addition, she speaks of mastery and power as available to all family members, including the female child. The sense of female power and competence that pervades this interview distinguishes it from the male-dominated, traditional model. Further, Sharon does not present herself as an authoritarian parent. She distinguishes herself as a sixties person into communication.' She does not want to 'exercise parental fiat' but wants Greta to understand that there is 'sense in relationships' and that there are reasons for any rules.

Sharon says she enjoys Greta's attempts to be as provocative as possible, seems to identify with her, and considers how to deter particular actions without 'taking all the joy out of her misbehavior.' In this, the provocative child is impish; aggression and anger are never mentioned. Similarly, Sharon never speaks of fighting with Jay or of anger and conflict as valuable to relationships.

Interestingly, Sharon never speaks of her relationship with Jay in terms of sexuality. The intimacy lost with Greta's presence is the opportunity for conversation. She contrasts her ability to be away from Jay with the 'passionate love affair' she has with her daughter. 'It's just a passionate kind of love. You know. I can't bear to be away from her.'

Reference measures

I Object relations: Assessment of Qualitative and Structural Dimensions of Object Representations (AQSDOR)

	Mother	Father	Husband	Daughter
Factor I – Nurturance				
Nurturant	6	5	3	2
Positive ideal	6	3	5	6
Benevolent	6	3	5	7
Cold–Warm	7	5	5	7
Degree of constructive involvement	7	2	5	3
Affectionate	4*	5	4	6
Weak–Strong	3	5	6	3
Successful	4	4	4	5
Factor II – Striving				
Judgmental	3	5	2	4
Ambitious	4	6	5	5
Punitive	4	5	4	4
Intellectual	5	4	7	5
Degree of ambivalence**	1	3	2	1
Successful	4	4	4	4
Weak–Strong	3	5	6	3
Conceptual level***	5	3	3	7

* 4 = uncodable, inadequate material
** Three-point scale
*** Scored on scale of 1, 3, 5, 7, 9

Sharon's scores indicate more ambivalence toward male figures and less sense of them as distinct people. Her mother and daughter are presented without ambivalence and as separate, although her mother is presented in terms of behavior and only Greta is presented in terms of her own feelings. Sharon presents her mother as a fearful but extremely admirable, nurturant figure who is loving, accepting, wise, and able to respond to Sharon constructively. Sharon's father is presented as a less admirable, somewhat malevolent figure. Although to some extent caring, loving, and strong, he is unable to respond to Sharon's interests, especially in terms of his ambitious investment in her career rather than motherhood.

Jay is presented as a strong, bright man who is able to respond to Sharon constructively. Although benevolent and admirable, Jay is less nurturant and involved in caretaking than Sharon would like. Sharon's presentation of her daughter suggests that she does not expect caretaking from the child. Greta is presented as a very admirable, satisfied, loving and benevolent figure although she takes rather than gives care and has little ability to respond to Sharon constructively.

II Relationality: Attanucci coding of Gilligan dilemma

Types of self-description	Number of responses by level			
	I	II	III	IV
Self in relation to daughter	0	2	0	0

Sharon's concern is how to make the best decisions for Greta; her own needs are never mentioned (Level II). Her dilemma concerns whether to send Greta to camp during the summer, earlier than she 'really thinks is right for her,' or send her to school in September when the baby is born and Greta would 'have a lot of things thrown at her at once.' While this situation revolves around her pregnancy, Sharon immediately says this dilemma is analogous to the decision to enroll Greta in the Children's Center. Sharon saw her daughter as a 'homebody type' who also needed the 'exposure to other children.' In both situations, staying home is 'easier' in the short run but is not necessarily 'better' in the long run.

The correctness of Sharon's decision depends on 'whether Greta seems to end up satisfied and content,' particularly whether 'her adaptation is smooth.' Adaptation here is contrasted with conflict: 'I hate to see her unhappy, I really do. And I hate to see her torn and conflicted and things like that much more strongly than I ever thought I would.' If Greta is content, Sharon says she will 'pat herself on the back even though it probably had nothing to do with what I did at all;' 'if she's unhappy, I'll be beating my breast.'

III Traditionality: Newberger dilemma

Issue	Final score
Resolving conflict	2
Meeting needs	2
Subjectivity	3(2)
	2: Global level

Sharon begins her response to the dilemma by discounting the child's 'every mother' argument as a 'slippery slope that leads you into trouble endlessly' and mystifies mothers' actual behavior. Instead, Sharon believes all four-year-olds need their parents and cannot understand their mothers' need to work. The mother must strike a 'balance' between her own needs and those of the child and protect herself from being 'at the child's beck and call.' Her position is scored at Level 2 because of its emphasis on fairness and generalized sense of the child's needs. Interestingly, although she finds the child's statement of her need to have her mother at home 'reasonable,' she also diminishes this desire; wanting your mother home is no better or worse than 'our desires to marry Paul McCartney.'

Sharon's elaborated sense of the mother's needs and conflicts is scored at Level 3. The mother who works is 'losing out on the best your child has to offer.' Like all people, this hypothetical mother has mixed feelings about working which are exacerbated by conflicting social pressures. At one point, Sharon frames the child's needs in terms of the necessity to absorb the family's values and be 'well integrated' into the household. This resolution via a single perspective and focus on control is scored at Level 1.

IV Thematic Apperception Test

Story I, Card 1

The child taking violin lessons 'drags,' but has 'no choice' but to practice even though he wants to do something else.

Clinical assessment

Import: when you've committed yourself to a task, you have no choice but to complete it.

Conflicts: spontaneity versus commitment.

Internal representations: child seen as mature, able to delay gratification.

Quality of relations: cannot be inferred.

Story II, Card 2

The girl sees farm work as drudgery and isolating, finds school 'mind broadening' and is going to be a teacher. She will send her parents money and visit the farm on weekends. Her parents have worked hard and can use the money.

Clinical assessment

Import: there is no conflict between one's needs to become independent and the needs of one's parents.

Conflicts: none can be derived.

Internal representations: parents seen as hard working and instrumental – thinking of goals and means to achieve them; daughter seen as compliant and cooperative.

Quality of relations: relationships appear conflict-free and cooperative but there is no mention of psychic needs, suggesting somewhat limited, superficial relationships.

Story III, Card 5

The immigrant mother is peeking into a room at her son studying for the baccalaureate. She tells him it is late at night and that he will 'wear himself out' if he keeps 'burning the candle at both ends;' he should get up earlier the next day. He will do 'brilliantly' and the mother will feel 'glad that she supported him.'

Clinical assessment

Import: when you work hard at something, you succeed.

Conflicts: concerns about the price of achievement.

Internal representations: mother seen as supportive, protective, concerned, instrumental; boy seen as ambitious, hard-working, instrumental.

Quality of relations: relationship centers around work and achievement. Mother is concerned with child's well-being but in the context of achievement.

Story IV, Card 7GF

The girl has been rejected by older girls with whom she wants to play. The girl is easily consoled by her mother who points out that this is not a 'crushing blow,' older girls often do this and should be ignored, and that she has a lot of friends her own age. 'They live happily ever after as in all my stories.'

Clinical assessment

Import: one can get over feelings of being rejected.

Conflicts: emotional vulnerability versus maturity. While the child is hurt, the mother sees young age as no reason for vulnerability and she minimizes the child's pain.

Internal representations: daughter seen as vulnerable but strong, mature; mother seen as concerned but unempathic.

Quality of relations: daughter trusts her mother, but mother has little empathy. Mother is more concerned with the outcome of what sounds like good adjustment than with the process of current feelings of hurt.

Overall clinical impression

There is little conflict in this subject's stories. This can be a function of the subject's guardedness – in the TAT or in general – or a reflection of a genuine lack of psychic conflicts.

The main concern of this subject appears to be achievement. There is no indication of serious conflicts over achievement but ambition and instrumental thinking overshadow feelings and interest in people's inner worlds.

It is possible to speculate that the subject's guardedness is a reflection of characterological repression and denial of vulnerability and feelings. Such defenses might be necessary if achievement in the work world is her main priority.

In general, relationships appear to be cooperative – people working together toward a goal. But there are no indications of empathy or interpersonal closeness.

Impulse control appears adequate.

Within-subject comparison of measures

This case is particularly striking because of the extent to which the reference measures conflict with and modify the case study. The most prominent contrast is that between the case study's analysis of Sharon as a relational woman who seems to be identified with her own responsive mother and the Thematic Apperception Test analysis which indicates that achievement seems to be Sharon's main concern. Sharon's early disinterest in full time motherhood, presentation of herself as a 'hard driven career type,' and her months of post-partum inadequacy become more important in the light of this reference measure.

In the light of the TAT analysis, the cross-pressures and lack of understanding Sharon feels may be understood as internal conflicts as well as reflections of social complexity. Sharon suffers from the loss of support from people who formerly admired her. Her own conflicts about working and feelings about the loss of her father's approval and interest have been exacerbated by contradictory social values and complex historical processes.

The reference measures suggest that avoidance of conflict is particularly important to Sharon and detracts from the quality of the interpersonal relationships she presents. Attanucci's notion that connection involves authentic attention to the terms of both self and other is useful here. The dilemma Sharon constructs at the beginning of the second interview is consistently oriented to the child's terms. While the summer will be a time of major transition for Sharon, signalling as it does the last trimester of pregnancy, Sharon never refers to her own needs or feelings about whether Greta is at home during the day. In contrast, in her subsequent response to the hypothetical Newberger dilemma, Sharon speaks in the mother's terms. Both the individual dilemmas and the sequence – concern for child in the Gilligan dilemma followed by concern for the mother in the Newberger dilemma – suggest some lack of interpersonal engagement, an idea supported by the TAT analysis as well.

In the light of these findings, Sharon's case becomes particularly interesting as an example of a woman invested in close, nurturant relationships but who, in order to avoid conflict and vulnerability, speaks of relationships which are in some sense impoverished. It may be that Sharon looks for safety in relationships and that in this sense relationships are instrumental to her feelings of comfort. The good mother's ability to ignore troubling circumstances is, in this context, an unfortunate ideal. Sharon's sense of her mother as scared of everything suggests that their relationship might have been more constricted than she allows. Her father's inability to be a dependable figure may have exacerbated this situation. Relationality here signifies both close connection and a defense against somewhat more dangerous relationships and activities. It is interesting that motherhood was hardly a 'welcoming meadow' at the outset; the maternal position has – and must – become safe and familiar.

INDIVIDUAL PROFILE: LINDA

Case summary

Linda is a forty-two-year-old woman from the Midwest. She has two younger sisters and a younger brother. Her father, a small businessman, died ten years ago. Her mother, a teacher, is still alive. Linda was a college professor for fifteen years and entered student services administration when her daughter was one year old. Her husband of thirteen years, 'Ron,' is a college administrator and a very active parent. In the last two years, Ron and Linda have each taken a one-semester job outside the New York metropolitan area; the other parent has spent weekdays as primary care-taker.

Their daughter 'Elizabeth' was twenty-eight months old at the time of the first interview, thirty-four months at the time of the second. She was enrolled at the university Center for Children.

I did not interview Linda the first time. She was immediately willing to participate in this extended research project and took great pleasure in helping with my study. Linda was both a playful and serious interviewee and enjoyed putting thoughts into carefully crafted language. During the second interview, Linda seemed particularly involved in finding a new way to talk about her relationship with her mother. She enjoyed having an audience but did not seem to expect any input from me.

Object relations

MOTHER At least in part as a result of becoming a parent, Linda says she has been moving 'from anger to acceptance' of her mother. This sense of movement and emphasis on acceptance and connection is clear in her effort to assert a relationship with her mother while attending to both positive and negative aspects of that relationship. Linda sees her mother as a hardworking woman, but also as a 'nagging,' 'restrictive disciplinarian' who tended to 'solve problems for her children.' While Linda says she set 'good priorities' in putting her children first, she sees her mother as so concerned about what other people thought that much of her extensive housecleaning was 'for show' and she could not seem to 'make values about herself properly.' Linda felt that she had to accomplish things to be 'accepted' by her mother. Upon questioning, she allows that she does not remember ever receiving positive feedback and goes on to say '[my mother] never under-stood what was important to me.'

> As a result, instead of telling her and beating my head against a brick wall, uh, I stopped telling her things that were important to me because they would either be confidences that would be broken as far as I could tell. Or, if she couldn't deal with it, she would simply lie and say I never told her something.

Despite these difficulties, Linda feels that women's mothers are the 'only model we've had for those intimate circumstances [like parenthood].' Linda expected to 'muck up' motherhood and to need courses in 'remedial motherhood' because of lack of a model or of advice from her mother and her similarly lacking, childless sisters. It is as Linda becomes comfortable as a parent that the connection to her mother seems to become less problematic. At least in part, this process seems to be occurring during the six-month interview period. In the second interview Linda makes comments like, 'It's good to know that one is connected back, even in ways that one doesn't have control over.'

FATHER Linda says that her father 'delighted' in his children. He sounds more accepting and playful but weaker and less insightful than her mother.

> He was a very, um [pause] generous, compassionate person. Um, not terribly articulate and not terribly insightful about things that he did that helped cause the circumstances he was in. I used to think of my mother as the head of the relationship and my father as the heart.

Perhaps because of his death, Linda does not voluntarily speak of her father. She seems unclear about his place in her life and, when asked, says, 'Nothing about him helps me right now. I suspect I will learn things, my memory will kick things forward when the need comes.'

GOOD MOTHER The good mother is a better mother than her own mother. She creates a 'warm, open, accepting environment that doesn't limit the child into certain areas of doing' and has 'fun' with the child. In contrast, the bad mother gets 'self-fulfillment through the accomplishments of the child' and depends on the child to do what she was unable to do. It is not clear whether Linda is speaking from the position of herself as child (who was depended upon) or herself as mother – who may well feel concerned about becoming hooked into the wonders of her own daughter.

Linda's response to questions about the embodiment of motherhood seems to come from a different register and focuses on breastfeeding. It is, she says, more clearly an 'image for myself rather than an image out there for somebody else.' It is 'totally physical,' 'a circle that is just you and the child.' Linda thinks of it now when she needs to relax.

> I guess I was thinking about an imagery in the sense of how it felt and all of that. Um [pause] if I were to explain it, um [pause] besides the comfort, the warmth, um [pause] my surprise at how it felt when she would breathe on me. And sometimes she would, she would touch whatever I had on. Her fingers would just go back and forth against the fabric and I thought, that's the beginning of sensuality.

In this image, both mother and child get the same satisfactions of warmth, comfort, and sensuality. The sustenance the child receives is unmentioned; instead, shared satisfaction obviates issues of giving and getting. Although the twenty-eight-month-old Elizabeth can be seen as having moved beyond this circle, the mother can rely on its image.

HUSBAND Linda speaks of a close relationship with her husband. In many ways, Ron seems to be a better mother than Linda's own. Linda can talk to him, he is good at establishing values, helps her put difficult work and child rearing situations in context, and reminds her to look for the comic in stressful work situations. Linda's appreciation of her husband as a parental figure has been enhanced by his active involvement with his daughter.

Interestingly, however, like her own less involved father, Ron is presented as the child's 'playmate' and as the more indulgent parent.

Parenthood has firmed but also led to loss of the marital relationship, especially the loss of 'evening rituals,' of 'coming together to talk at the end of the day.' This relationship was 'counted on' by both husband and wife but 'it's very difficult when you're exhausted to find time for it.'

DAUGHTER Elizabeth is presented as 'separate,' powerful, and resembling both her parents. Like her father, she enjoys adventure, play, and treats. Like Linda, she is judgmental, evaluates situations before becoming involved, is talkative, and enjoys being in charge.

> I think of her as a bright china thing when I just see her from afar. By that I mean almost colors, almost a visual sense that whenever I see her it's against a sort of ordinary background and she just glows. Um, when I think about her interaction with my husband and myself and she's very aggressive and she sort of likes to. I think of her as holding court almost over dinner.

Presenting Elizabeth as a child who makes aggressive demands, Linda at times has to 'shunt her off' to complete household tasks and has felt frustrated enough to 'whack' Elizabeth when she could not sit still on a car trip. Linda feels she overreacts but she experiences her daughter as pulling on her and ignoring her needs.

Elizabeth's beauty adds to Linda's self-esteem but gives the child access to a different female position to Linda, who describes herself as having more ordinary looks. Striving to see Elizabeth as 'a Lily Tomlin rather than a Marilyn Monroe,' Linda is teaching her the importance of humor, strength, and kindness so that the child does not rely on her looks. Elizabeth's intelligence and verbal ability make her less threatening. Linda describes instances of togetherness when she uses the Socratic method to help Elizabeth build increasingly abstract concepts. Mother and daughter also converse, joke around, and are able to be what Linda describes as 'silly' together, skipping and singing down the street.

Linda sees Elizabeth as 'totally accepting me' without demanding accomplishment. The child here functions as the good mother and seems to be helping Linda to accept herself. Linda speaks of seeing things in Elizabeth that are reflections of her own 'foibles.' Because she loves them in her child, she has come to love them in herself. This self-acceptance may well contribute to acceptance of her own mother.

Relationality

Linda values close connections with others but her close relationships with women reflect ongoing concern with issues of acceptance and neediness. The relationship with her husband, Ron, is described in strikingly unproblematic terms; they enjoy each other's company and Ron is able to respond to Linda's needs.

For Linda, separation has been a way of dealing with unmet needs. Linda speaks of keeping her needs to herself when interacting with her own mother and now has to 'shunt the child off,' separate from her own child, in order to protect herself and spare Elizabeth a potentially violent response. Separation is also part of the way Elizabeth is expected to deal with her own problems; she is to 'tough out' daily separations and has been encouraged to 'get angry at her toy airplane' alone in her room in order to deal with feelings about Linda's commuting to a distant workplace.

Linda speaks explicitly about her interest in helping others when she describes helping her sisters get along with their mother and about helping colleagues. 'I like helping people get into circumstances in which they feel [pause] valued.' In both cases, her goal is helping others feel accepted. Significantly, it is her own needs that are problematic.

> Sometimes where I need something out of a relationship, it's harder for me to [be nurturant]. And when I find that I, that there's a relationship that seems out of sync with all the other ones, then I, I know that there's something I'm needing out of it. That I'm not allowing that other [pause] nurturing kind of relationship to show up.

Linda goes on to legitimatize but mask her own needs by speaking in terms of what can be described as a more masculine sense of reciprocity, a 'quid pro quo,' stressing that 'everybody's got to play team.'

Traditionality

Linda is a highly successful professional woman who seems to accept her need for achievement and willingly shares child rearing responsibilities with her husband. Her ability to 'separate [her]self' from the traditional woman seems to be enhanced by the fact that her own mother worked and 'did things for herself.' However, Linda also emphasizes that she has a 'domestic instinct' and says that having time to sew and knit would be 'bliss.' Linda very much wanted to have a child and strives – for personal reasons and to be a role model at work – to incorporate a sense of herself as mother into her vision of herself as a 'competent' and 'trustworthy' professional. She speaks to colleagues about Elizabeth, displays family pictures at work, finds planning skills useful at home, and acts 'silly' when with her daughter in the university neighborhood. Perhaps projecting her own difficulties, she feels people cannot easily 'accommodate' her combination of work and motherhood. 'I'm the same person who brings certain strengths to a professional circumstance that loves having her daughter there and for me that's all of a piece.'

Despite efforts to break what she experiences as a distinction between public and private life, Linda believes that it is in the private realm – in the home and in close relationships – that 'you really find out what you are made of' and deal with more that is unspoken, physical, and impulsive. Linda is interested in language but says that, because words transform experience, they cannot always be used. Anger is particularly problematic. Although Linda says she grew up in a family in which people got verbally angry and she likes 'levelling' with Elizabeth, her anger is not easily contained and can spill over into more violent reactions.

Linda's feelings about breastfeeding suggest that physicality can enable deep, comforting connection. However Linda does not want to be a 'clinging mama' holding her child back or, I think, having a sensuous relationship with a girl child. Especially because of many miscarriages, the child is able to 'avert' Linda's sense of a 'failed female body.' Femaleness here depends on children rather than heterosexuality.

Reference measures

I Object relations: Assessment of Qualitative and Structural Dimensions of Object Representations (AQSDOR)

	Mother	Father	Husband	Daughter
Factor I – Nurturance				
Nurturant	4*	5	7	3
Positive ideal	2	5	6	6
Benevolent	2	7	7	6
Cold–Warm	3	6	6	6
Degree of constructive involvement	1	4	7	3
Affectionate	4	4	4	5
Weak–Strong	5	4	6	6
Successful	5	4	4	4
Factor II – Striving				
Judgmental	7	4	4	5
Ambitious	6	4	5	5
Punitive	4	4	4	3
Intellectual	5	2	6	7
Degree of ambivalence**	2	1	1	2
Successful	5	4	4	4
Weak–Strong	5	4	6	6
Conceptual level***	9	1	5	9

* 4 = uncodable, inadequate material
** Three-point scale
*** Scored on scale of 1, 3, 5, 7, 9

Scoring suggests that Linda represents her mother and daughter at the highest conceptual level, as separate people with their own feelings and activities. She treats both with moderate ambivalence and is troubled by their demands, judgments, and inability to respond to her constructively. Despite their similarity, these female figures also differ in important ways. Linda presents her mother as a rather strong, successful woman who has had an extremely negative effect on her life. Elizabeth is presented as admirable, benevolent, and accepting.

Linda's presentation of her father is unambivalent, positive, and focused on nurturant characteristics. However, the extremely low conceptual level indicates that Linda sees him exclusively as need satisfier and not a separate person. Her husband is presented more positively. He is extremely nurturant and the only object she presents as able to respond to her constructively. He is also bright, strong, and wise enough to endure difficult situations and ambitious and responsible enough to drive himself a bit. However, the conceptual level of 5 indicates that Linda presents Ron in terms of his behavior toward her rather than in terms of his own feelings and needs.

II Relationality: Attanucci coding of Gilligan dilemma

Types of self-description	Number of responses by level			
	I	II	III	IV
Self in relation to colleagues	0	1	0	0
Self in relation to mother	0	2	1	0
Self in relation to daughter	0	1	0	0

Linda begins by speaking about two kinds of situations in which she attends to the terms of others and watches to find out what the 'expectations are' (Level II). As a professional, she is aware of not wanting to 'embarrass the institution;' a great deal is 'at stake' because people are depending on her. In social situations, she prefers to observe before participating. Asked to describe a specific situation, Linda speaks of taking Elizabeth to a child's birthday party where, since she is not a 'practiced mother,' she was not sure what was going to go on. Linda felt that she 'should' pay attention to the other mothers but felt outside of their circumstances with 'nothing to offer' them. While she chose to take advantage of the rare opportunity to play with the children, her attention to the expectations of other mothers is scored at Level II.

Linda speaks at some length about being an outsider uncomfortable with 'identifying [her]self as a mother.'

Partly because I spent so much of my professional life not identifying myself as a mother, when I get into circumstances where motherhood is the only card by which you enter the circumstances, it's not clear to me. Um. I don't like making motherhood negotiable in that sense, as though key to getting into a social group.

Linda goes on to say that nothing drew her out of the group with the children and these comments, focusing on her own terms, are scored at Level III.

It is not until the end of her discussion that Linda introduces Elizabeth's needs (Level II). It is here that Linda finds a way to justify her choice of affiliation. She let Elizabeth sleep late because she wasn't feeling well, they arrived at the party late, and Linda 'was aware of her need and sort of being accessible for her' because she only knew one other child there. She ends her description of the dilemma by justifying her choice and indicating that Elizabeth accommodated herself better than Linda had expected.

III Traditionality: Newberger dilemma

Issue	Final score
Resolving conflict	3
Meeting needs	2(3)
	3(2): Global level

Linda's response to the dilemma focuses on the Level 3 notion that no one person's needs and feelings should dominate the needs of another. In particular, children are not 'fragile' and it would be 'unhealthy to keep them from the real world of other people's needs and desires.' She 'votes for Mrs Stewart,' recognizes that mother's mixed feelings, and indicates that her interest in working has been stimulated by Susan's going to school.

A good deal of Linda's discussion focuses on the communication between Mrs Stewart and her daughter (Level 3). She stresses the value of taking Susan to see where her mother works so she can begin to understand the satisfactions of work. She also emphasizes the importance of 'acknowledging the reality of the child's feelings.' 'The emotions that the child has that she's going to talk about are real. And you ignore them at her peril. Your peril. Both of those.' In particular, she suggests that the child may feel 'abandoned.' Linda emphasizes that going to work is 'not the same behavior after you've already acknowledged [the child's] feelings. It is a different kind of behavior. It may look on the surface like it's the same, but it's not.'

Interestingly, while Mrs Stewart is presented as a particular person, Susan is presented as every child who wants her mother home, feels abandoned, but also has a need for a 'diversity' of adult figures in her life. Although this is a complex presentation, the generalized discussion of the child's needs is scored at Level 2.

82

IV Thematic Apperception Test

Story I, Card 1

Linda's story is based on something that happened to her own husband. His grandfather dies and the boy is given his violin. He doesn't play but wants to keep it with him throughout life. His mother has the 'bitter-sweet awareness that the generation that comes after cannot be the same as the generation that came before.'

Clinical assessment

Import: one can use symbols to cope with loss.

Conflicts: none can be inferred, partially because it is based on true story of someone else.

Internal representations: boy seen as sad, happy, reflective; mother seen as loving and insightful.

Quality of relations: there is a suggestion of closeness. People are important to each other, feelings of loss are evident as well as empathic understanding of others.

Story II, Card 2

Linda tells the story of her own mother, who was gifted in school and left the farm to go to college. She is part of a large, close-knit family who work hard, are satisfied, and proud of her. She goes back to 'return labor in kind' by teaching farm children.

Clinical assessment

Import: families stay together.

Conflicts: difficult to derive because based on a true story but there are indications of feelings of guilt over separation.

Internal representations: daughter seen as grateful, committed, appreciative, conflicted, gifted; mother seen as hardworking, proud of her daughter; father seen as hardworking, committed to his children.

Quality of relations: there is mutual appreciation, feelings of love, concern for each other, understanding of differences, and a flavor of closeness in the family.

Story III, Card 5

The wife is ready to go to bed and is worried that her husband, who is still reading, has fallen asleep and is uncomfortable in his chair. 'She'd like to have him warm in bed next to her.'

Clinical assessment

Import: marriage should involve (not necessarily sexual) physical closeness.

Conflicts: none can be derived but there is a suggestion of unmet dependency needs.

Internal representations: wife seen as emotionally needy and concerned; husband seen as self-involved, intellectual.

Quality of relations: there is concern and need for closeness on the part of the wife. Husband seems somewhat aloof.

Story IV, Card 7GF

A mother and child are 'happily waiting' for father who is late getting dressed for a party although this is 'not to imply that he dislikes going.' They are 'happy with each other,' pleased that the daughter was invited although she is somewhat apprehensive, and have a good time.

Clinical assessment

Import: families are all happy.

Conflicts: there is no direct suggestion of conflict but an apparent denial of 'normal' negative feelings suggests a conflict about negative feelings such as anger.

Internal representations: mother seen as happy, passive; daughter seen as happy and apprehensive; husband as passive–aggressive.

Quality of relations: there is concern for the unity of the family. There is no communication and the 'happiness' has a rather superficial quality; the togetherness seems to mask a lack of relatedness among individuals.

Overall clinical impression

This subject appears to be rather concerned with the issue of closeness in her family. Her stories portray close, inseparable families. There are many unmet dependency needs and associated anger which she denies. There is also fear of loss. Separation implies loss and, therefore, there is a great effort to keep families together. These families are emotionally close as groups, but there is little relatedness among the individual members in them.

Some of the subject's stories are taken from real life events of other people which suggests that this summary should be taken with caution. Additionally, there are indications of empathy, love, loyalty, insight, and interest in others. Her ability to capture emotions in symbols suggests a mature organization of psychological defenses. There are no indications of impulsivity.

In sum, this subject appears to have a great deal of capacity for intimacy. But this is also associated with unmet dependency needs and related anger, which are denied.

Within-subject comparison of measures

In this case, material from the Gilligan and Newberger dilemmas is particularly rich. It seems that Linda found the opportunity to present a problem and come to closure particularly meaningful. Linda's response to the Newberger dilemma underscores the importance of the mother openly dealing with her own needs as well as accepting and acknowledging her child's feelings. The parallel with Linda's sense of her own childhood is clear: in ignoring Linda's feelings, Linda's mother put herself and her child in jeopardy.

In her response to the Gilligan dilemma, Linda describes ongoing issues of affiliation with other mothers. This response suggests that Linda's affiliation with her own mother and, it seems, other women is rooted in shared, public competence. Connection with women as mothers is considerably more problematic. The construction of the dilemma is interesting, focusing on Linda's own feelings of distance combined with her sense that she should affiliate with these mothers. She introduces Elizabeth and her needs only at the end of the presentation and relies on the child's interests to explain her own behavior.

The lack of relatedness among individuals in this dilemma is central to the clinical analysis of the Thematic Apperception Test stories. That analysis indicates that Linda is loyal, empathic, and interested in others but that she may be denying considerable anger and unmet dependency needs. While the case study suggests that Linda has made some valuable achievements in moving from anger to acceptance of her own mother, the TAT analysis nevertheless suggests Linda's investment in denying the needs that make her angry.

This denial of negative feelings is most apparent in relation to her father and her husband, both of whom are presented as positive figures. Interestingly, Linda introduces men into TAT stories that more commonly focus on parent–child relationships and also constructs scenarios in which wives' needs are unrecognized by the husbands they nurture. These stories suggest that Linda's relationship with Ron may be more problematic than the interviews indicate. Interestingly, scores on the Assessment of Qualitative and Structural Dimensions of Object Representations indicate a substantial difference between presentations of male and female figures and lend support to the idea in which Linda is more able to see women as distinct figures and to express frustration with them. Men remain idealized but less separate.

Although the TAT analysis indicates the way that separation implies loss, the case study suggests ways that Linda also uses separation to keep relationships together. To be more precise, Linda seems to maintain relationships by keeping angry and needy feelings to herself. Concern about loss in the TAT analysis relates to the concern about acceptance mentioned in the case study. Linda feels she must be accepting and acceptable to others or she will lose those relationships. It is significant that, although in most instances connection is furthered by achievement and by helping others to be accepted, she looks to her daughter for a more basic bond exemplified by the intimacy and mutual satisfaction of breastfeeding and by full acceptance. The child's presence seems to have contributed to Linda's feelings of well-being in terms of self-acceptance, pleasure, and increased connection with others, particularly her mother. At the same time, the child's demands and her femaleness are complicating and threatening.

INDIVIDUAL PROFILE: LAUREN

Case summary

Lauren is a thirty-five-year-old child of a corporate executive and grew up on the east coast. Her mother died when she was nine months old and she was brought up by her grandmother until her father re-married two years later. Lauren has an M.B.A. from a prestigious institution and says she was a high-powered finance executive until her daughter was born. Conception, pregnancy, and childbirth were somewhat difficult and the child was born by Caesarean section. Lauren now describes herself as a 'twenty-four-hour mother' and is beginning to consider ways she might start her own business in order to work on a more flexible schedule. Her husband, 'Tom,' is an attorney.

'Jacqueline' was seventeen months old at the time of the first interview, twenty-three months at the time of the second. She was enrolled at the university Center for Children.

I did not interview Lauren the first time. She is very willing to participate in this study, and hers is the first of the follow-up interviews I conduct. Lauren arrives with a bad cold and seems intent on talking non-stop before her voice gives out. In addition to the effect of illness, she seems to have a brash style, rarely pauses, and speaks with certainty without having to deal with what I might think or say. The standardized measures pose a problem for her; she indicates they are 'too black and white' and would like more guidance than they provide. The TAT cards are most troubling. Starting the interview with a dilemma rather than with a point of certainty also seems disconcerting. In response to her physical and psychological discomfort, I hesitate to probe. Instead, I become an audience for her breezy but generous discussion.

Object relations

MOTHER Lauren speaks of her stepmother as her mother. Lauren says she is not an 'encouraging, supportive person.' She could not 'sit back and detach herself from her opinions and listen to your needs or your wants.' Instead, her reactions were 'classically wrong.' She pushed – 'Why weren't you first?' – regardless of Lauren's achievements. Overly invested in propriety, she is 'myopic in her vision of how things should be with a child,' wants Jacqueline to stop doing anything she finds 'ridiculous,' and sees breastfeeding as 'animal.'

Lauren does allow that her stepmother 'must've had something to do' with how well Lauren turned out. As a mother herself, Lauren has 'so much more appreciation for some of the things that I just couldn't deal with when I was growing up.'

In addition, having a child has made her miss her real mother and 'think back to what it was like being a child.' She is 'becoming aware of [her own] needs.'

> It makes me very sad that my – that [inaudible seven words] my mother, that my mother didn't know me. I – I look back on that whole thing. And to, to me it's such a tragedy. It makes me terribly sad. And it also makes me so aware of how, what an effect my relationship with my stepmother must have had.

Unfortunately, while Lauren makes a number of such statements, she does not speak further of her mother and the first interviewer and I do not push her. The gap in Lauren's life is reproduced in the interview process.

FATHER Lauren stresses that there is 'a different dimension to my relationship with my father because he's my father. I mean, you know, it's just that simple.' Lauren says she and her father are 'just about identical in looks and temperament.' He is 'wonderful,' especially because he is 'smart' and able to 'put aside' his own feelings, 'step back and be objective and fair.' For example, Lauren felt he was responsive when she decided to cancel her first engagement days before the wedding. His reaction was 'Love first. I want you to be happy.'

Lauren does not present her father as affectionate. When she sees him privately kissing Jacqueline on the head, Lauren says she is moved by his tenderness and says this behavior is unlike his typical, chairman-of-the-board demeanor.

GOOD MOTHER Lauren says she has many 'fantasies of family life' but they are visions of Tracy and Hepburn, of an achieving woman who has 'romance' and a 'glamorous life.' Despite the prominence of this fantasy, Lauren contends that she has no fantasies of motherhood: 'I don't have those preconceptions or things to live up to.' While Lauren may not have a vision of what it is like to *be* the Mother, it seems that to imagine 'the Mother' is to imagine her own dead mother and face her loss. This is harder for Lauren to speak about directly. The interviews do provide indications of Lauren's views of the present 'Mother' and, in particular, an image of a mother–child relationship that is close, intense, and secure. It is based on instinctive, unconditional love merged with the intelligence, objectivity, and fairness Lauren associates with her father.

While not occupying the same domain of fantasy or desire, questions about her image of motherhood are answered in terms of standards Lauren uses to evaluate her own behavior. She and her good friend 'always have discussions about how we're being bad mothers today.' The good mother is 'loving' but also 'teaches her child to be autonomous to a degree, um caring, educating, disciplining.' She will

> exert the time and energy that is necessary. I mean a child doesn't just grow by itself or learn by itself. I think it needs time spent. And you have to be selfless, you have to be willing to ss-teach, teach and love and care. And I think a lot of people don't do that.

While the bad mother is 'impatient,' the good mother can also 'sort of step back and always at least maintain a calm semblance' rather than be angry.

HUSBAND Lauren speaks of Tom as 'understanding me like a book,' as 'sensitive' to Lauren's needs, and able to 'fulfill a lot of the fantasy.' 'We have a very communicative relationship and he takes a lot of time and effort to make sure I feel loved and I feel happy and I feel secure.' Tom is also presented as aggressive, independent, and strong-willed like Lauren's father, Lauren, and Jacqueline. He is playful, physical, and athletic, all qualities Lauren admires.

Tom is a busy executive who disliked Lauren's career, said it was debilitating to her well-being and to the marriage, and encouraged her to give it up to have a child. His most effective argument was, 'If you quit, three years from now nobody would remember that you had ever been here.' However, there are tensions involved in being a full time mother. Lauren sometimes 'resents' Tom because he can be with Jacqueline when he wants and is not 'on call.' She is concerned that Tom sees her differently than he did when she too was an executive. However, she also sees him differently, as less 'realistic' about Jacqueline's interests and having 'absurd fantasies,' such as the threesome being able to gallop on the beach when Jacqueline was a newborn baby.

DAUGHTER Lauren says she felt 'immediate bonding' with Jacqueline, and got 'sucked into loving her' because the child was so precociously 'responsive.' The child tapped into and responded to Lauren's feelings concerning the loss of Lauren's own mother.

> Through Jacqueline I'm realizing so much the importance of that relationship, um, what it does for her and what it does for me. And I think in a lot of ways, this is getting very psychological, but I think it's like coming all the way around, that her relationship with me is giving me something that perhaps I didn't have when I was younger.

Lauren thought the newborn baby resembled her own family but quickly realized that Jacqueline was, in surface ways, 'more his' because she looked just like Tom and shared his physicality. Lauren has a hard time seeing Jacqueline's character as different from her own. In response to questions about differences between the child and herself, she says, 'traits aren't developed enough' to tell. However, Jacqueline is described in detail and in ways that befit this family. She is strong-willed, independent, communicative, and extremely bright. She is 'intrepid' and 'fearless,' active and enthusiastic rather than 'easy.' Lauren distinguishes the seventeen-month-old child from Tom in terms of a developmentally advanced trait: her intellectual curiosity.

> He's very bright in a different way. Um, and I think she's got more of the interest in books and learning conceptually. But I mean, it's very hard to tell. You know, she's just talking, beginning talking. So I can't tell what she thinks or is that well at this point.

Lauren continues to emphasize mother–daughter similarities when she speaks of Jacqueline as a girl child and her contemporary. Mother and daughter are 'good buddies' who 'hang out,' play, and 'kid around' and also comfort and take care of each other. A moment of 'clicking' takes place in Bloomingdale's department store: 'I smiled at her and she smiled back and it was, clearly, it could have been a grown-up. We were friends smiling at each other. It was just, "Isn't this great?"' In Lauren's presentation, the sharing of care and friendship are most prominent; only incidentally does Lauren talk about asymmetrical aspects of the relationship, the 'classic parent–child' discipline and the purposive teaching.

Relationality

Lauren wants to be deeply connected to Jacqueline, to be her inside 'core' and outside 'focal point,' and to provide her with that 'love and security' that will make Jacqueline more confident, secure, and independent than she is herself. For Lauren, connection is necessary for independence – for the stepping back and not being subjected to the judgments of others that she values. This connection is also decribed in terms of considerable mutuality.

> I think there's tremendous caring between both of us. I mean if I cry, if I'm really tired or get upset, and I cry – which clearly doesn't happen very often – she will get very upset and try to come over and pet my face and try to comfort me.

Lauren looks to the child for the kind of mother–daughter relationship she never had. In reflecting on her own need for care, Lauren says she does not 'abuse' the child but clearly voices some concern about depending on her too much.

Lauren has more problems dealing with how Jacqueline 'takes.' 'It's relentless, it's just if you're tired, if you're sick, um, if you're hungry, if you're moody, you know. Um, Jacqueline doesn't go away.' The combination of wishing to be the child's focal point, wishing to be cared for by her, and wishing for her to go away is particularly problematic. For Lauren, it is clear that there is a difference between being a mother and a person. She needs time away from Jacqueline as time to 'restore my personality, to make me feel like A person outside of being A mother.'

When speaking of marriage and friendships, Lauren consistently emphasizes her need to feel loved. Lauren has five or six close women friends, one from each stage of her life, and is in weekly contact with them. Despite the prominence of these relationships, Lauren feels she does not have many friends and that there are not many people whom she trusts and respects enough to have as friends. Instead of feeling an affiliation with other people, she feels 'insecure,' overly 'concerned about what people think,' and struggles to fulfill 'obligations' while 'steaming the whole time.' Her need to be 'independent' can be seen as a way of dealing with her dependency needs and others' demands without feeling angry or depleted.

Traditionality

A self-described 'yuppie' who values pragmatism and achievement, Lauren presents herself as a woman who in her 'heart of hearts didn't want to be a mother' and admired women who were 'achieving type persons.' She presents herself as an 'opinionated' woman who compensated for her own insecurity by relying on accomplishments and began to question her career when she felt she was not 'political' enough to make it all the way to the top. She distinguishes herself both from working mothers who do not know their children and from 'earth-mother,' traditional women. Lauren sees herself as 'very into being a mother,' a 'relentless', twenty-four-hour task, but 'not as much into being a typical wife.' She eschews domesticity, wants an egalitarian marriage, but also wants to be the object of romance. She loves it when Tom does things like buy her champagne and never speaks of ways she takes care of him.

Lauren's discussion of motherhood involves a combination of the love and security she values and a vision of progress. In her presentation, the child is maternal, playful, and also is 'unmarked,' 'raw material' to be 'chanelled.' Privileged parents like Lauren and Tom can help a child 'reach the moon'; at the same time they may expect too much and be misled by their child's brightness.

Lauren is openly ambivalent about her daughter's strong-willed qualities and about presenting herself as a disciplinarian. She prefers not to 'lock' with her daughter, makes tasks into games, but feels she must win the battles of will, be the 'tough guy,' and 'decide the limits of Jacqueline's life.' Interestingly, Tom is never mentioned in the context of these battles; he is associated with play and fantasy, a captain of industry rather than powerful at home.

Lauren voices two 'modern' messages: that it's okay to get angry; that parents are people too. Her wishes contradict these messages. She says she would like to be selfless enough to step back and focus on the child instead of allowing her own reactions to interfere with the relationship. Every time she speaks of anger, she interjects something like, 'I wish that I could not have that happen,' and seems to feel the need to undo some damage.

Reference measures

All four figures are presented as somewhat nurturant. Lauren's stepmother is presented most negatively, as a highly judgmental, malevolent, unloving, somewhat weak individual who has been thoroughly unable to respond to Lauren constructively. All other figures are admired, presented as benevolent, loving, bright, and able to respond to Lauren constructively. Despite their similarity, in other ways they are somewhat different. Lauren is unambivalent in her presentation of her father and speaks of him as extremely bright and strong. Tom is more loving and affectionate but pushes Lauren more than her father does. Jacqueline combines the qualities of both her father and husband; she is extremely bright, strong, loving, affectionate, and ambitious. She is the only figure presented in terms of her own feelings.

I Object relations: Assessment of Qualitative and Structural Dimensions of Object Representations (AQSDOR)

	Mother	Father	Husband	Daughter
Factor I – Nurturance				
Nurturant	5	5	5	5
Positive ideal	2	6	6	6
Benevolent	2	6	6	7
Cold–Warm	2	6	7	7
Degree of constructive involvement	1	6	6	5
Affectionate	4*	5	6	6
Weak–Strong	3	7	6	7
Successful	4	4	4	4
Factor II – Striving				
Judgmental	7	3	4	4
Ambitious	4	4	6	6
Punitive	4	3	4	4
Intellectual	4	7	6	7
Degree of ambivalence**	2	1	2	1
Successful	4	4	4	4
Weak–Strong	3	7	6	7
Conceptual level***	3	3	5	7

* 4 = uncodable, inadequate material
** Three-point scale
*** Scored on scale of 1, 3, 5, 7, 9

II Relationality: Attanucci coding of Gilligan dilemma

Types of self-description	Number of responses by level			
	I	II	III	IV
Self in relation to daughter	0	2	5	0

Lauren's dilemma concerns a 'battle of wills' between herself and her daughter. Lauren must find the 'right balance between encouraging Jacqueline's inherent, strong-willed personality and controlling it somewhat.' Most of Lauren's responses are scored at Level III and deal with her own need to 'establish who's the boss' and to 'socialize' and 'get through' to her daughter in order to make life 'manageable.'

Lauren also says that children should know that their parents get angry and that, although she wishes she did not get angry, 'that's just the way life is.' 'I wouldn't yell if I wasn't absolutely at the end of my ropes,' that 'I couldn't do anything else at that point.'

After speaking of times when she has 'had it,' Lauren shifts to a consideration of Jacqueline's needs. Comments about the child getting upset and not learning anything from Lauren's anger are scored at Level II, as is her final statement that after she gets angry, she must say, 'I love you but love has nothing to do with what's happened, you can't always have your way.'

III Traditionality: Newberger dilemma

Issues	Final score
Resolving conflict	3
Meeting needs	3(2)
Learning and evaluating parenting	2
Subjectivity	3(2)
	3(2): Global level

Lauren's response to the dilemma involves considerable attention to her own feelings about not working. Lauren begins her response by stipulating that there is no definition of a good mother and presenting the mother as person: 'Every person has an obligation to do what's best for them,' 'for their entire psyche.' Arguing that 'what's best for me is inherently best for Jacqueline,' she does not consider the child's needs directly or make a distinction between mother and child (Level 3(2)). When Lauren considers Mrs Stewart and her daughter, she does move to focus on 'balancing' the child's feelings of unhappiness with the mother's needs, considering whether the child has 'deeper needs' or is being 'manipulative,' and whether the child could understand the concept of working. Comments about the hypothetical child are more advanced (Level 3).

As Lauren reintroduces her own child, her response becomes somewhat less complex. She says that a mother is 'damned if you do, damned if you don't work,' and indicates that she herself has mixed feelings about staying home but does not elaborate on those feelings. She argues that every child 'in her heart of hearts would rather have her mother there.' Lauren tries to end the dilemma with a point of certainty: 'the parent would have to be home, the child didn't ask to be here, the child comes first.' Motherhood must be a 'relatively selfless act.' Lauren then reintroduces the mother's needs; if Mrs Stewart is really unhappy it will have a negative effect on her child (Level 2(3)).

IV Thematic Apperception Test

Story I, Card 1

The boy practices the violin, gets bored or tired, and stops.

Clinical assessment

Import: work is boring and you don't have to do it.

Conflicts: no specific conflicts are seen, but subject might have a great deal of self-doubt and insecurity because she is unsure what is in the picture.

Internal representations: boy seen as bored.

Quality of relations: there are no significant others in the child's world.

Story II, Card 2

Reminds Lauren of a student in a museum looking at a painting because the student doesn't fit into the situation. It does not look as if she is standing at a farm. Lauren can come up with a different story, of a book-oriented person who leaves a more earthy home, but she goes back to her first reaction and wants to know how other subjects responded.

Clinical assessment

Import: no import can be derived, there is little plot.

Conflicts: belonging or 'fitting in.' Concerns with this issue are evident in the plot and in the subject's need to know how others responded to the picture. Self-doubts about her perceptions are evident.

Internal representations: woman seen as book-oriented; people seen as static, unreal, detached.

Quality of relations: there are no real people in character's world, suggesting detachment and alienation.

Story III, Card 5

Mother checks in to see what child is doing and if child is all right. She is happy the child is not doing anything wrong.

Clinical assessment

Import: mothers are preoccupied with their children's safety and happiness.

Conflicts: none can be derived, suggesting a constriction of emotional experience.

Internal representations: child seen as psychically absent, potentially in peril, or acting up; mother seen as warm, loving, preoccupied, concerned.

Quality of relations: there is virtually no meaningful interaction between mother and child in the story. The relationship appears to be a routine task, with no interest in each other's inner world, and no indication of empathy or closeness.

Story IV, Card 7GF

A 'quiet, intimate moment' between a mother and her daughter. Child may have been playing with dolls and they are talking about the dolls.

Clinical assessment

Import: no import can be derived.

Conflicts: none can be derived, suggesting emotional constriction.

Internal representations: mother seen as loving.

Quality of relations: on the surface, the relationship is described as loving. But the intimacy in the story consists of either silence or abstract discussions. There are no differentiated feelings and no interest in each other's inner worlds which gives the relationship a superficial flavor. There is no sense that mother and child are individuals with different developmental needs: they are 'discussing' the dolls as if they were two adults (or two children).

Overall clinical impression

This subject failed to follow the test instructions. This can suggest either a situational variable (e.g. subject was tired), or a certain character style. In terms of the latter, the cause could be either a passive–aggressive disposition or a constricted, repressed emotional and cognitive style.

With this in mind, as represented by these stories, subject appears to feel detached, unrelated to others, and deeply insecure. She might have low self-esteem and a great deal of self-doubt. She might be unsure about her perceptions of reality or about the difference between reality and fantasy (seen in the second card).

She might be emotionally repressed and cognitively global. That is, she may have little insight about others' feelings, and she may view the world in a superficial, stereotyped manner.

This subject's defense organization is rigid. However, at times, her defenses may be ineffective (as seen in the disorganized response to the second card) and therefore, under stress, there is a potential for impulsive acting out.

On a more speculative note, subject may have had a severe loss. The absence of people in her stories is striking and she has assumed a schizoid, detached style of relatedness to protect herself from the underlying rage.

Within-subject comparison of measures

Lauren's case is interesting because of its complexity. She speaks of a close relationship with her female child as having a profound effect on her and providing a previously missing mother–daughter relationship. She is a full time, responsive mother who has close relationships with other women, with her husband, and with her father. However, Lauren speaks primarily of needing care and support from others. She also values the ability to 'step back' and be objective, contain anger, and avoid dependency.

Scores on the Assessment of Qualitative and Structural Dimensions of Object Representations demonstrate the value Lauren places on strength, success, intelligence, and on the ability of people to care for and respond to her needs. She does not consider their own feelings about their lives. The Assessment is valuable in exhibiting the similarity between Lauren's husband, father, and daughter but also illuminates the fact that Jacqueline combines the best of the male figures.

Analysis of the Newberger and Gilligan dilemmas and of the TAT stories supports those aspects of the case study that focus on Lauren's own neediness and lack of responsiveness to the needs of others. The Newberger dilemma is interesting because it demonstrates Lauren's ability to consider hypothetical characters in some depth. However, when speaking of her own situation, Jacqueline's needs are presented as identical to her own. The dilemma Lauren presents in response to the Gilligan questions outlines a contrasting situation, one in which Jacqueline's will is opposed to her own. Here, Lauren's emphasis is on the importance of getting her own point across. Interestingly, Jacqueline is presented as her equal rather than as particularly childlike. Only when she speaks of her own anger does Lauren consider the child's feelings and the importance of repairing the damage of her own outbursts. As the Attanucci coding indicates, self and other are not present and engaged simultaneously, thereby suggesting inadequate connection.

The TAT analysis adds to this assessment. It must be stated here that two situational variables may have affected Lauren's response to the TAT cards. She had a bad cold and she was the first subject seen for the second time; stories were not probed freely. Despite these qualifications, the independent clinical assessment is of great value in focusing on Lauren's self-doubts, her inability to be sensitive to the feelings of others, her reliance on stereotyped responses, confusion between fantasy and reality, and use of a detached style to protect herself from underlying rage. The idea that Lauren relies on detachment to protect her insecure and raging self further explains why 'stepping back' is so important to her.

However, while Lauren can be seen as immersed in her own needs and unable to engage with real others, the case study also suggests that she is involved with a number of others, especially with her daughter. Without underestimating Lauren's need for love and security and her seeming inability to focus on the real characteristics and feelings of others, Lauren's struggle to act as the good mother whom she feels she never had, to give as well as to get, is an important one. The fact that 'testing' evoked constricted responses and self-doubts is also important and contributes to a sense that Lauren must feel supported and loved in order to be engaged with others.

INDIVIDUAL PROFILE: ANNA

Case summary

Anna is a thirty-six-year-old woman who grew up in California. Her father was a teacher and her mother a full time homemaker. They have recently divorced. Anna has two siblings, born when she was ten and twelve and she helped her mother take care of them. Anna was a political science major and met her husband, 'Eddie,' in college. They married after living together for years and have what can be characterized as non-materialistic, non-achievement-oriented values. Eddie now manages a large video equipment store. Anna worked in a nursery school and then became a chef. When she approached the age of thirty, she very much wanted to have a child. Pregnancy and delivery were described as easy. Despite financial difficulties, Anna is a full time mother.

'Elise' was thirty months old at the time of the first interview, thirty-six months at the time of the second. She is the only child in this population who does not participate in any organized toddler activity. In addition, she is still breastfed.

Anna meets the requirements of this study, but is, by virtue of income, activities, and values, unlike any of the other mothers. In a sense, after talking with her, it was impossible to ignore her story. Anna is a very forthright, down-to-earth woman whose long hair, wire-rimmed glasses, and Indian clothing are reminiscent of the 1960s. Once considered radical, she feels devalued and has to 'fight against' what she perceives as the lack of respect for full time mothers like herself. Anna answers all questions carefully and uses the interviews as an opportunity to think through her current situation. By the time of the second interview Anna is deeply troubled by her isolation and uniqueness. Anna never asks me anything about my own situation and I have the sense that she does not want to reckon with the possibility that I am different. She seems to treat me as a benign and supportive figure. Despite the need to pick up her daughter from a neighbor's house, it is clear she does not want these discussions to end.

Object relations

MOTHER Anna presents her mother as a good mother and tries not to speak of her in any way that is troubling: 'I have a lot of positive feelings for my mother so it's not hard for me. But that's, I try to keep it on that level more than anything else.' When asked how she wants to be unlike her mother, Anna speaks of her mother's difficulties as a wife. While particular 'frustrations' were tapped by the feminist movement, the marriage was never 'maintained real well' because Anna's mother could not express negative feelings. 'If my mother had been able to express that stuff all along, it would have worked out a lot better. As it came up. Instead of just, hanging on.'

When considering her mother as a parent, Anna describes her as appropriately 'mild' and 'relaxed' without considering the value of expressing anger to her children. Anna also emphasizes that her mother was 'not judgmental' and that she 'always felt accepted.' 'I didn't have to be a certain way to get her to like me. Just felt like she always liked me.' It is only incidentally that Anna allows that her mother was 'suffocating' and 'isolated' from other mothers.

FATHER Anna does not mention her father voluntarily, nor does she speak warmly of him. When asked, she introduces him as a man who is 'not good at opening up' or being 'close to people.' He is the 'angry one' who insisted on routines such as proper dinner-time behavior and used conventions to control against disruption.

> I think he would have anger at my mother and, or anger at his job, and who. It would always be excused, 'Oh, he had a bad day' or something. (Your mother would excuse it?) Yeah, you know, after a while we all knew. I don't think it was ever really excusable.

Anna says her father was 'physically daring' and encouraged her to do things she felt timid about. Her discussion suggests a pleasing and provoking physicality in this relationship.

GOOD MOTHER The question of what is a good mother is very important to Anna. She wishes to see her own mother as the continuously good mother but sees that her own image of motherhood has been challenged by her daughter's changing needs 'The all-giving Mother looked really good' and 'seemed to be working' when Elise was a baby. Being all-giving has become 'irritating' for the increasingly self-sufficient child. It is never presented as a problem for the Mother.

Anna also tries to put motherhood in a larger, timeless perspective. Nursing is a privileged activity representing the transcultural model of the generous, comforting Mother who 'helps the world's children.'

Anna says she used to define the bad mother as 'suffocating' – a quality she attributes to her own mother – but now defines her in terms of the opposite quality – the mother who ignores her child. In both cases, the mother says one thing and does another. Anna gives an example of a friend who remembers being toilet trained harshly. Taking the vantage point of the child, Anna implies that control expressed underneath an ethic of acceptance is damaging.

HUSBAND Eddie is presented as a secondary figure in the interview although his opinions are important and he and Anna share many values. The object of considerable attention from his own 'all-giving' mother, Anna says that Eddie was not a 'motherly boy,' was not interested in having a child, and it seems, does not function as a maternal figure for Anna.

Perhaps as he anticipated, Eddie has been replaced by Elise, with whom Anna is 'as close as when I first met my husband.' Although Anna contends that the marriage is not 'real different' now than before Elise was born, the couple rarely spends time alone and parents and child sleep in the same room of their three-room apartment. Further, Eddie has said that Anna has become 'devious' and 'manipulative,' a comment Anna finds perceptive and extremely disturbing.

Anna does feel marital stress owing to the fact that she no longer works. While Eddie overtly says, 'Stay home, it's good what you're doing,' Anna believes he feels that he is 'bearing the whole burden' and feels 'You won't do anything for me.' Anna sees this as a purely financial issue and never considers that Eddie might feel displaced by Anna's involvement with Elise.

DAUGHTER Anna speaks of 'feeling very one' with Elise but also feels that Elise has a 'different personality.' She focuses on Elise's confidence and strength, on how she has always 'known what to do,' 'takes charge,' and pats Anna on the back 'like the boss.' The child's power is presented as a source of guidance rather than a depleting demand.

Anna also sees Elise as a cautious, 'life-preserving,' 'dependent' child who 'wants to be with her mother.' Although she allows that nursing 'keeps her there' and that she is 'grateful' to Elise for continuing to be a 'strong nurser,' she presents nursing as Elise's need for 'comfort.' She sees the child as 'sick with worry' when she cannot breastfeed and increasingly troubled by situations in which nursing in public is no longer appropriate. She does not know how to make sense of Elise's resistance to going to the group meetings of La Leche, an organization that encourages breastfeeding.

Anna sees Elise as 'picking up on what we are wanting,' knowing if her parents are happy, and sensing her parents' 'disappointment.' Anna tries to 'contain' her own expectations but does not consider her demand for closeness problematic for the child. Instead, she locates difficulties in 'separating out' mother's and daughter's angry feelings. 'When I'm angry, she's angry;' 'emotions between us have to be matched.' Attempts to repress anger lead to a 'circle of whining' in which mother and daughter react to each other.

Throughout the interviews, Anna struggles to deal with Elise's moves toward differentiation, reviews the child's attachment history, and speaks of wanting to 'return' to the original relationship 'underneath.' At the same time, she knows that 'there's babyhood and there's not babyhood' and recognizes Elise's pleasure in the outside world, her 'fulfillment' and 'putting on airs' when going shopping and being treated like the grown-up 'she should have been treated like all along.' In addition, Elise is described as precociously verbal. For Anna, speech disrupts the earlier, physical relationship. Anna can no longer 'relax' and has to be careful not to explain or promise too much.

Shared female 'body parts' provide a basic similarity. 'I know from my own experience how, how I f-feel about my body and I, you know, I don't have to go one step further and imagine how it feels.' At the same time, Anna is ambivalent about herself as a model and does not want Elise to be compelled to be a full time mother.

Relationality

Although deeply connected to her mother and her daughter, Anna is not the quintessential all-giving, connected woman. Instead, she also can be defined by her 'cool exterior,' her attention to differences between people, her way of judging and distancing herself from others, and by her need to 'take in' and be cared for.

Anna likes 'being all by herself,' says she enjoyed working 'silently and steadily' with foreign kitchen help and that she can spend 'whole days not talking to anyone but Eddie and Elise.' Being out of the apartment is 'exhausting' for her because she believes people blame and judge mothers and have 'expectations' of children.

When asked for five adjectives to describe the relationship between herself and Elise, Anna immediately says, 'close,' and then says, 'How to describe a relationship besides close? [laugh] Close or far away?' Anna describes close relationships in terms of a 'calm' 'family feeling.' Although she has some close friends, she does not speak of doing things for and with these women but of how they 'may include you in a kind of reality' of mothering.

Anna characterizes herself as a motherly woman who has no 'conflict with the giving part of it.'

> The time I spent with her as a baby, doing, doing that for days on end were, were very good for me. Very good. And I think of them often. And I feel it's good. And I feel that's a good way to return. I would like to return to that, feel good about that.

Anna speaks of being 'plunged into a world of womanhood' but it is a secret world in which the mother is in a privileged position of receiving care from other women. This vision is particularly clear when Anna is asked if she feels differently now about being a woman than she did before she had a child. She says yes, this 'must be what all the rest of it flows from. Because the feeling of sitting somewhat incapacitated, fairly still, asking people to do things for you, being pampered yourself.'

Traditionality

Anna presents herself as a 'homebody' who has the same communal values that were once considered 'radical' and are now held by 'stodgy' older people. Although she has moved away from anti-motherhood, pro-work values and back to her earlier motherly feelings, Anna feels the 'ideology' of the working woman is socially dominant. She feels increasingly alone and that she has more in common with Third World women.

Anna and Eddie want to provide 'unstructured freedom' and to keep Elise at home as long as possible. While Anna never speaks of teaching Elise, increasingly she feels she must be the planner, 'balancing' Elise's week, and providing the social interaction and outings Elise desires.

Anna herself desires a 'calm' relationship and would rather that 'people just, you know, didn't, didn't behave in a way where you had to tell them what to do.' Perhaps like her own mother, desiring to have 'things go smooth,' Anna continuously focuses on not getting angry and, at the end of the second interview, begins to consider this stance 'counterproductive.' 'The mother is the center of the world kind of feeling. Like you're controlling and manipulating everybody around you.'

Discussion of anger pervades these interviews. Anna speaks of how Elise has moved from physical aggression to 'inhibition,' tantrums and whining. The problem is that it is hard to define the continually present but 'bottled up' anger.

> I know in my family, in my relationship with Eddie, it was a lot. I had a lot of trouble knowing when somebody *wasn't* angry any more. Or was. You know. What exactly it was. It's the anger that you don't know what it's for that drives you crazy.

Anna uses the word pleasure throughout the interview. The pleasure she describes is not wild or playful. Instead, it is a pleasure that is 'calm,' 'smooth,' a symbiotic, archaic satisfaction that may well depend on the presence of a girl child. This discussion of pleasure excludes discussion of (hetero)sexuality and seems to obviate the need for any other satisfaction. When asked if having a child has affected her sexual relationship with Eddie, she tells me that it has 'worked out fine.' Anna and Eddie can go to the living room to be alone. The possibility of Elise sleeping in the other room is never mentioned.

Reference measures

I   Object relations: Assessment of Qualitative and Structural Dimensions of Object Representations (AQSDOR)

	Mother	Father	Husband	Daughter
Factor I – Nurturance				
Nurturant	5	4*	5	2
Positive ideal	6	2	5	6
Benevolent	6	2	6	6
Cold–Warm	7	2	5	4
Degree of constructive involvement	5	2	3	2
Affectionate	4	4	4	5
Weak–Strong	6	2	6	7
Success	4	2	4	5
Factor II – Striving				
Judgmental	1	5	4	5
Ambitious	4	6	5	5
Punitive	1	4	4	6
Intellectual	4	4	4	5
Degree of ambivalence**	2	1	2	3
Success	4	3	4	5
Weak–Strong	6	2	6	7
Conceptual level***	3	3	3	9

* 4 = uncodable, inadequate material
** Three-point scale
*** Scored on scale of 1, 3, 5, 7, 9

Anna presents her mother, husband, and father as minimally differentiated, need-gratifying figures. She is moderately ambivalent about her mother and husband and unambivalent but negative in her presentation of her father. In contrast, she presents her daughter with great ambivalence but at the highest conceptual level, in terms of her feelings and behaviors.

Except for her father, figures are admirable, benevolent, and strong. Anna's mother is particularly loving, accepting, and to some extent able to respond to Anna constructively. Eddie is presented more negatively, as a fairly warm figure who pushes Anna to satisfy his needs, and is not very able to respond to her constructively. Elise is presented as unusually strong and as the only affectionate, intellectual figure of the four. However, she is not described as warm or nurturant and is a somewhat judgmental figure who responds punitively when Anna does not do what she wants.

Anna presents her father as malevolent, weak, unhappy, unloving, unable to respond to his daughter's needs, and as driving Anna to respond to his standards and encouraging her to to be physically bolder.

II Relationality: Attanucci coding of Gilligan dilemma

Types of self-description	Number of responses by level			
	I	II	III	IV
Self in relation to other mothers	0	2	3	0
Self in relation to daughter	0	4	3	0

Anna's dilemma concerns whether she should continue to hold Elise's hand when crossing the street or, like other mothers, let her walk by herself. Anna moves back and forth between Level II concerns for adhering to the terms of other mothers and forcefully stating her own belief in the importance of being 'strict' about safety issues. Similarly, she vacillates between feeling guilty about being 'over-protective' (Level II) and arguing why her terms are better (Level III).

Anna expresses particular concern about 'being in the minority' and feeling distant from other mothers. She says 'I don't have so many close, sharing, exchanging type relationships' and tries to 'avoid situations where I have to play the bad guy to other people's children.'

Anna is also concerned that 'my whole way of life is leading me to be over-protective and I'm holding Elise back.' While she explains her rules and knows Elise complies (Level III), she is concerned that Elise might feel that she is 'not as good as [the other] children' (Level II). While Anna feels she must 'compromise' by letting Elise hold onto her stroller, the larger issues are unresolved by this solution.

III Traditionality: Newberger dilemma

Issues	Final score
Resolving conflict	3
Meeting needs	3
Subjectivity	4(3)
	3: Global level

Anna's response to the working mother dilemma is complex and involves attention to the feelings of Mrs Stewart and her daughter, and to communication between them. Interestingly, the child is more elaborated than her mother and Anna suggests that Mrs Stewart must 'separate her own feelings' from the child's and watch the child to figure out which needs are 'really deeply felt.' Verbal statements are presented as less clear; the child who says 'Don't work' might be saying 'Nursery school is not for me.' Similarly, while Mrs Stewart can explain the value of work to her daughter, it would be better to take the child to see where she works. Anna sees the child as a 'bundle of ambivalence,' picking up the cues of people around her; this is scored at Level 4(3) because of the complexity of interaction.

103

Anna ends by saying that we 'should make more allowances for the child's needs,' that children need 'intimacy and closeness,' and that emotional distance may be created by the mother's absence. Anna's final comments concern the mother doing the 'right thing' and are scored at Level 2.

IV Thematic Apperception Test

Story I, Card 1

Boy would like to be able to play the violin well but can't 'get very good sounds out of it,' so he can't 'bring himself to pick it up.'

Clinical assessment

Import: it's hard to learn when you are a perfectionist.

Conflicts: learning versus performing. One can only learn if one is willing to make mistakes; the boy wants to learn but also wants to perform beautifully immediately.

Internal representations: boy seen as self-critical, serious, conflicted.

Quality of relations: cannot be inferred.

Story II, Card 2

The woman is leaving the farm, is apprehensive and unsure about her future, and is 'not interested in the life of the other woman.' The other woman – who may be a mother or sister – is very tired and 'not excited or scared' about her unchanged life. Hard to know what the man – who may be a brother – is feeling.

Clinical assessment

Import: the future and making choices are scary and exciting.

Conflicts: cannot be inferred because there is no real plot. But there are suggestions about fear of the future, and being different from others. Issues of identity are prominent.

Internal representations: women seen as either excited but apprehensive or bland, tired.

Quality of relations: there is a sense of alienation and lack of relatedness. Subject can't decide how people are related to each other, and they all go in 'different directions' with no care or concern for each other.

Story III, Card 5

A mother 'in charge of the good and bad' has surprised a child, animal, or thief who is doing something 'vaguely improper,' that she has already said 100 times not to do. She is angry and is not going to 'stop before she does something' that is 'verbally or physically abusive.' Anna says she herself is usually less sure and would hesitate.

Clinical assessment

Import: it is impossible to control a misbehaving child and one's own anger.

Conflicts: self-control versus aggression. Subject states she herself cannot be as sure as the character, suggesting a conflict about controlling aggressive impulses. Obedience–defiance. Child's repeated transgression is defiant but brings repeated punishment. Concerns with identity are evident in subject's vacillation in assuming the child's and mother's viewpoints and in vagueness about child's gender.

Internal representation: child seen as rebellious, defiant, curious, controlling, an animal or thief – suggesting a 'bad' child; Mother seen as angry, impulsive, punitive, abusive, ineffectual.

Quality of relations: the relationship consists of a bonding power struggle. Closeness is experienced in the modes of rebellion and punishment. There are no indications of empathy.

Story IV, Card 7GF

A mother is waiting for her daughter to pay attention before she begins reading. There is a lot of 'distance' between them. Daughter wants to 'get away,' but mother has 'enforced' this as instructional time. Daughter will stay 'like a good girl' but will go and 'do something nasty to the doll.'

Clinical assessment

Import: when expressing one's anger is feared, it is acted out aggressively on a powerless object.

Conflicts: obedience versus defiance and self-control versus aggression.

Internal representation: mother seen as manipulative, distant, unempathic; daughter seen as alienated, conflicted, scared, aggressive.

Quality of relations: distant, alienated, unloving, unempathic. Based on demands and reactions to those demands.

105

Overall clinical impression

This subject might have considerable conflict about authority. She might engage in power struggles with those she perceives as authority figures. She needs to comply and achieve but also to rebel, and she experiences a great deal of anger.

She may feel quite alienated from other people and might have some confusion about her own identity. Her TAT characters can relate only in power struggles. Otherwise, they are distant, aloof, going off in different directions. Anger is the only emotion expressed, and it is a dangerous one, leading to aggressive acting out.

Taken together, the subject's somewhat obsessional storytelling style, the predominance of conflicts about obedience, and two instances of aggressive acting out suggest a struggle to contain impulses, if not a potential for impulsive acting out.

Within-subject comparison of measures

The reference measures illuminate the extent to which Anna is concerned with issues of anger and control. Interestingly, they provide little evidence of the symbiotic connection to the still nursing daughter so central to the case study.

Anna's response to the Newberger dilemma indicates her ability to think in complex fashion about hypothetical characters. Interestingly, in resolving the dilemma, Anna moves away from this complexity, focuses on the importance of the mother doing the right thing for her child, and obviates the importance of communication and of dealing with both the mother and child.

The absence of interaction between characters in the Newberger dilemma is supported by the scoring of the Gilligan dilemma. Anna vacillates between the terms of others and herself. While she communicates with Elise and finds a compromise, she is unsure whether she is harming the child or whether the other mothers' terms are better than her own.

The TAT analysis emphasizes Anna's identity confusion and suggests that Anna's own development from motherly person, to anti-motherhood feminist, to pro-motherhood woman should be considered more carefully and may be seen as a shift from rebellion to compliance. Anna's hope that Elise will not feel that she has to become a mother suggests Anna's ongoing ambivalence about her own decisions and that she does not want her daughter to follow her out of compulsion.

While Anna's presentation of her mother as loving and accepting is suppported by the scores on the Assessment of Qualitative and Structural Dimensions of Object Representations, the TAT analysis suggests the extent to which this presentation is idealized. Instead of support and connection,

Anna may feel considerable conflict with authority figures while at the same time she feels suffocated and needs to comply. Power struggles provide the only mode of relating in the stories. Otherwise characters go in different directions. The case study supports this sense of alienation and focus on power issues but also suggests another mode, a more symbiotic, 'calm' connection in which mother and daughter or mother and other women are in tune and willingly heed each others' demands. Based on the TAT analysis, this can be seen as a wished for mode of connection, one which involves considerable compliance without struggle between inherently distinct terms.

As both the independent clinical assessment and the case study suggest, this mode involves considerable anger. The TAT analysis suggests the attraction of physicality and aggression to Anna. It is possible that nursing acts as a form of physical and symbiotic connection and is used to defend against other forms of aggressive but differentiated connection. At the same time, nursing has become the ultimate separator, distinguishing Anna from the community of mothers and leading to a struggle between mother and growing child.

Anna wants to feel one with the world. However, to experience this, people must act as she wants them to without her having to assert herself. Her own concern that she is becoming manipulative suggests the difficulty of becoming demanding in pursuit of her desire for connection and control.

INDIVIDUAL PROFILE: JULIA

Case summary

Julia is a forty-four-year-old woman who grew up in the West with her parents and younger sister. At the age of thirty-five, after years of work as a financial expert in a major corporation, Julia had a what she calls a 'breakdown.' She says she became aware that work and dating were not enough; she had been 'programmed' to have a child. Within three years, she left her job and married 'Irwin,' a highly successful real estate investor with grown children from a previous marriage. During two years of difficulty conceiving a child, Julia enrolled in an M.B.A. program with emphasis on human resources. Pregnancy, birth, and breastfeeding were described as pleasurable. Julia spent one year at home with her son and then 'forced herself' to spend afternoons completing her graduate work. Irwin provides considerable paid domestic help but is not involved in any child care activity.

'Max' was twenty-one months old at the time of the first interview, twenty-six months at the time of the second. He was involved in a one-morning-a-week pre-school program.

Julia arrives for the first interview in a sophisticated suit and matching

107

accessories. In appearance and manner she is very mature. Her formal appearance contrasts with the intense, rambling, disorganized, dramatic and humorous way she responds to questions. Because of her lengthy responses, the first interview spanned four hours and two sessions within a one-week period. At the completion of the interview, Julia said that she valued the opportunity to 'go on and on' rather than be engaged in the more familiar 'give and take.' I experience Julia as in charge of the pace of the interview. I feel she enjoys the way I function as an audience and is looking for a sympathetic response and for respect rather than advice. The second interview is somewhat different. Julia arrives with a strict two-hour time limitation, perhaps because we went too far during the first interview. She introduces a child rearing issue in response to the Gilligan dilemma and seems to be looking to me for advice. My lack of advice is frustrating and it seems hard for us to find the right ground for this interview. The interview process is not as meaningful for her and, I think, does not have the same richness as our earlier discussions.

Object relations

MOTHER Julia both admires and distinguishes herself from her mother. She emphasizes the value of her mother's 'aggressive' world view, her ability to answer questions and give advice based on her individualistic, do-for-your-self mentality. Julia speaks of her mother as attentive and supportive: 'I don't ever remember being put off or not treated well or pushed aside.' Yet she also speaks of her mother as self-absorbed and unable to attend to her daughter's needs

> My mother's not really interested in [understanding]. She's interested in what *she's* interested in [small laugh]. (Uh huh.) And, uh, tends to jump to conclusions about what other people are interested in.

In particular, Julia presents her mother as 'bad-tempered' but overly invested in propriety and impulse control. Julia gives an example from her adolescence. Her mother responded 'inappropriately' and restricted Julia from going to school carnivals because she saw them as questionable events. More recently, Julia sees her mother as expressing the same invest-ment in propriety in relation to her grandson. She has been appalled by Max's interest in playing with muffins at the breakfast table. Julia speaks of resisting childhood prohibitions by colluding with her friends, secretly doing what she wanted, and 'wearing my mother down.' 'Mother would get angry, then be sorry, and give in.'

However, Julia was unable to resist her mother's 'fearfulness' and became concerned about her own well-being. Julia's mother seems to have capitalized on this fearfulness by making threats when she felt unable to control her daughter. For example, when Julia was ten, her mother said that if she 'wasn't good, daddy was going to leave,' a memorable comment that raised the threat of separation and suggests her mother's need to break up the father–daughter relationship.

FATHER Julia says she has come to see her parents very much as a couple who 'really lived very much for each other' even though they focused considerable attention on their children. Her father is described as the more loving, 'gentle,' 'patient,' and 'understanding' parent, a man who could listen to people and be attentive to their ideas. This loving quality is associated with his ability to 'mend the fences' and 'put up with' his difficult wife. It is also associated with a problematic lack of confidence and assertiveness. 'His view towards things is more of a, a protective, cover the bases – this sort of thing. Rather than to take an aggressive, an ambitious viewpoint, which is more my mother's permutation.'

GOOD MOTHER Julia says it is easier to focus on the 'bad things' she doesn't want to do as a mother. She first focuses on her own mother's way of manipulating children to get them to comply with her 'projections' and her idea of appropriate behavior. Julia then presents the Mother as person. She emphasizes that the central quality in all relationships is honesty. Consequently, the Mother's relationship with her child should be based on responding to the child's questions and also on being truthful about Her own interests rather than being self-sacrificing.

> You know, people have to learn to live in the world with other people who also have needs, even though *they* have needs, and their needs may be more pressing at the moment. But it's not like you just totally obliterate your Mother's needs as a person. I mean, she still is a person.

In Julia's discussion, both Mother and child have the potential to relate without recognition. However, it is the Mother who suffers in two instances. She either 'pays a terrible price for expecting compliance' or She can be obliterated by the child. Although seeing the Mother as a person, Julia locates Her within the mother–child dyad. She is vulnerable and dependent on her resilient, yet punitive and needy child.

HUSBAND Julia speaks of her husband frequently and seems to be both understanding and critical of him. She presents him as a 'patriarch' as well as a child; he is a successful but demanding, non-nurturant figure. Irwin shares her mother's determination and values as well as her bad temper. In relation to him, Julia is loving and patient, a position that is similar to the role her father played in relation to his wife.

Julia indicates that Irwin is 'deeply loving' even though he 'acts like he doesn't care.' She also emphasizes that she and Irwin share the same 'basic values.' While having considerable strength of character, Irwin is presented as a very needy man who suffers from 'tremendous emotional problems that are narcissistic in nature.' Despite his achievements, 'there's no real happiness inside' and he is incapable of accommodating his son. In one example Julia heard about through their maid, Irwin ignored Max when the child was pounding to get into his locked study. Julia was at the opera that evening. She feels Irwin ignored Max because he felt deprived of his wife's attention. As Julia sees it, 'it's not an altogether selfish thing. I mean, he really, really needs my attention.' Julia wants to be the good mother she believes Irwin never had and also to partake of his well-to-do life. However, she feels an ongoing and difficult 'pull between my husband and my child.' SON Julia describes Max as determined, bright, and quick-tempered like her mother and husband but also as uniquely loving. The sensuousness, intensity, and peacefulness of the relationship is clear when Julia speaks of how Max gets her bed jacket when he wants to be held.

> We both know what's going to go on. That he's going to lie in my arms. And he's going to rub his face against this jacket, and drink his bottle, and close his eyes, and just be. (Uhuh.) You know. That I will. It'll be quiet and there won't be any other distractions.

Throughout the interviews, Julia emphasizes Max's ability to make intense connections and to 'make associations.' He puts ideas together and is presented as uniquely capable of responding to his mother. Julia speaks with awe of how during pregnancy the active Max would immediately become quiet whenever she was going to sleep. He now completes her sentences and reminds her of things she has forgotten. Because Max 'gives as good as he gets,' his attention to Julia makes her feel that he deems her uniquely worthy of this responsiveness.

The quality of Max's judgments is enhanced by the fact that he is presented as a wondrously insistent, powerful child who cannot be 'bribed' or told what to do and who uses charm and anger to get what he wants. His overt protests contrast with what she describes as her own covert maneuvers. Through Max, she has a vicarious experience of directness. Julia is, however, concerned about Max 'shutting you out' when determined not to respond to her requests. For example, he doesn't always say the alphabet when asked and sometimes doesn't let her touch his toys. Julia is concerned that Max may be 'pushed' too much by her efforts to teach and 'harness' his intelligence and that he may be overwhelmed by too many toys. However, she focuses more attention on her feelings of exclusion from Max's world and anticipates that, like her own mother, it will be 'hard when he asserts his independence from me.' As one indication of this difficulty, despite her portrayal of Max as competent and powerful, she cannot picture him as a grown up.

Relationality

Julia speaks of a variety of connections to other people, often mentioning women friends, neighbors, and relatives as well as members of her immediate family. She appreciates difference, seems to look for similarities underneath different personalities and lifestyles, and is intent on salvaging what is valuable in difficult relationships. Throughout what are described as caring, responsive relationships to others, Julia expresses a level of self-involvement and vulnerability.

Her metaphor of mending fences suggests that relationships are supported both by fixing breaks and by maintaining boundaries. The boundary can be used to differentiate between self and other or, as in the case of mother and child, it may be placed around the dyad and used to 'shut out' others. Julia also uses boundaries to deal with worry and her propensity to 'think of every possibility for everything.' She shuts out ideas to 'put things out of [her] mind.'

Although advocating an individualistic, do-for-yourself stance, Julia associates separation with a purposive break in connection. Julia identifies with Max's growing understanding that he is 'separate and different' and a person with the 'ability to operate independently.' However, she also emphasizes the 'fear of doing that, and the wanting not to, you know, to wipe it all out.' In Julia's view, individualism and the assertion of one's needs can lead to 'obliteration' of the other.

Traditionality

Julia became a career woman at a time when such achievements were unusual. She depicts the traditional woman in negative terms and says that she 'never thought in terms of great, loving, intentful, caring, mothering kinds of things,' and did not feel a sense of affiliation with other women until she had faced the 'subtleties of discrimination' at the workplace.

Julia's devotion to her child, support of her patriarchal husband, and current lack of career involvement are highly traditional. At the same time, she advocates the modern notion of mother as person and sees the traditional woman as 'mired down' in motherhood and as 'dull, plain, and unattractive.' This is an inevitable consequence of motherhood. 'How can you be all that you can be with those distractions? And the needs of other people.' The needs of husbands and children are 'taxing.' They pull the woman away from herself, specifically from being attractive and lively. Nowhere in this presentation does Julia question this sense of motherhood as taking away from self-actualization. Throughout, Julia's own painful need for care is apparent. She is in a difficult situation. She feels Max needs her to be attractive, but in her view to be the caring mother she must turn into the 'hag' her son will reject. Interestingly, Irwin is more dependable; he would rather have her be a 'hag' than neglect him.

Attractiveness is not associated with heterosexuality. Julia associates sensuousness with symbiotic closeness and with care of her own body. It has a primitive, intense, pregenital quality. Similarly, while loving to play with Max's toys, Julia does not seem to see play as wild, silly, or physical. She describes herself as a 'serious,' practical person who associates impulsivity with outcome. She enjoys Max making a 'mess' with food. It reflects a useful 'driving need to know,' an intellectual achievement rather than a physical pleasure. Max's saying 'No' is seen as contributing to his development and self-esteem rather than as some inherent pleasure. Here, Julia enjoys his power: 'He almost gets bigger while he's saying no.' While attaching importance to her own ability to say no, Julia never accepts her own anger. Instead, she feels most 'righteous' and adult when she 'doesn't allow personal frustrations to take over.'

Reference measures

I Object relations: Assessment of Qualitative and Structural Dimensions of Object Representations (AQSDOR)

	Mother	Father	Husband	Son
Factor I – Nurturance				
Nurturant	5	6	2	3
Positive ideal	5	5	3	5
Benevolent	5	6	3	6
Cold–Warm	6	7	5	7
Degree of constructive involvement	2	6	1	6
Affectionate	4*	4	2	7
Weak–Strong	5	3	5	5
Successful	4	4	2	6
Factor II – Striving				
Judgmental	7	3	7	4
Ambitious	6	2	7	6
Punitive	6	4	6	5
Intellectual	5	6	4	6
Degree of ambivalence**	3	1	3	2
Successful	4	4	2	6
Weak–Strong	5	3	5	5
Conceptual level***	5	1	7	9

* 4 = uncodable, inadequate material
** Three-point scale
*** Scored on scale of 1, 3, 5, 7, 9

Julia presents her father unambivalently, as an undifferentiated, need-satisfying figure. In contrast, she describes her mother with a great deal of ambivalence but presents her at a higher level, as a separate entity, and in terms of her behavior. Both mother and father are rather benevolent, admirable but contrasting figures. Her father is weaker but more nurturant and able to respond to Julia constructively. Her mother is a stronger, judgmental, pushy figure who does not respond to Julia constructively.

Julia presents her husband and especially her son as considerably more distinct figures and focuses on their feelings as well as their behaviors. Like Julia's mother, Irwin is judgmental, strong, punitive, and highly ambitious. However, his nurturance scores differ substantially from those of Julia's parents; although quite loving, he is an extremely needy, unhappy, undemonstrative man who is thoroughly unable to respond to Julia constructively.

Max is the only object whom Julia presents as affectionate or happy with himself. He is benevolent, warm, and, like her father, extremely able to respond to Julia constructively. He is also bright, strong, and ambitious. However, he is demanding and somewhat punitive, characteristics which detract from his nurturance.

II Relationality: Attanucci coding of Gilligan dilemma

Types of self-description	Number of responses by level			
	I	II	III	IV
Self in relation to son	0	3	5	3
Self in relation to experts	0	4	0	0

Julia's dilemma concerns how to respond when Max deliberately urinates on the floor. This situation is confusing because 'everything [she] has read' says that toilet training has lifelong impact and that parents should be 'low key.' Julia wants to follow expert advice and be the best mother for Max. When Max deliberately urinates on the carpet, she does not know whether to be low key or to see this act as more like biting or deliberately spilling cereal, acts she sees as meriting a stronger, more punitive response.

The scores of self in relation to child represent various ways of seeing this situation. In the three instances coded at Level II, Julia focuses on Max's need to 'regress' as well as his desire to be a big boy going to the bathroom without assistance. The material coded at Level IV is introduced later and concerns both the child's 'ambivalence' and Julia's own mixed feelings: 'I don't want to hold on to him, or keep him little. But it's still nice to hold him and have those moments.' The five statements coded at Level III, many of which come at the end of the dilemma, focus on the specific situation and Julia's need to convince Max that he is a big boy who must not urinate on the floor. At the end of the dilemma, Julia is confident that she must transmit her own terms or Max will be 'uncontrollable.'

III Traditionality: Newberger dilemma

Issue	Final score
Resolving conflict	2(3)
Meeting needs	3(2)
	3(2): Global level

Julia begins by focusing on how the effect on the child of the mother working depends on how she feels about herself (Level 3). While constructing a complex and varied scenario that is dependent on the mother's history and life circumstances, Julia does not elaborate on the situations of the hypothetical Mrs Stewart and David. Instead, she focuses on her own situation and needs (Level 2). For example, while asserting that Max's happiness is a 'prime ingredient of [her] own happiness,' Julia focuses on her own need to 'enjoy his growing up.' Graduate school has allowed her to be away and 'still feel good about it.'

When Julia tries to reckon with the needs of mother and child, she describes a complex 'individual equation' in which the needs of one person cannot outweigh those of the other. Here, the mother must pay attention to the child's adjustment and his expression of needs over time.

IV Thematic Apperception Test

Story I, Card 1

A child has positive feelings about the violin, is feeling 'pensive,' but continues to play even when he wants to do other things or after his performance has been criticized.

Clinical assessment

Import: when you feel strongly about something, you can stick with it despite resistances and disappointments.

Conflicts: ambivalence about achievement or work; doubts about abilities versus ambition and determination.

Internal representations: boy seen as pensive, ambivalent, mature, hardworking, sensitive to criticism.

Quality of relations: cannot be inferred directly. However, attachment to the violin and sensitivity to criticism suggest the ability to empathize.

Story II, Card 2

At first unsure whether female characters are the same person in different roles, Julia then sees them as mother and daughter. Daughter sees her mother as 'mired down,' is 'sad' but 'determined' to leave. Mother feels 'resigned' to 'losing the daughter' but she sees her as doing what she might have done. Husband is 'doing what he wants to do.'

Clinical assessment

Import: the process of separation between mother and child is conflictual but inevitable.

Conflicts: concerns about separation. There is a determination to separate yet a desire to remain at one with the mother.

Internal representations: mother seen as conflicted, stoic, passive, resentful; father seen as content, sensual; daughter seen as determined, sad, empathic.

Quality of relations: care, empathy, and the fear of loss. There is 'preverbal' closeness and sense of shared destiny. There is no overt dialogue or communication.

Story III, Card 5

A wife is called by her demanding husband. He expects his needs will be met, she responds and accepts her mundane role. Both 'play the roles' and do not expect 'intimacy,' 'spontaneity,' or 'joy.'

Clinical assessment

Import: a wife can accept the role of a housewife.

Conflicts: cannot be derived from the story but Julia's comments suggest that she is concerned with intimacy and, possibly, about her role as a wife or housewife.

Internal representations: women seen as wives, submissive, self-accepting, passive, reactive; men seen as entitled, dependent, demanding.

Quality of relationships: flat, mundane, fixed in roles. Action-oriented as opposed to feeling-oriented. However, Julia's criticism of these relationships suggests a capacity for greater depth and relatedness.

Story IV, Card 7GF

A young girl is daydreaming about being older and more glamorous, wondering whether she will be a mother or a movie star. Her mother is understanding. Like most people, 'she'll grow up within the norms.'

Clinical assessment

Import: childhood dreams of glamour are unlikely to be fulfilled.

Conflicts: grandiosity versus self doubt; fame versus safety; conformity versus non-conformity.

Internal representations: mother seen as thoughtful, curious, observant, understanding, passive, calm; daughter seen as pained, future-oriented, mature, passive.

Quality of relations: there is intuitive understanding, empathy, and insight. But there is no overt dialogue.

Overall clinical impressions

As represented by these stories, the subject's main concerns appear to be the regulation of self-esteem and intimacy. In terms of self-esteem, she might have doubts about her abilities and might be sensitive to criticism (rejection?). As for intimacy, she appears to have the capacity for closeness and empathy but, because of the passivity of female characters and lack of dialogue, there is a question as to whether she is able to actualize these capacities in relationships.

Defenses are primarily intellectual in nature. Her characters think a lot, do little, and accept their roles. There are no indications of impulsivity.

Within-subject comparison of measures

The reference measures highlight the diversity and complexity of Julia's responses. Scores on the Assessment of Qualitative and Structural Dimensions of Object Representations indicate that Julia's object representations vary considerably. The coding of the Gilligan dilemma indicates that Julia's focus on Max varies depending on whether she is considering his needs and conflicts about growing up (Level II), or considering her own need for Max to be a controllable and acceptable child (Level III). Responses scored at Level IV are interesting and suggest Julia's ability to consider both her own terms and her child's at those exquisite but fleeting 'warm and cuddly' moments. Interestingly, Julia's response to the Newberger dilemma suggests that she may be less prone to consider the child in situations when needs conflict.

The independent analysis of Julia's TAT stories emphasizes her capacity for closeness and empathy and also suggests that she may be too passive to actualize these capacities. Julia experiences moments of calm, sensuous, symbiotic connection as particularly meaningful; she may be less able to relate through activity and dialogue.

This analysis is particularly striking because Julia admires striving characteristics and presents herself as an ambitious, persevering woman who is capable of resisting her mother's control and of having enduring relationships with difficult people. The TAT stories suggest that while Julia may wish to be strong and vital, underneath she may feel inadequate, 'mired down,' subjected to restrictive demands and norms. In particular, family life is mundane, lacking in intimacy and excitement. Women are particularly subject to the demands of men. Daughters share their mothers' dreams but are unable to actualize them.

These stories lend support to the traditionality analysis in the case study and suggest that while Julia may find motherhood to be deeply meaningful, she also feels weighed down and seems concerned about being obliterated by it. While her TAT stories indicate Julia's close association with the unfortunate traditional woman, they also may reflect the extent of Julia's identification with her father, a loving but passive man who lacks self-confidence and puts up with his wife. This underlying, primitive connection with her father is also supported by the low conceptual level Julia's presentation of him received in the scoring of the AQSDOR. While admiring her mother's more masculine and aggressive stance, Julia's do-for-yourself mentality comes to make particular sense as a way of caring for herself when no one else can or will. However, Julia's stories and discussion also suggest a degree of hopelessness which contrasts with her considerable effort to persevere, enjoy Max, and gain satisfaction from her ability to care for her husband.

INDIVIDUAL PROFILE: DENISE

Case summary

Denise is a forty-two-year-old Jewish woman who grew up in the South with her eastern European immigrant parents and two older brothers. She has been married to 'Ted' for four years. Denise had established a successful career in marketing before her son, 'Joshua,' was born. She worked part time from the time Joshua was two to nine months old, then resumed full time work at her employer's request so she could 'appear to be trying it.' Denise found this arrangement unsatisfying, left her job a short time later, and has done freelance work in order to spend time with Joshua. Ted is a sports attorney who encouraged Denise to work and has become very accepting of her decision to stay home. The family has a daytime house-keeper who takes care of Joshua when Denise is working.

Joshua was seventeen months old at the time of the first interview, twenty-three months at the second. Denise takes Joshua to a one-morning-a-week 'mommy and me' art program.

Denise is a very engaging interviewee who talks in a somewhat dramatic, enthusiastic, open, and humorous style. Having been in therapy for years, Denise respects psychologists. She seems to see me as a wise friend and likes building a relationship in the context of motherhood. While comfortable, Denise also is concerned about how she fits into the 'matrix' of mothers I have interviewed. She also wants me to tell her story to a public that she feels does not listen to her.

Object relations

MOTHER Although Denise believes that her mother 'must have done something right' because she and her brothers are decent people, she says she feels unable to define or reproduce her mother's goodness. Her mother's negative qualities are more apparent. Denise describes her mother as a 'tenacious,' 'disapproving' woman who did not appreciate her daughter's uniqueness and wanted Denise to be an 'ordinary,' 'sweet and agreeable' girl. 'I always felt that though I didn't have her love, I could rely on her to harangue me some more I guess.'

Denise always felt that she was the 'bad seed' who could not make her 'tense, fraught, angry' mother happy.

> She would be more concerned about cleaning up the house than letting us play with the broom. Um, that she had this agenda, and that was of paramount importance. And part of her achievement was to achieve it in spite of us.'

FATHER In contrast, Denise says that her father took 'enormous pleasure and delight in young children' but that kids lose the 'sanction of being a child' at about age six or seven. Denise then experienced

> terrible abandonment. That [my brothers and I] must have been doing something horrible. Why would our father lose interest in us that way? And then he becomes sort of more judgmental and um – which is a word I realize I ascribed to myself earlier. Um you sort of have to win his approval. It's not so ready. He can withdraw it if you do something that he doesn't like, even though that might be objectively a fine quality for you to have.

In addition to the shift from acceptance to abandonment, Denise speaks of her father as lacking self-esteem and social skills, as a 'superficially gregarious' but 'guarded and antisocial' man who had few friends.

PARENTAL COUPLE Both parents are described as hard-working immigrants who did not understand the 'rules' in their new country, depended on Denise to make a place for them here and 'projected their feelings of badness' onto her. Instead of showing tolerance for the 'evolution of a child into a socialized adult,' Denise's parents felt they had to 'stamp out' any problems.

> I had this sense of being rushed when I was with my parents. I never had the feeling they took pleasure or delight in me. Um. That I was always somebody that had to be reared, corrected, cleaned up, straightened out, disciplined, organized. Da, da, da. As opposed to somebody who was an intrinsic delight.

GOOD MOTHER Denise speaks of trying to 'compensate' for the mothering she 'sorely missed' by not becoming the bad mother – a woman who, like her own mother, is suspicious of her children and cannot enjoy them.

Denise describes the embodiment of motherhood as a 'paradigmatic relationship' in which the Mother is the 'tolerant, accepting partner.' While speaking from the vantage point of the child who continues to seek the acceptance she herself missed, Denise also speaks from the vantage point of the mother who may become 'glommed on' [overly connected] to her child. She says that the Mother must have a 'separate and parallel existence' or she will suffer 'attrition of herself.' Work provides a form of feedback that Denise finds 'ego-enhancing.' Without this experience of individual effectiveness, Denise says it is possible to 'lose it here' and 'drift.'

HUSBAND Denise speaks of Ted as an erotic, powerful, 'rigid' male figure who 'dominates the marriage' and is the source of 'order and predictability' in Joshua's life. Like herself, he is a 'bright, determined, inquiring, empathic' person who also had a troubled childhood and is in psychotherapy.

While presented as a person and husband, Ted is also presented as troubled by being a father. Denise describes him as feeling displaced by Joshua and as emotionally dependent on her; 'It's not very kind and perhaps it's not even very accurate to characterize it as a more infantile kind of desire for closeness.' Although Denise is disturbed that Ted does not share her close bond with Joshua, Ted's interest in her is also pleasing; she is still loved even though she is a long-term wife and mother. Both the adoring relationship with her husband and her concern about its loss parallel Denise's relationship with her father.

SON Joshua is described as 'bright,' 'determined,' and 'empathic' like both parents but as more like Denise because he is 'gregarious.' Most prominently, Joshua is presented as an adored and adoring male child. He is 'charming,' has a 'pleasing' body, and Denise 'cannot resist' kissing him. Denise describes the threesome as a 'ménage à trois' rather than the 'family' a second child would create, suggesting that she experiences somewhat taboo, highly sexualized relationships with two men.

Joshua is distinguished from his father in the unique quality of his 'life-giving' love for Denise, 'the purest form of unquestioned, unqualified love' for 'being' rather than for achievement. Joshua here is like the good, loving, accepting parent and also 'like the child I can barely recall. And that was really quite screwed up by my parents.'

> I was so thoroughly taught that I was sort of the *bad* seed that it was difficult for me to say that I was going to reproduce myself. So I feel *vindicated* that not only have I reproduced myself, but it's such a nice um, child.

In Denise's case, this resistance to reproduction is actually doubled. She is concerned about reproducing both her mother and herself.

Denise does not describe Joshua solely in positive terms. She says she has 'mixed feelings' that he is aggressive with other children and hits and bites her. However, she does not experience Joshua as demanding or damaging and, rather, sees him as making contact and as able to protest at intolerable situations. Denise is more concerned that Joshua is a 'child who goes his own way' instead of playing with other children. She says she cannot help but 'project' her own feelings of loneliness and is concerned that his solitary activity is evidence of her own lack of sociability. It also seems that Denise wants to keep Joshua to herself. Notably, Joshua's attempts at comforting other children – especially a baby girl – are presented as Joshua going his own way rather than Joshua being sensitive to others.

Relationality

Denise speaks of caring connections to significant others and of trying to be supportive of her husband, parents, and child. She seems to want to make them feel better, but is also worried about either damaging them by being overly critical like her parents or ruining the relationship by acting 'authentic' rather than 'entertaining.' Although Denise says she has a number of long-term relationships characterized by 'mutual affinity,' she adds that 'nothing about these relationships makes me happy.'

> I was lonely for big parts of my life, and look at me, I'm still, here I am now kind of plugged into a social system [of mothers] I don't feel entirely at ease with. And suddenly I'm friendly with women. Not friendly with women. I don't know what I'm doing with them.

Denise says that what she wants is 'gritty, earthy, frank kind of friendships' but is afraid to be herself. It is easier for Denise to be charming with men; sexuality provides the desired intensity. However, Denise worries about those relationships ending as the 'mystery' wears off.

Although the relationship with Joshua is different, she again indicates the possibility of loss. She would like to 'freeze' the relationship at this moment when both mother and child are 'happy with each other.'

Denise seems to accept the idea that, as a parent, you 'give on one level and get back on another.' She does not find Joshua inordinately demanding and enjoys the fact that Joshua recognizes her as the person with whom to share interesting things. She feels that this is a model relationship because the 'fall out from just his being who and what he is is gratification enough.' He adores her and she does not have to demand more of him.

Traditionality

In many ways, Denise wants to be the available, accepting, never angry mother. These are traditional maternal qualities which Denise's own mother lacked. In an interesting addition to these traditional qualities, Denise's sense of motherhood also includes an edge of 'otherness' and sensuous pleasure that is at odds with the conventional notion of the asexual mother. She relates sex and motherhood by saying both 'are not trivial and I think they put you very much back in touch with what's good and wholesome and innate in life.' Denise's feels 'out of step' but generous and wiser than what she sees as the more conventional, career-oriented 'superwoman.' She also believes that people see her as 'narcissistic' and unattractive for leaving her job and feels further 'debased' by building her schedule around her husband's demands.

In her desire to be attractive and acceptable to a complex range of others, Denise can analyze critically but not reject social messages. Instead, she feels she 'leads two or three lives,' each with its own clothing and mode of behavior. Denise says the only time she has ever felt really beautiful is as a mother and she is 'dazzled' by watching mothers' postures as they care for their children. At the same time, Denise is aware that 'society' sees mothers as 'ordinary.' Denise 'resents' this and criticizes the notion of 'superwoman' as stunning, but does subscribe to the image of attractive, male-oriented woman she sees represented in *Cosmopolitan* magazine. However, she is in a trap: to be this *Cosmopolitan* woman while being a mother would be to be a 'cunt,' a woman more involved in satisfying herself and her adult male partner than 'sacrificing' for her child.

When focusing directly on the relationship with Joshua, Denise prefers to see herself as a benign and powerful figure. Denise's image of the relationship includes herself 'playing God,' both helping Joshua and 'molding,' 'arming' him for 'assault' in a less benign world. In pointed contrast to her own mother's practice, Denise feels that children deserve 'boundless approval.' They are appropriately 'antisocial' and only need a modicum of socialization. Instead of imposing her will, Denise wants unspoken negotiation: if she 'indulges' Joshua and gives him space to play with whatever intrigues him on the street, he ought to accommodate her schedule and move along.

While she finds the position of limit-setter unappealing, Denise is particularly conflicted about whether she wants to be associated with comforting, easy-to-provide 'routine' or with more complex and exciting 'adventure.' This issue seems to relate to impulsivity. Play has been a lonely, unhappy experience for Denise; she is not comfortable engaging in active, aggressive play with Joshua. She prefers to 'accompany' Joshua, 'hang out' with him, and take 'childlike' pleasure in things like colors. These pleasures are less wild and messy, less dependent on personal initiative than is play. Further related to impulsivity, Denise associates anger with her own mother and never says that it is all right to get angry at her child. While she seeks intense positive emotions, her emotional range is limited. It is in terms of sexuality with an adoring male that Denise is freest of these restraints and seems to experience the greatest pleasure.

Reference measures

I Object relations: Assessment of Qualitative and Structural Dimensions of Object Representations (ASQDOR)

	Mother	Father	Husband	Son
Factor I – Nurturance				
Nurturant	3	3	3	4*
Positive ideal	2	3	5	6
Benevolent	2	3	5	7
Cold–Warm	1	5	6	7
Degree of constructive involvement	2	3	3	5
Affectionate	4	5	6	6
Weak–Strong	2	2	6	6
Successful	2	2	4	5
Factor II – Striving				
Judgmental	7	6	4	4
Ambitious	7	6	7	5
Punitive	6	5	4	2
Intellectual	4	4	5	5
Degree of ambivalence**	2	2	2	1
Successful	2	2	4	5
Weak–Strong	2	2	6	6
Conceptual level***	9	7	7	9

* 4 = uncodable, inadequate material
** Three-point scale
*** Scored on scale of 1, 3, 5, 7, 9

Denise's representations of her mother and son are at the highest conceptual level and include integration of feelings and behavior. Representations of the two adult males, husband and father, focus on their feelings and are at the slightly lower, internal iconic level. Except for the unconflicted representation of her son, objects are presented with a moderate degree of ambivalence.

The scores indicate that Denise presents her parents as rather similar, although she sees her mother in consistently more negative terms. Both are presented as malevolent and as needy, weak, unsuccessful figures who are judgmental and punitive and push their daughter without responding to her constructively. Denise distinguishes her father from her mother by presenting him as warm and affectionate; her mother is presented as cold.

Denise presents her husband and son in considerably more positive terms. In contrast to her parents, both are presented as admirable, benevolent, loving, affectionate, strong figures. Although ambitious for themselves, they are not presented as driving, judging, or punishing Denise. Joshua, in particular, is seen as non-punitive, extremely warm, and benevolent. He is the only figure that Denise presents as happy, undemanding, and able to respond to her constructively. Although strong, his striving characteristics are more moderate than those of other objects.

II Relationality: Attanucci coding of Gilligan dilemma

Types of self-description	Number of responses by level			
	I	II	III	IV
Self in relation to children	0	0	1	2
Self in relation to own parents	0	1	0	0
Self in relation to other mothers	0	4	2	1

Denise's dilemma revolves around the 'peer pressures' of motherhood and the difficulty of dealing with the conflicting messages of other mothers. She portrays these other mothers as judgmental. Denise wants to 'look like a socially responsible mother,' but feels 'unbelievably confused' because some mothers find her 'overbearing and interfering' and others find her 'lackadaisical and irresponsible.' In particular, she gets no consistent message about how to behave when her son is aggressively grabbing toys from other children.

Denise explains the salience of this issue by saying that her own mother and father 'didn't know how to get along outside of the family.' Her mother was confused about what people wanted or meant; her father was 'remote' and had few friends. As their most charming child, Denise felt a great deal of pressure to carve a niche for the family. 'When I failed, I felt doubly bad, because I felt I was letting down this whole family.'

While this discussion of her parents and other mothers is at Level II and focuses on satisfying the terms and needs of others, Denise's presentation changes markedly when she speaks of herself in relation to Joshua and when she speaks about a good friend, the only mother she does not present as judgmental. Denise describes herself as 'refereeing a situation' and imposing her rules once when Joshua is grabbing a toy (Level III). She also speaks of having 'good instincts' as a mother and as being able to 'read' her child accurately and respond in terms of his needs as well as in terms of values she wishes to transmit (Level IV). Her discussion of how she and a friend differed about the appropriate kind of birthday party for a two-year-old is also scored at Level IV.

However, Denise closes the dilemma by reiterating her 'self-doubts' and speaking of the 'wear and tear' on herself as she agonizes over decisions. In terms of the central issue of the dilemma, Denise scores at Level II. She is unsure of herself, focused on the terms of others and on striving to be helpful and deemed good by them.

III Traditionality: Newberger dilemma

Issue	Final score
Resolving conflict	3
Meeting needs	3
Subjectivity	3
	3: Global level

While Denise begins to resolve the Stewarts' dilemma in terms of the more conventional, Level 2 focus on fairness, she quickly moves to the subjective–individualistic Level 3 and considers David and his mother as people involved in an ongoing, communicative relationship. Denise sees Mrs Stewart as a caring, responsive mother who has gotten her child off to a good start and now needs to return to work for her own well-being. David is in 'pretty good shape 'cause [he] can verbalize' his interest in having his mother there.

Denise's resolution of the dilemma focuses on the fact that both mother and child have 'distorted perceptions' and mixed feelings. While the mother is legitimately unhappy and 'romanticizes' the value of work, she is not fully able to understand what work means to her. David wants his mother at home but also 'wants his mother somewhat to have what she wants.' He understands in a 'visceral' way what satisfaction is, but does not have the capacity to understand what work means to his mother.

In Denise's view, David 'fears making his mother unhappy' and feels that her anger 'could come back to haunt him.' While outlining a scenario scored at Level 4 because of the complexity of the emotional transaction between mother and child, Denise focuses on the child's concern about his mother's anger and unhappiness. Denise resolves the dilemma at Level 3 with the child 'cooling it.' He keeps his worries to himself but has enough 'self-worth' to handle his mother's absence.

IV Thematic Apperception Test

Story I, Card 1

A boy who would rather be playing outside is 'forced' to play the violin by his mother who wants him to be 'cultured and refined.' His father does not intervene. The boy survives, stops playing as he gets older, and tells funny stories about it.

Clinical assessment

Import: a child can survive his mother's imposition of her own needs.

Conflicts: vulnerability versus strength.

Internal representations: mother seen as unempathic and narcissistic; father seen as passive; child seen as strong, healthy, mature, detached.

Quality of relations: mother-child relationship seems to consist of unrealistic expectations, an absence of empathy, and little by way of communication.

Story II, Card 2

A researcher is studying a more primitive people. Denise says she 'identifies' with both women but sees the researcher as sexually 'repressed' and 'worried' that she will not have children; the other woman is a 'primitive earth mother' who is happier and more sensuous. The man is a sexy 'hunk' who 'does what has to be done' without great dissatisfactions or aspirations.

Clinical assessment

Import: in the conflict of choosing career versus motherhood, the latter choice is more gratifying.

Conflicts: career versus motherhood; mind versus body.

Internal representations: women seen as thoughtful, preoccupied, sensual, sexually repressed, voluptuous, worried, conflicted. Men seen as sexual, content, thoughtless, animalistic, sensitive.

Quality of relations: emphasis is on the fulfillment of motherhood. The man is essentially dismissed as a thoughtless beast and the wife–husband relationship is primarily sexual.

Story III, Card 5

A woman peeks in a room. If it were a bedroom, she would be seeing a masturbating son. But she is looking in the living room at her husband who has lost his store, is struggling to find a job, and has returned home drunk again. She is a 'victim' and 'victimizer' who struggles to be 'respectable' and yells at him. Both feel disappointment with themselves and each other and go to bed without speaking. Their children 'grow up to feel sad and write novels.'

Clinical assessment

Import: when parents don't resolve conflicts, their children grow up to be sad but creative.

Conflicts: guilt versus externalizing the blame. Concern over sexuality.

Internal representations: mother seen as intrusive; son seen as autoerotic; wife seen as uptight, panicky, angry, proud, victimized; husband seen as a loser, a schmuck, passive, out of control, a victim.

Quality of relations: relationship between mother and son is sexualized. Relationship between husband and wife consists of a compulsive re-enactment of hostility. There are expectations in their relationship – husband and wife are not withdrawn from each other – but their only interaction is hostile in nature.

Story IV, Card 7GF

A mother and a pubescent daughter are sitting what seems 'unusually close to each other' but the closeness is caused by 'distorted perspective.' The daughter is thinking of her future. Because she has had a loving mother, she will have an 'interesting life' filled with 'passion' and fulfilled 'potential,' an abortion and an affair as well as marriage and family. While her life is different from her mother's, her mother is 'accepting,' 'loving and content.'

Clinical assessment

Import: when a mother and a daughter have an unusually close relationship, the daughter will grow up to be a separate person and lead an exciting life.

Conflicts: although there is no conflict in the story, there are some subtle suggestions about conflicts over the sexualizing of relationships.

Internal representation: mother seen as loving, accepting, gracious, content. Daughter seen as interesting, sparkling, passionate, adventurous, sexy.

Quality of relationship: mother–daughter relationship seen as exceptionally close, loving. Mother allows daughter to separate but remains close.

Overall clinical impression

As represented by these stories, subject appears to have a very rich, creative inner life. She has concerns about her role as a woman, wife, and mother. She might be able to have emotionally close and meaningful relationships with women – which might be underlain by unconscious homosexual wishes. Her relationships with men are intensely sexual, but underneath there appears to be a great deal of ambivalence and hostility.

She also might have conflicts about pregnancy and she may sexualize her relationship with her child. She has sex on her mind, but probably longs for emotional intensity which, in non-sexual terms, she can only find with women.

There are indications of impulsivity, but in general, a higher order defense organization suggests no acting out except perhaps where sex is concerned.

Within-subject comparison of measures

The issues of judgmentalness, desire for closeness, and satisfaction with motherhood highlighted in the case study are supported and extended by the reference measures. The scoring of the Gilligan dilemma indicates that Denise is capable of close connection to others, especially to children and to the rare woman who is not judgmental. However, Denise's presentation of other mothers as judgmental and pressuring suggests that she sees in other women those characteristics she found so troubling in her own mother. Interestingly, while she feels her own judgments are good, she feels she must listen to and satisfy these other women. This material lends support to the idea that Denise may feel unable to say no to her own mother and to reject social messages.

This desire to satisfy others is further elaborated in Denise's response to the Newberger dilemma. Denise's scores demonstrate a high-level ability to focus on particular people and on emotional transactions. However, the material she presents indicates her own considerable anxiety and the burden she has felt in trying to make her mother happy. Denise's response to the hypothetical dilemma adds a sense of how she herself may have been 'haunted' by the possibility of her mother's anger and how, like David, Denise had to 'cool it' rather than get angry or demanding.

Scores on the Assessment of Qualitative and Structural Dimensions of

Object Representations support the case study, highlight the extent to which Joshua is a new and distinctly good object, and make clearer the extent to which Denise feels that she herself has not been cared for by her father, mother, or husband. The TAT stories seem to suggest that children with demanding and troubled parents can survive and be creative and charming. However, an exciting and fulfilling modern life comes to the daughter who has had a loving and accepting mother and real contentment comes only to the primitive earth mother. The pull between traditional and modern pleasures described in the case study is elaborated here. The clinical assessment of Denise's stories extends the case study analysis considerably in suggesting that Denise is capable of emotionally close relationships with women. The TAT analysis indicates the possible presence of homosexual wishes and that ambivalence and hostility are involved in her sexual relationships with men.

Her relationship with Joshua is distinguished by her sense of his goodness and belief that his love for her is unqualified. Denise experiences these qualities as the source of considerable personal change. For Denise, motherhood provides pleasure and profound and much desired change.

INDIVIDUAL PROFILE: HARRIET

Case summary

Harriet is a thirty-four-year-old Jewish woman who grew up in the New York metropolitan area with her parents and her younger brother. Her father was an optometrist and her mother a full time homemaker. Harriet spent twelve years as an elementary school teacher in Manhattan. She married 'Charles,' a chiropractor, five years ago. While pregnant, Harriet left her job as a social worker and the couple moved to the outskirts of a smaller city in the New York metropolitan area. Harriet is a 'full time' mother who wants to return to work when her son, 'Seth,' is in elementary school but also wants to have a second child.

Seth was twenty-four months at the time of the first interview, twenty-nine months at the time of the second. He is enrolled in a two-morning-a week toddler program and goes to a play group with his mother. Harriet feels it is hard to find good babysitters and, consequently, spends more time with Seth than she would like.

Harriet is a very pleasant woman who takes the interview seriously and also responds humorously to questions. As much as she is willing to participate in the study, she seems uncomfortable with the intrusion into her time and personal life. In particular, she does not seem clear about whether the interviews are for her, for me, or for some more amorphous purpose. She seems uncertain about how to balance full time motherhood with her own needs and unclear about what story she wants to tell. Harriet seems detached, concerned about doing a good job, and, as indicated by the fact that she wonders so much about whether the tape is picking up her comments, about making an impact.

Object relations

MOTHER While referring to a 'happy family situation,' Harriet does not mention her parents until asked about them toward the end of the first interview. Then she speaks about her mother's availability in a way that resembles Chodorow's overly involved mother.

> She wanted to be there for everything, she didn't want to let anything slip by. I mean I, my standing joke was that I was always afraid to call the operator for a phone number so she did that for me. (Uhuh.) And it's something that now in later years I kind of resent. I mean it's *great* that she was always there but I just want Seth to be able to *do* things on his own, to go places a lot more than I was able to do.

Harriet's mother became the interface with school officials and mediated Harriet's moves into the outside world. Harriet sees her mother's behavior as 'unhealthy' but she is also sympathetic to her mother. She explains that her mother needed to be so present because her own mother died when she was a teenager and was absent from her life. Harriet also takes responsibility for her own dependency: 'It was always too easy to do things like belonging to the brownie troop my mother led instead of doing it on my own a little bit more.'

Throughout, Harriet speaks of herself in a way that suggests a lack of agency – a lack of energy and will to achieve things. In contrast, her mother is a powerful figure who has had substantial impact on her life, 'probably took charge of things more at home' than her father, and is 'able to get her point across to Seth' in a way that Harriet cannot.

FATHER Harriet's profile raises the possibility of substantial father–child similarity even within a family with a strong mother–daughter connection. Harriet says, 'I have my father's personality' and – interestingly – focuses on shared negative qualities and on his means of dealing with aggression.

> My father can be very stubborn. And I've picked up a lot of that. I think that I'm getting a little bit better with it. Just, uh, stubborn and very [pause] he holds a lot of things in and lets them build up. And that's something I'd like to get rid of. You know that's something I'd like to be most unlike my father.

When she speaks positively about her father, she focuses on characteristics he shares with her husband. Both are 'very loving' men who spend a lot of time with their families. The emphasis is on closeness rather than on activity; Harriet provides no sense of what her father did.

GOOD MOTHER Harriet's good mother is an improved version of her own mother.

> I think a good mother is somebody who is there for their child when they need them, doesn't smother them, and gives them some space to be themselves. And, uh, just creates an atmosphere that's *happy* and, uh, not pressurized.

This Mother is not overbearing. Her goodness is defined by the child's response. She is 'just somebody that can put a smile on the child's face. Then you know you're doing something right when you get that smile back or the hug.' Throughout this discussion, Harriet does not articulate what it is like to be the Mother. Instead, it is as if the child's satisfied response is supposed to take care of Her.

Interestingly, Harriet does not speak of the bad mother as over-available. Instead of focusing on her problem with her own mother, she focuses on the opposite extreme. The bad mother is one who is never there and who 'ships [children] out to other people to babysit for the whole time.' This notion of the bad mother can be understood to include the working woman who relies on a babysitter. In contrast, the full time, stay-at-home mother is more likely to be a good mother. Harriet's presentation suggests both the danger of over-involvement with the child and the appeal of shipping the child off.

HUSBAND Harriet speaks of her husband often and presents him as similar to her father and to herself. 'My husband and I are, as I say, so much alike that it's almost scary. We're almost too much alike.' She goes on to speak of how they are both 'even-keeled' people who do not get 'too hot and bothered.' Interestingly, she never considers how Charles feels, his needs or activities outside the family setting.

Instead, there is considerable emphasis on how Charles is 'understanding' and 'extremely supportive,' he gives her 'that lift [she] needs at the end of the day' by frequently taking the family out to dinner. Harriet is concerned that she is 'relying on [her] husband for everything.' There is no indication that Charles encourages Harriet to get out by herself.

Before Seth was born, the couple travelled, went out a great deal, and could 'be free and easy and do what we wanted to do.' While Harriet hopes they can stay 'young at heart,' she is very concerned about 'slowing down' and becoming 'middle aged.' There is a sense of loss of marital excitement, although the couple go out to dinner by themselves once or twice a week, have vacationed without Seth, and seem to enjoy being parents together.

SON Harriet speaks of Seth as a 'real combination of my husband and myself.' She emphasizes that 'he's a real member of the family. He fits in very well.' He is a loving and lovable 'cute little guy,' 'has a great personality,' is 'easy-going,' and able to joke and laugh. Although mechanically inclined like his father, in response to questioning, Harriet says she 'never thought about' Seth as different from herself.

Most prominently, Seth is presented as the provider of feedback. 'Look, you're getting the so-called right responses. You have to feel good about it. Uh, if your child seems to be happy, it's got to make you feel good.' Although Harriet 'has to' feel good, she never says that she does feel good.

Harriet enjoys watching Seth grow, explore, and make discoveries and she enjoys exposing him to things. However, she finds two a 'difficult,' tantrum-filled age. She tends to see Seth as bothersome and frustrated rather than as terribly demanding or powerful. She sees him as 'apprehensive' around other children and thinking before acting rather than 'taking chances.' She is concerned that she may have inhibited him by being 'overbearing' when he was aggressive with his friends. Harriet does not identify with Seth's persistence or wish that she too could have tantrums. Although she seems to wish Seth were more impulsive, she tries to find the 'magic thing' to shift his behavior to a more 'easy-going' mode.

It is in terms of her child's interest in food that Harriet identifies most with his needs She would like to 'give him what he wants' but also feels that she must monitor his food intake. This is particularly difficult when Seth has been good or needs comforting; withholding food feels like a punishment.

Relationality

Although Harriet has numbers of friends and is very involved with her family, there is something flattened about Harriet's presentation that detracts from a sense of interpersonal engagement. For example, Harriet is not sure what she does for Seth and is particularly concerned about her psychological availability – 'I hope I'm being there for my child – as much as I should be.' In addition, she does not speak of responding to the needs of the adults in her life.

Instead, Harriet values a relatively undifferentiated and more primitive sense of comfort and togetherness. Throughout, she seems to need to have her own needs met. Connection means the comfort of a happy atmosphere at home and having a friend who is 'somebody to really talk to when you need someone,' 'someone that can make you happy to be with him or just talk to him.'

Connection also means being 'tied down' and 'held back.' Separation offers Harriet some relief. In this, she indicates that she is like her father and says, 'if I didn't like something I would just get very quiet, remove myself from the situation and go into my room or something.' As a child, Harriet hid in her closet. Now she sends Seth to his room when his behavior is bothering her so he 'doesn't get [her] boiling point up quite as high.'

Although this separation allows both mother and child to 'cool off,' Harriet is not clear about whether separation is good or punitive.

Traditionality

Harriet takes as her reference group other women who stay at home until their children are in school. She makes no explicit mention of the substantial changes in women's lives but is not fully satisfied with this traditional stance. 'There are times that I feel that I would like to go back to work *only* because it would make me feel a little bit more of myself. Right now, I don't feel 100 per cent myself.' The sense that motherhood diminishes her self and the association of work with independence and with selfhood are at odds with the traditional belief in fulfillment through motherhood.

Although not fully happy, Harriet cannot move out of the maternal position. She feels 'consumed' by motherhood and that her 'world is revolving around a much smaller area.' Harriet feels that she is now 'middle-aged;' 'there are a lot of things that you want to be doing that you can't be doing and that makes it harder now.' For example, Harriet would like to get out with friends during the day but seems to have difficulty getting out of the house unaccompanied by either her son or her husband. While she says quality child care is a problem, she has no difficulty leaving Seth with a fourteen-year-old when she goes out with Charles.

Staying at home is supported by Harriet's notion of child development: 'If I'm not there at the right time, you know, if I don't do the right thing, it's going to show up later on and be detrimental to him.' While she knows there are no 'guaranteed results,' Harriet tries to be 'understanding,' to set up a 'good environment' that makes Seth happy and provides 'good guidelines.' Harriet is concerned about being infantilizing or being the pushy teacher. While she can articulate a less overbearing position, like her mother, she 'falls into' doing too much for Seth and worrying, 'Have I missed a whole day or a whole week in his life when I didn't provide this or that?'

Throughout the interviews with Harriet, questions of her effectiveness relate to issues of impulsivity. Harriet never mentions sexuality directly but speaks of a loss of vitality in relation to her husband. She also demonstrates considerable difficulty in locating and owning angry feelings. While saying 'It's better to let things out' than to hold things in like her father, anger is a particularly dangerous emotion. Instead of indicating that Seth's whining makes her furious or frustrated, Harriet says, 'I couldn't decide what was bothering me.' Her response is to send Seth to his room – 'looking for the magic thing that will change things,' bring back the sweet child and the more comfortable mother.

Harriet does speak of herself as athletic and this interview is characterized by considerable humor and playfulness. She sees the childish part of herself as playful but also feels relieved that the fourteen-year-old babysitter provides play when she cannot.

Reference measures

I Object relations: Assessment of Qualitative and Structural Dimensions of Object Representations (AQSDOR)

	Mother	Father	Husband	Son
Factor I – Nurturance				
Nurturant	5	4*	5	4
Positive ideal	3	3	6	6
Benevolent	3	5	7	5
Cold–Warm	6	6	7	6
Degree of constructive involvement	1	4	7	4
Affectionate	4	4	4	6
Weak–Strong	5	3	4	5
Successful	4	4	4	4
Factor II – Striving				
Judgmental	4	4	4	4
Ambitious	4	4	4	4
Punitive	4	4	4	5
Intellectual	4	4	4	6
Degree of ambivalence**	2	2	1	1
Successful	4	4	4	4
Weak–Strong	5	3	4	5
Conceptual level***	5	5	3	5

* 4 = uncodable, inadequate material
** Three-point scale
*** Scored on scale of 1, 3, 5, 7, 9

Harriet describes her mother, father, and child in terms of their behaviors rather than in terms of their feelings. All four objects are described primarily in terms of their nurturant qualities and their ability to make Harriet feel loved. Her husband is less differentiated and presented primarily in terms of those behaviors and qualities that satisfy her needs. Except in her representation of her son, descriptions do not include physical affection or material scorable in terms of primary striving characteristics. These scores suggest more ambivalence and less admiration of parents than of her husband and child.

Harriet presents a particularly negative representation of her mother who, although loving, somewhat nurturant, and strong, is presented as somewhat malevolent, smothering, and unable to respond constructively. Her father is more benevolent although not nurturant and a negative ideal because he holds anger in. Harriet presents her husband without ambivalence and emphasizes his extreme benevolence, warmth, and ability to

133

respond constructively. Notably, this positive representation is based on reference to few qualities; it does not include physical affection or any striving characteristics. In contrast, Harriet includes many more characteristics in her positive representation of her son and emphasizes his affection, intelligence, persistence, and successfulness. Harriet presents her child as moderately punitive, giving indications of the way he would only stop doing something 'after he made me feel guilty.'

II Relationality: Attanucci coding of Gilligan dilemma

Type of self-description	Number of responses by level			
	I	II	III	IV
Self in relation to son	0	3	6	1

The dilemma Harriet presents revolves around issues of discipline. Harriet begins by considering her son's terms, focusing on whether to 'hold back' or 'give in' to Seth's requests for food when she believes he has had enough to eat but has been good; she does not want him to feel punished (Level II). She quickly moves on to consideration of when Seth has done something wrong and, specifically, whether she should hit him and whether hitting through the cushioning of a diaper is effective. Her construction of the dilemma revolves around her need to 'get the message across,' 'to make some kind of a dent that he knows that I'm finally really mad about something.' Throughout, Harriet is concerned with communicating her terms (Level III). At one point, she expresses particular concern about how Seth will understand her message since he is worried that his mother is mad at him rather than mad at what he did (Level IV). However, Harriet moves back to a Level III response, 'I, you know, tell him that I love him and give him a kiss and a hug, and that I'm sorry, and it usually helps me feel a little bit better.'

Harriet's scores reflect a concern for the self (Level III) with vacillation to concern for others (Level II). Attanucci's research suggests that such scores often reflect inadequate connection between self and other.

III Traditionality: Newberger dilemma

Issue	Final score
Resolving conflict	1.75
Meeting needs	2
	2: Global level

Harriet's initial response to the dilemma is scored at Level 1 because of the lack of a mechanism for resolving conflict between Mrs Stewart who has 'problems' being home and David who 'feels bad' when she works. Harriet then moves to a consistent Level 2 response to the dilemma. She indicates that it is 'better [for some mothers] to go out and work' and makes references to full time mothers 'going a little crazy.' However, she quickly counters these indications by saying that she believes that children do 'lose out' and know that 'something just is not right.' The emphasis on identifying *the* correct behavior and subordinating parental comfort to parental responsibility, central to Level 2 thinking, is reiterated in comments like, 'I just feel that once you make the commitment to having a child, that's got to be a top priority.' Harriet speaks of her own commitment to Seth: 'It wouldn't be good, as far as he went, to go back to work.' Characteristic of Level 2 thinking, Harriet never elaborates on the boy in the story or on Seth's feelings or responses.

In Harriet's case, response to the dilemma focuses much more clearly on Mrs Stewart and on the issues mothers face and should resolve in terms of fulfilling their commitment. She does present the possibility, again at Level 2, of explaining work to the child by emphasizing what Newberger calls fairness: David goes to nursery school because he likes it and his mother works because she likes it.

IV Thematic Apperception Test

Story I, Card 1

Harriet begins with a story about a boy 'drawn to' the violin and changes to a story in which a boy would rather be playing but is being pushed to practice the violin by a family member. He doesn't practice as much as he should but 'will play a little bit.'

Clinical assessment

Import: when you don't feel like doing a task which needs to be done, you compromise.

Conflicts: initiative versus (inferiority?); productivity versus fun.

Internal representations: boy seen as curious and compliant.

Story II, Card 2

A girl is going off to school but feels a 'certain closeness' to her family and looks 'guilty' and 'ambivalent.' Harriet first saw other characters as slaves and then as the girl's parents who are working hard to 'provide the best for her.'

Clinical assessment

Import: it is difficult to separate from one's parents.

Conflicts: autonomy versus guilt.

Internal representations: mother seen as 'backbone,' 'rock of the family.' Parents seen as self-sacrificing; father seen as hard-working; daughter seen as concerned, guilt-ridden.

Story III, Card 5

A mother has returned home from work exhausted and is 'not totally happy' that her child is watching television instead of doing homework.

Clinical assessment

Import: a woman's job is never done.

Conflicts: initiative versus rest (depression?).

Internal representations: mother seen as overworked; child seen as bored.

Story IV, Card 7GF

A mother is 'putting [her daughter] through the paces' of 'extra literary development.' Daughter would rather be doing something else but is 'trying to fit into her mother's image' and is 'not her own person.' Daughter 'resents' it, stares into space, and, someday, will make her mother feel 'rebelled against.'

Clinical assessment

Import: when a mother 'creates' a daughter in her own image, the daughter will act out in anger and the mother will feel rejected, perplexed.

Conflicts: separation versus symbiosis; identity.

Internal representations: mother seen as unempathic, rigid, self-centered; daughter seen as compliant, angry, rebellious.

Overall clinical impression

As represented by these stories, the subject appears to feel overburdened and unable to mobilize energy to initiate or produce. Her central conflicts seem to be with respect to separation–individuation. Guilt is the price of autonomy, and the attainment of individuality jeopardizes the desired symbiosis with the mother.

A concern with psychological and physical boundaries, a certain loss of distance from the TAT cards, and the use of idealization suggest narcissistic features.

Impulse control or the regulation of affect might be difficult at times.

Within-subject comparison of measures

Scores on the Assessment of Qualitative and Structural Dimensions of Object Representations support the case study analysis. The scoring distinction between qualities of nurturance and qualities of striving is particularly useful. The absence of material codable in terms of striving characteristics is striking and supports the case study analysis of Harriet as 'flat' and unable to deal with aggressive feelings. The idea that Harriet is self-involved and needing love is supported by her lack of attention to qualities like ambition, intellect, and success, qualities that might reflect the relationships her significant others have with the world.

The flattened sense of relationships, lack of engagement, and lack of nurturant response to others emphasized in the case study are supported by the Attanucci scoring. Harriet, the seemingly traditional full time mother, is scored in terms of an unconventional, but equally problematic focus on her own needs. Harriet's dilemma reflects her need for recognition of her presence and of her impact. She is focused on others but dependent on them to make herself feel better.

Although Harriet addresses the subject of loss of vitality and sense of self, and attributes this loss to motherhood, her representation of her mother's smothering quality and her emphasis on the importance of feeling loved suggest a more enduring sense of emptiness. This sense of emptiness is supported by Chodorow's analysis of the effect of the over-dependent, inadequately differentiated mother on her daughter. However, Harriet's sense that hitting Seth is essential to being heard suggests that aggression and control are related to the need for recognition.

The Thematic Apperception Test emphasizes the difficulties Harriet faces in differentiating self from other and in asserting an autonomous position. In her stories, Harriet assumes the position of a person constrained by others. In response to the Gilligan dilemma, she speaks of the problem of constraining her son. In both, Harriet suggests the difficulty of saying 'No' without harming another. The potential difficulty with impulse control mentioned in the TAT analysis suggests that negative feelings may break out despite efforts to contain them.

The Newberger coding supports the idea that Harriet can be seen as a fairly traditional woman, especially in terms of this research sample. Her Level 2 responses are consistent with the lack of engagement emphasized throughout this analysis. However, more must be said about the Newberger material and coding in order not to misrepresent Harriet's conventionality. First, although Harriet consistently exhibits Level 2 thinking when she argues that the mother must do the right thing and make her child her first priority, Harriet indicates that doing the right thing is at odds with the comfort of the mother who may be 'going crazy.' The case study, Attanucci coding, and TAT analysis suggest the degree to which Harriet's sense of duty does not resolve her own conflicts. Instead, while she enjoys being a full time mother and believes that commitment to Seth is right, she feels a substantial attrition of herself. Notably, in the dilemma she constructs, there is no sense of a conventional, right response to the issue of how to get her message across.

INDIVIDUAL PROFILE: KAREN

Case summary

Karen is a twenty-five-year-old woman who grew up in the Midwest. She is the oldest of four siblings and helped her full time mother take care of the brother and sister born by the time she was three years old and the sister born when she was thirteen. Her father was an electrician; he died about one and a half years before the first interview.

Karen works part time in a museum office and is studying fabric design. Her husband, 'Peter,' is European, ten years older than Karen, and is completing doctoral work in international relations. He felt that having children was 'one of the purposes of life' and convinced Karen – who says she was less interested in having a child, 'nonchalant' during her pregnancy, but felt 'immediate love' when 'Alex' was born.

Alex was twenty-four months old at the time of the first interview, twenty-nine months at the time of the second. He was enrolled at the university Center for Children. Peter takes care of Alex when Karen works and goes to school.

Karen has long hair, delicate features, and gentle voice and is intensely interested in questioning who she is and reflecting on her vulnerabilities and desires. I did not interview Karen the first time but she begins the second meeting by discussing her experience of the first session and reflecting on what she considers her inability to 'generalize' in response to questions, living instead from 'moment to moment.' Although she invites me to assess her previous performance, I talk instead about how other mothers share her experience of being bound in the present. She seems to find my comments supportive and is ready to start the interview.

Object relations

MOTHER Karen introduces her mother when asked about her image of a good mother. At that point in the interview, she presents her mother as a 'loving,' 'physically demonstrative' woman who 'did too much' for her husband and children.

Later in the first and throughout the second interview, Karen speaks of her mother in very negative terms, as 'obsessed with housework,' dreary, and 'just left, left us to grow ourselves' without responding to many of her children's emotional or physical needs, talents, or interests. Karen is most bitter when speaking of how her mother did not encourage her interest in reading and how she left Karen to walk home from a friend's house in a blizzard. Throughout, Karen speaks of her mother as 'superficial' and she fears being like her.

> I think my mom tends to be kind of superficial. And you know I kind of fear that in myself. You know, I *do* tend to be like that. I think, in a way. Um, and even um, in my relationship with Alex.

Numerous comments suggest that through her relationship with Alex Karen is confronting the lack of support she felt as a child. Karen speaks of a 'looking back' and – from the simultaneous vantage points of mother and child – dealing with a changing sense of her own mother. In particular, she is struggling to accommodate considerable negative feelings which she used to rationalize by understanding her mother's difficult farm background. Karen has few memories of her childhood but she is surprised that her 'generalized' sense of the past includes only 'bad memories' associated with her mother's lack of responsiveness and playfulness.

FATHER Karen speaks of her father in positive terms, although she limits her discussion to his paternal activity and does not describe his background, marriage, or other interests. In contrast to her mother, Karen presents her father as a man who delighted in his children. 'He just made it clear we were the most important thing in the world.' He is associated with celebrations and 'making special things' for his children. He had 'infinite patience' and 'nurtured' Karen's interest in reading.

He is a 'liberal in every way,' a man who 'didn't discipline us much at all.' Karen herself would like to engage in a more structured approach to discipline, although she shares her father's interest in 'freedom.' When Alex was born and soon before her father's death, Karen was surprised to find that he had 'conservative' ideas about the mother's place being in the home. Now that she is involved in taking care of Alex, she says she has 'come around' to his point of view.

GOOD MOTHER According to Karen's image, the good mother is,

> a pretty selfless person. I would like to be more selfless. And that's not to say she doesn't have her own interests. Every person should.

But I think your child should really come first. My mother was like that. And I guess you tend, maybe you accept your parents' values and standards. My dad was like that too.

Here, Karen mentions both her father and her mother and speaks of them in idealized fashion. While she introduces the idea of Mother as person, Karen values selflessness and presents an image of female maturity, insightfulness, and concern that supersedes her own mother's inadequacies. The focus here is on the Mother's being and selflessness rather than on her doing anything in particular. There is no mention of any behaviors or results of caretaking. The bad mother is 'not interested in her child.'

HUSBAND Karen mentions Peter often. He comes from a culture of 'in-depth,' 'stronger' relationships and is 'tenacious,' 'strict,' and criticizes American superficiality. He seems to voice Karen's own concerns and, in many ways, seems a parental figure. 'He's ten years older than me. And I tend to anyway feel [pause] um unequal is not quite the word. But [pause] you know, younger. And I kind of leave the leadership up to him.' Although Karen continues to feel like a shy, awkward child, she believes that with Peter's encouragement and with her maternal experience, she has become more 'responsible,' 'self-assured,' and self-reliant. She feels that this maturity has strengthened the marriage.

Although a parental figure to her, Peter is presented as less the parent to Alex. She speaks of Peter's 'babysitting' solely in practical terms and emphasizes that, although he has 'unbounded love' for his son, he lacks experience with children, gets overly concerned about Alex developing 'bad habits,' and is impatient and tends to treat the child as a 'little adult.' This picture of Peter as the lesser parent is extended by the sense of Peter and Alex as 'pals and playmates.'

The pre-child marriage is described in terms of 'unstructured' time to do what they wanted 'whenever we felt like it.' Although sex is not mentioned, this seems a matter of propriety rather than lack of physicality. Alex has transformed this relationship, 'refocused attention,' and led to the establishment of routines. Although Karen looks forward to getting out more when Alex is older, she does not focus on the losses involved in having a child.

SON Karen describes Alex as a 'mama's boy' because they are so close. Asked how Alex is different from herself, Karen says, 'I can't analyze him like that.' Instead, she lovingly describes shared but problematic qualities. Like her, Alex is a 'shy,' 'easily frustrated' child who tends to 'give up at things.' Karen also mentions that both have 'warmth' and a 'good sense of humor.' She sees no resemblance to Peter except that 'when Alex scowls he looks just like him.' Alex belongs to Karen, is her 'incredible treasure.' Their relationship is 'intense, emotional' and probably closer than it will ever be again.

But he just needs me so much. And I'm so *happy* that he needs me [small laugh]. And um later he will become more independent. But right now he's just very dependent on me. And, and, we just *love* each other so intensely.

Karen says this love makes her feel 'cuddly' and 'confident' and that she enjoys being treated as Alex's 'nourishment,' 'protection,' and as his 'home base.' These qualities are important for the child and also seem to make Karen feel magical and bountiful.

At the first interview, Karen says that Alex is quite cooperative and no longer a 'terrible two.' During the second, Karen says she and Peter have mixed feelings because the Children's Center Director says that Alex is 'too civilized.' Karen tends to present Alex as childlike and provocative and gives numerous examples of Alex 'driving me crazy' climbing over kitchen counters. She seems to see this behavior from Alex's point of view, often seeing him as 'chipper' (i.e. in a good mood, cheery and energetic) and 'enjoying himself.' At other times she speaks of 'power struggles' and is upset that she is too strict and overreacts; she does not blame Alex for these confrontations.

While his provocations can be upsetting, Karen also speaks of having a 'childish side' that can come out with Alex; she can 'become really silly and just be a total wild woman.' With Peter she can 'clown around' but 'there's always a barrier and you don't want to make a total idiot of yourself.'

Relationality

Karen sees relationships as the 'meaning of life,' takes pleasure in 'deep connection,' wants to be able to 'give and give and give' and to 'care about strangers.' In this, Karen desires the kind of deep connection she feels she never had. It seems that her mother's superficiality has made her feel unknown rather than filled with intrusive projections or demands; Karen does not see connection as dangerous. 'I guess it makes me happy when I feel a deep connection to someone and I really feel that we're on the same wavelength. And that's a pretty rare experience.' This feeling is present in relationships that have been 'tested' and 'solidified' by their 'ups and downs.' Superficiality is contrasted with giving and represents an inability to hold onto relationships or to get below the surface.

Close connection with Alex depends, in part, on his recognition of Karen's needs and being 'in tune' with her. Otherwise, 'I can just um, become cold. Almost. And feel like, "Look, I've got my *own* needs. You're just demanding too much."' She wants Alex to 'care about me in the same way I care about him. I mean, well maybe not exactly.' Karen does not want the relationship to be 'one-sided' and likes the way Alex gets 'concerned' if she gets hurt. Karen wants him to 'figure out the needs of a particular situation.' Notably, the mutuality she advocates is presented as helpful to her; selflessness is best for the child. Here she suggests the polarization of the positions of giver who needs to receive and receiver who benefits from not giving.

Karen does not value separation or speak of a need to get away from her child. Maturity is defined by 'responsibility' to the household rather than by independent activity. Separation is always presented as a problem. She is concerned about 'cutting Alex off,' about being rejected, 'left out' by people who do not like parts of her. Karen is also concerned that she and Alex are likely to become less close as he develops; she does not envision a relationship rooted in greater separateness.

Traditionality

Karen says that she is 'not a feminist exactly' but believes in women having all the rights and privileges of men. Even though she and Peter now share parenting responsibilities, Karen speaks in traditional terms and sees her decision to be a mother as a private decision to follow a role that her father defined and Alex proved important. Interestingly, although other women are presented as benign, there is no sense that Karen feels part of a network of mothers.

Karen wants Alex to have 'freedom to express his personality,' to have as much latitude as possible so he will not feel 'squashed and humiliated.' In order for Alex to be free, however, Karen has to contain herself. 'Good days' depend on Karen 'exercising self-control and making things run smoothly,' bad days happen when she cannot 'control [her]self.' Karen never says that it is all right to get angry and she associates anger with 'helplessness' and with the feeling that she is 'losing it,' 'stops listening,' and, it seems, acts like her own mother.

Karen does speak with pleasure about Alex's play and how the family 'touches a lot in games.'

> I'm having almost as good a time as Alex is. Although I think I'm not as good at playing with him really as his father. I'm never sure why. I guess my attention span is shorter or something. I lose interest.

Karen suggests an association between play and following Alex. The idea of play requiring attention span rather than innovation suggests an image of Karen as an apprentice rather than as a wild woman.

Reference measures

Karen's representations show considerable variety. Her description of her mother is highly ambivalent and particularly negative and differentiated. She is presented as a malevolent figure who is not at all nurturant and cannot respond to Karen constructively. She is also an affectionate, some-

142

I Object relations: Assessment of Qualitative and Structural Dimensions of Object Representations (AQSDOR)

	Mother	Father	Husband	Son
Factor I – Nurturance				
Nurturant	1	5	3	5
Positive ideal	2	6	6	5
Benevolent	2	7	6	6
Cold–Warm	3	7	5	6
Degree of constructive involvement	1	6	3	3
Affectionate	6	4*	4	6
Weak–Strong	5	5	7	5
Successful	4	4	4	4
Factor II – Striving				
Judgmental	4	5	5	4
Ambitious	5	5	4	3
Punitive	4	2	4	5
Intellectual	2	5	6	5
Degree of ambivalence**	3	1	2	3
Successful	4	4	4	4
Weak–Strong	5	5	7	5
Conceptual level***	9	5	5	3

* 4 = uncodable, inadequate material
** Three-point scale
*** Scored on scale of 1, 3, 5, 7, 9

what strong woman who pushed Karen to do housework but is not presented as judgmental or punitive.

In contrast, Karen presents her father without ambivalence, as a less distinct figure, and as a particularly warm and benevolent person who is able to respond to her constructively. He is not characterized in terms of affection but is described as an encouraging, intellectual man with standards. Peter is also described as an admirable and benevolent figure, although he is not nurturant or able to respond to Karen's needs very well. While stronger and more intellectual than her parents, he is not presented as either ambitious or punitive.

Karen presents Alex quite positively but his scores do not reach as high as those of her father and husband. Karen speaks of him with moderate ambivalence, as a less distinct and need-satisfying figure. He is moderately benevolent, warm, affectionate, and nurturant but does not respond constructively to Karen's needs. He is fairly strong and bright, but he seems to lack some ambition and acts punitively at times.

II Relationality: Attanucci coding of Gilligan dilemma

Types of self-description	Number of responses by level			
	I	II	III	IV
Self in relation to others	0	2	0	0
Self in relation to son	0	4	2	0

Karen describes an incident the day before the second interview when she had to take Alex home from the park so that she could go to work and he 'was just having a fit.' Karen first focuses on her own need to leave, her insistence that Alex meet her terms, and efforts to manipulate and force the child to cooperate (Level III). However, throughout this discussion, Karen is uncertain, self-blaming, and feels responsible for failing to keep the relationship on a 'good level.' Although she sees that Alex 'reacts against my anger and he's gonna do everything possible to make me more angry,' she does not consider that he is acting like a two-year-old and that, at times, mother and child are going to be in conflict. Karen's sense of uncertainty and of being out of control is prominent as she speaks of feeling 'humiliated' and 'being made a fool of' in front of other people (Level II).

Karen then shifts to focus on the child's terms, sees Alex as enjoying himself, aware of his impact, but also as 'upset' by her anger (Level II). Karen says that she should have turned his 'misbehavior' into a 'joke' and been more 'flexible.' She felt 'terribly, terribly guilty' and called the Children's Center Director who suggested that Alex was upset that his stroller had broken the day before. Karen then realized that the 'real difficulty' was an even deeper issue – Alex does not like her to go to work and the lack of his stroller made leaving more difficult. That night, she 'tried to do everything' to 'show Alex how much [she] loved him.' She concluded the discussion of the dilemma without reaching a resolution by saying she still felt a 'little guilty' because she 'wasn't understanding of what was going on inside him.'

III Traditionality: Newberger dilemma

Issue	Final score
Resolving conflict	2
Meeting needs	2(3)
	2: Global level

Karen's responses focus on the conventional Level 2. In her discussion, there is a correct answer: the mother's first responsibility is to her children. Like all children, this child wants his mother home and his 'whole future may depend on his good relationship with her, and how happy his childhood is, and his sense of security that, that she loves him and everything.' Karen does present a more complex distinction between the mother's needs and the child's needs; the only thing the child sees is that 'she's not there for him' while the mother knows how much she loves the child and that work is only one facet of her life. While these comments are scored at Level 3, Karen does not consider the kind of communication that Newberger suggests is central to dealing with these different perspectives and complex feelings. Instead, Karen returns to the notion that the most important thing is that the child is 'happy.' The mother 'has the rest of her life to work.'

IV Thematic Apperception Test

Story I, Card 1

A boy wants to be a musician like his mother, feels 'somehow left out of her world,' and is looking at her violin. The mother is loving and gives him piano lessons so he will not feel competitive with her. He becomes a great musician and she does not feel competitive.

Clinical assessment

Import: success is a function of good mothering.

Conflicts: separation–individuation. Boy wants to be like his mother and she is concerned that he excel in his own way; competition; unmet dependency needs.

Internal representations: mother seen as concerned, loving, protective, insightful, separate, empathic, rejecting; child seen as admiring, respectful, gifted, ambitious, longing for mother.

Quality of relations: there is a great deal of closeness, empathy, concern, mutual admiration, and idealization. But there is also some rejection.

Story II, Card 2

A young woman leaves her parents' farm to become a school teacher. Her mother does not understand her love of books and wishes this oldest and most responsible daughter would stay and help with her new baby. Her father is proud and understanding, but feels somewhat rejected. The daughter loves her family and visits often but knows they 'will never quite accept her.'

Clinical assessment

Import: the process of separating from one's parents is fraught with mutual rejection.

145

Conflicts: separation–individuation – girl can only separate by rejecting the parents who can then not accept her. Sibling rivalry.

Internal representations: mother seen as loving, insecure, sensitive to rejection, rejecting; father seen as loving, hurt, proud of daughter, ambivalent; daughter seen as loving, rejecting, responsible, ambitious; siblings seen as irresponsible.

Quality of relations: openly conflictual. Feelings of rejection dominate.

Story III, Card 5

A girl in her twenties brings a 'gentleman' to her room for tea. The landlady is nosy and 'caught them kissing.' Landlady kicks the 'kind and innocent' girl out but the 'honorable gentleman' marries her immediately. They 'live happily ever after.'

Clinical assessment

Import: when it comes to sexuality, men are more trustworthy than women.

Conflicts: sexual expression versus guilt seen both in plot and in portrayal of girl as kissing, then as 'kind and innocent.'

Internal representations: girl seen as innocent, upset; woman seen as rigid, rejecting, unpleasant, gossipy, nosy, intrusive, punitive; man seen as honorable and committed.

Quality of relations: conflict over sexuality dominates the relationship between the two women. The girl's relationship with the man is pleasant, romantic, sexual.

Story IV, Card 7GF

A girl has been close to her widowed mother and feels 'pushed out' when she re-marries and has a new baby. Girl 'copes' by 'look[ing] outward' to new friends and boyfriends. Her mother doesn't understand and tries to draw her back by interesting her in holding the new baby. It will take years before they can understand each other.

Clinical assessment

Import: new arrivals in the family can disrupt the mother–daughter relationship.

Conflicts: dependence versus independence. Separation is forced rather than natural or progressive, suggesting a conflict. Also, mother experiences her daughter's independence as a loss. Conflict over sibling rivalry evident in daughter's disinterested handling of the baby.

Internal representations: mother seen as self-involved, lacking in empathy; daughter seen as rejected.

Quality of relations: there is closeness between mother and daughter but the abrupt interruption creates conflict. There is little empathy in the relationship.

Overall clinical impression

This subject appears to be concerned primarily with conflicts about separation. There is a sense of great closeness and intimacy with the mother which was abruptly and prematurely terminated. As a consequence, subject might have very intimate but very conflicted relationships with women. She might feel more comfortable with men, who are seen as more reliable. There is a suggestion that the subject has sexualized her unmet dependency needs, channeling them to her relationships with men. There is also an indication of guilt over sexuality and competition.

Subject's stories indicate little by way of resolving her separation conflicts, primarily because female figures are seen as consistently rejecting. On a more speculative note, it is possible that subject assumed a counter-dependent style, if indeed the separation was too abrupt.

It is interesting that separation issues are seen not only in child figures but, perhaps even more, in the parental figures *vis-à-vis* their children. This suggests that subject might project on her children her own separation conflicts.

There is some indication of impulsivity in the third story in which marriage is the quick solution to not having a place to live.

Within-subject comparison of measures

The reference measures shed further light on the relationship between Karen's own unmet needs, her desire for deep connection, and her interest in being selflessly giving to others. In response to the Gilligan and Newberger dilemmas, Karen asserts the importance of the mother taking care of the child and of seeing issues in the child's terms. The Gilligan dilemma is particularly interesting because Karen presents an incident in which she herself is subject to constraints and has needs. She is torn between manipulating Alex to keep things going smoothly or focusing on his interests. Karen cannot move to what Attanucci sees as the connected response involving a focus on her feelings and the child's simultaneously. Instead, she feels guilty for not recognizing Alex's real feelings, for being superficial like her own mother. Her own feelings and the need to get to work are presented negatively; she is self-centered, unempathic, rejecting, as well as humiliated, overreacting, confused, and desperately manipulative.

The Thematic Apperception Test analysis is particularly helpful in understanding how these feelings may relate to her own mother. Superficiality now comes to sound increasingly like being rejected, being cut off, ignored, unappreciated. It signals a break in connection. The TAT stories and analysis suggest that Karen's mother may have been more responsive when Karen was a baby and that an abrupt and premature break in their connection occurred with the births of two siblings. The case summary makes a different point and proposes that Karen's interest in deeper relationships might have something to do with her mother's lack of intrusiveness.

What becomes striking in Karen's case is that she turns to men as dependable figures and subscribes to the traditional female position of selflessly giving mother. Giving to others becomes the opposite of being like her own mother. This giving depends on the ongoing presence of an other. Karen gives Alex her attention and her love and does not mention the toys, books, lessons, or symbols that might be part of but also mediate the relationship and provide some independence. In return, Karen wants Alex to be caring and responsive. When he is 'out of tune' with her needs, she gets angry and feels that her anger disrupts the relationship. Within this dynamic, the relationship is either good or bad. When it is not good, Karen feels she can 'kiss it goodbye.'

In the TAT stories, separation is problematic – there is no way for characters to differentiate at their own pace and still be accepted by others. As the clinical analysis suggests, separation issues may be particularly problematic for Karen in relation to her child. However, the case material does indicate Karen's efforts to see Alex as a two-year-old and to accommodate his needs. In addition, the case material suggests the extent to which Karen is now struggling to deal with her own mother. While Karen's way of monitoring her behavior and feelings in terms of a notion of selfless giving is unfortunate, there is a sense that motherhood provides some opportunity for Karen to deal with issues of separation, to satisfy her need for a non-superficial relationship, and to feel herself a mature woman.

INDIVIDUAL PROFILE: ELLEN

Case summary

Ellen is a forty-two-year-old woman who grew up in the West and has a brother four years younger. Her father comes from a working class family and advanced to a managerial position in a shipping company; he died nine years prior to the interviews. Her mother is a retired teacher. Ellen is an academic administrator at a college and her husband, 'Don,' a university grants officer. Both have doctorates.

Ellen married when she was thirty-eight, much later than if her life had 'gone according to plan.' She says she no longer expected to have a child and does not 'take children for granted.' Childbirth was difficult and 'Neil' was delivered under anesthesia. Breastfeeding was also difficult initially. Ellen took a job 'off the university fast track' to spend more time with the baby. While the new job was not inordinately demanding, Ellen rarely returned home before 6 p.m. The family live near Don's employer and, except when he has been away on work-related travel, he has been responsible for late afternoon child care and dinner preparation. Ellen has recently shifted to a higher level position closer to home and she and Don work at the same college.

Neil was twenty-nine months at the time of the first interview, thirty-three months at the time of the second. He was enrolled at the university Center for Children.

Ellen speaks warmly and seems to work very hard to present her feelings. She is forthright about the way her child has disrupted her marriage and friendships and about her own struggles to become less 'nice' and more assertive. A self-described feminist, Ellen weaves in political views and sense of historical context throughout her discussion. I feel a bond between us. Ellen remarks on how much she enjoys the first interview. At the beginning of the second interview, Ellen describes a dilemma concerning the Children's Center Director. Despite my support and assurances of confidentiality, Ellen seems very upset and less comfortable than during our first meeting; I experience her as pulling back from me and the interview process. She is most open when speaking of her own experience indirectly, through discussion of traditional women.

Object relations

MOTHER Ellen does not mention her mother voluntarily but, when asked, introduces her as a 'very interesting person,' a hard worker, a teacher who is still interested in learning. Ellen stresses these as admirable qualities she has 'incorporated in [her] life.'

Ellen also presents her mother in terms of historical/personal circumstance, as the child of divorced parents whose own mother worked and who yearned for a 'traditional family.' Although a teacher, Ellen sees her mother's 'identity' revolving around being a wife and mother, 'worrying about other people.' When middle-aged, she became deeply affected by the women's movement, realized that this 'traditional model' was not completely good for her, and began to be 'independent.' Ellen sees this independence as 'destroying my parents' marriage,' but she appreciates what her mother was doing. In fact, the women's movement has created a

149

satisfying bond between mother and daughter as people. The connection as parent and child is more difficult.

While Ellen speaks of positive changes in her mother, she simultaneously refers to earlier difficulties.

> Actually she is more loving and affectionate with Neil than I think she was with us. So that while I saw a quality that I think I've experienced a lot – I don't know that it was missing actually – there's a warmth about her now.

In this statement and in others, Ellen refers to things missing in her childhood. She indicates that 'My, my first memories are not, uh, much that was fun or anything other than lots that was painful.' When asked to elaborate on the pain, Ellen says 'I was just routinized, scheduled and did things every four hours kind of thing.' Ellen's discussion suggests that this routinization made her feel constricted rather than free to play and feel masterful.

In addition, Ellen feels that she has suffered lifelong difficulties from the lack of 'important conversations' with her mother. 'My sense is that I could have been encouraged to talk about some things, or just think some ideas that I wasn't.' She does not place full responsibility for this lack of intimacy on her mother, but indicates that she herself was an overly 'nice girl' with a 'narrow world view.' 'I was so traditional as a child that I don't think I was ready to tell her anything.'

FATHER Ellen does not have the same difficulty talking about her deceased father. His ongoing sensitivity to his humble background contributed to his ability to establish good values. He 'gave me an acceptance of other people,' especially homosexuals and old people, and was 'more understanding of other people's foibles' than her mother was.

> He was a funny kind of wanting to get, get ahead but, but not ever forgetting where he came from. And in some ways that didn't help his work but he always remembered the disenfranchised. It was a strange ideal but when I grew up I really learned to be respectful of other people because of that.

In Ellen's presentation, her father's advancement was a mixed blessing; the move beyond his more humble beginnings was difficult and led to a drinking problem that she sees as related to these pressures.

GOOD MOTHER Ellen interprets the question of what is her image of a good mother as one concerning working versus non-working mothers. She advocates the acceptability of women working and tempers her position by describing the bad mother as one who goes too far and doesn't 'adjust her lifestyle to *somehow* be with the child.'

For Ellen, questions of the embodiment of motherhood tap a deeper concern for the importance of the mother 'encouraging a child to say what's, he or she is feeling' rather than constraining the child's very being and ability to raise questions. For Ellen, this constraint is socially supported and gender related and, in this sense, concerns Ellen and *her* mother more than Ellen and her male child.

> A nice girl was pretty well defined [by culture]. And so that a daughter would not be encouraged to tell her mother that she is having thoughts that were not within the realm of what being a nice girl was.

Together, the mother and daughter perpetuated female niceness and left unspoken issues – especially anger and sexuality – that might disrupt the tradition.

HUSBAND Ellen speaks of her husband, Don, throughout the interview. He is supportive of Ellen's career, an involved father, and is presented both as her 'complement' – as someone different from herself who completes her – and as someone who thinks and acts in the same way as she does, especially in relation to Neil. Interestingly, Don is differentiated by what can be described as his maleness; he is more 'strong-willed,' 'more secure about his place in the world' than she or Neil, and is inherently 'interested in ideas,' something Ellen feels she has to work at. Ellen does raise some questions about Don's values: his expectations are 'very high' and he tends to encourage Neil to accept conventional values rather than to 'stand up for his own values.'

Despite these differences, Ellen says that she and Don 'function pretty much the same way with Neil.' Most comments about child rearing are spoken of in terms of 'we,' suggesting the closeness of the parental couple. Interestingly, she does not speak of Don and Neil's relationship despite the substantial amount of time they spend without her, suggesting a concern about exclusion from a close father–son relationship.

While Ellen says she and Don feel 'very together' when with Neil, the child has also put 'real strains' on the marriage. The couple spend all of their free time with Neil and have had few 'intimate moments' for either 'physical closeness' or 'sharing of ideas.' Even more problematic,

> Having a child brings out the essence of one's own being and so we've had [pause] some, some, times when we've had to listen very hard to each other because, because we were coming from such different perspectives.

Time together with Neil does compensate for some of these disturbing differences. However, despite concerns about the marriage, this couple has not taken the opportunity to spend time together, even now that they work at the same institution and have a babysitter willing to stay late. It seems difficult for this husband and wife to separate themselves from the trio.

SON Early in the first interview, Ellen says that she is 'working to make Neil different than me. Although I think of myself as being sensitive, insightful, caring, and those kinds of things and I'm hoping he's that also.' Ellen says 'I depend on him for expanding my world and increasing my ability to love.' For Ellen, this experience of relationship with the child satisfies a need for self-definition. As she puts it, 'I depend on him to define me.'

Interestingly, Ellen tends to focus on Neil's phallic qualities and to make a parallel between Neil and Don, strong-willed, 'independent minded' males. Neil comes most to life in these interviews when Ellen speaks of him as an 'explorer,' climbing, taking things apart and putting them back together, and reading. She speaks with great pleasure of the family playing basketball in their apartment and golf outside. Ellen also speaks of Neil as big and says 'people have said he's going to be expected to do things that he can't do just because he looks so big or so much older.' While she never fully owns these expectations, when she speaks of Neil as frustrated, she is concerned 'maybe we're expecting too much' and is uncertain of how to view him.

While Ellen appears certain about Neil's phallic qualities, in other ways she presents him tentatively. Perhaps cautious about projecting qualities onto him, she describes Neil in terms of what he 'seems to be' in response to questions about his appearance and interests and rarely volunteers information in a way that distinguishes this child. She 'thinks' he is happy, inquisitive, affectionate, humorous, and outgoing.

Relationality

Ellen speaks in terms of close, nurturant connections to significant others throughout the interview. Ellen's notion of connection involves two rather distinct characteristics: 'being together' and sharing thoughts and ideas without capitulating to the opinions of others. Ellen speaks of 'being around' her family often. Despite the importance of conversation, most often Ellen does not talk about what they do or say to each other. Instead, this togetherness has a more primitive, undifferentiated and timeless feel. This togetherness has, for Ellen, led to changes in the marriage and detracted from important and long-term friendships. Ellen sees friendships as requiring ongoing 'work;' she feels she is 'not being a good friend right now' because she lacks time and energy to maintain relationships. Although concerned about these long-term relationships, Ellen never speaks of newer relationships with other mothers or colleagues.

Ellen wants to be connected but different and yearns to be autonomous in the sense of being able to take a stand and hold onto her own opinions. However, she feels she is 'insecure,' likely to 'acquiesce,' and concerned that disagreement signals an end to relationship. Mutuality – each person has a responsibility to recognize the other – provides a solution and model for relationships.

Ellen's interest in mutuality is exemplified when asked for five adjectives describing the relationship with her child. Ellen begins to speak of 'responsibility' and then shifts to five that 'work both ways,' 'interdependent,' 'responsive,' 'basic,' 'teaching,' and 'affectionate.' Her attention to mutuality is impressive, although it also may suggest some difficulty with the asymmetrical mother–child relationship.

Ellen feels that the 'enormity' of the parent–child relationship is 'hard.' She wants to respond to Neil's needs 'immediately' but feels the limits of giving. 'Come Sunday night, uh, I may be very much looking forward to going back to working outside of the house. And so this feeling, "Okay, I've given and I've given and I've given."' While speaking of her own limits, Ellen also seems uncertain of what she gives Neil and has to get recognition back to know that she has given. In this context, Ellen's response to the question, 'Could you describe a moment where you and Neil really clicked?' is important. Ellen speaks of Neil doing a puzzle and there was a piece missing. 'It happened that I saw it first and he 'found' it. And uh, uh, the sort of real pleasure that doing something for him and he found it.'

Traditionality

Ellen is a feminist who sees gender equality as necessary but not sufficient for a move beyond traditionality. She focuses on the importance of moving beyond constricted niceness in order to be a full, strong person. Although Ellen never considers this a woman's problem, all the people she describes as strong-willed are men.

Not surprisingly, Ellen values intimate conversation with Neil. In her examples, both mother and child share dislikes, doubts, and concerns. However, neither is portrayed as speaking of pleasure or fantasy.

Ellen wants to encourage Neil to explore and be masterful and to give him the latitude she missed. However, she also seems afraid to provoke Neil's frustration and aggression and, at times, feels too insecure to set limits. By not setting limits, Ellen (and Don) continue to be subjected to someone else's power. The still unfixed stereo that Neil broke the year before is emblematic of the restriction of their own pleasure. Being 'really on his schedule to a large extent' means the parents' own freedom continues to be restricted.

Although Don has been very involved in child care, Ellen feels she has been 'much more full time' and feels 'responsible' for the child: 'Feminist that I am, I still haven't worked out feelings in terms of mothers' responsibilities.' In this context, work is defined as a place where Ellen is supportive of colleagues but doesn't have to 'give and give and give.' However, instead of fully distinguishing work and home, Ellen feels that career, home, and friendships require 'work.' The public realm is distinguished in some sense as the locus of experts and judgment. Ellen would 'abdicate' rather than yell at Neil in public, 'I just know I'm capable of feeling that I'm subject to other people's judgments.'

Although Ellen says that she can be very angry at her child, she says that she is usually 'indifferent' in terms of anger. Asked if she was allowed to express anger as a child, she speaks of how anger was turned into sadness, 'Well I was allowed to cry for sure. But that's the only way I learned how to express anger. And that's what I think was too bad.' In addition, the threat of anger limited discussion and debate. Ellen feels she continues to 'avoid disagreement. I might acquiesce too quickly because I am afraid of what might ensue.'

Ellen speaks of Don being romantic and supportive and is clearly moved by his sending her two roses when out of town at a job interview. Interestingly, mention of jumping, tickling, and rolling around with Neil as well as references to how she is enjoying herself are only volunteered in response to probing. There appears to be a pattern whereby pleasure and physicality are often unspoken until legitimized or given space within the interview process.

Reference measures

I Object relations: Assessment of Qualitative and Structural Dimensions of Object Representations (AQSDOR)

	Mother	Father	Husband	Son
Factor I – Nurturance				
Nurturant	5	5	6	5
Positive ideal	5	6	6	6
Benevolent	5	7	6	6
Cold–Warm	5	5	6	6
Degree of constructive involvement	2	6	6	5
Affectionate	5	4*	4	6
Weak–Strong	6	3	6	5
Successful	4	3	5	6
Factor II – Striving				
Judgmental	5	1	5	4
Ambitious	6	5	4	6
Punitive	4	4	4	4
Intellectual	5	4	6	5
Degree of ambivalence**	2	1	1	1
Successful	4	3	5	6
Weak–Strong	6	3	6	5
Conceptual level***	9	7	5	7

* 4 = uncodable, inadequate material
** Three-point scale
*** Scored on scale of 1, 3, 5, 7, 9

Ellen's representations are at moderate to high conceptual levels. She presents her mother at the highest level, as having her own constellation of behaviors and feelings. She speaks of her father and son with no scorable ambivalence and presents them at a slighly lower level, focusing more on their feelings than on their behavior. Her treatment of Don is also unambivalent but is at a lower conceptual level – she concentrates on his behaviors rather than on his feelings.

All four objects are presented as admirable, loving, benevolent figures. These figures do differ considerably. While Ellen presents her father, husband, and son as able to respond to her constructively, her mother is distinguished by her inability to respond, by her judgmentalness and driving of her daughter. While Don is also somewhat ambitious and judgmental, he is not presented as pushing or judging Ellen. In contrast, Ellen's father is presented as completely accepting but as weaker. Neil is presented as strong and very happy with himself, but as vulnerable to becoming weaker as he gets older. Notably, while Ellen sees her mother and especially her son as affectionate, she does not mention physical affection when speaking of her father and husband.

II Relationality: Attanucci coding of Gilligan dilemma

Types of self-description	Number of responses by level			
	I	II	III	IV
Self in relation to experts	0	4	1	0
Self in relation to son	0	1	4	0

The dilemma Ellen presents concerns how she and Don are to deal with the Director of the Children's Center's view that Neil is not 'aggressive' enough, that he is 'docile,' shares too readily, and shows dissatisfaction indirectly by stamping his feet in the corner. Ellen and Don respect this woman and want to 'defer to the experts,' especially this one who sees Neil interact with his peers. Ellen and Don do see Neil as aggressive at home and had not really thought his peaceful interactions with peers were problematic: 'We had not thought he was un-normal.' They do follow the director's advice not to 'interfere' and to let Neil be 'possessive' (Level II). Most of Ellen's comments in relation to Neil are scored at Level III and focus on her assertion of the parental couple's values: 'It's not bad to have Neil share, for a period of time;' 'We don't want him to be obnoxious, um and just, that it's not bad to be a nice child.'

While Ellen is concerned that the child may be getting mixed messages, she does not worry about Neil's indirect expression of anger. Her dilemma concerns family values in relation to those of the expert and the question of what is appropriate child behavior. The dilemma is particularly salient because the day before the interview Neil's babysitter reported that the director was happy that Neil had thrown a block at another child. Ellen says, 'From my perspective, that's *nothing* to get excited about! So that's my problem.'

III Traditionality: Newberger dilemma

Issues	Final score
Resolving conflict	3
Meeting needs	3(2)
	3: Global level

Ellen's response to the dilemma revolves around the notion that Mrs Stewart should 'weigh a variety of factors,' make sure that David is well cared for, and then do what's best for her. Ellen fleshes out the family's history: Mrs Stewart felt she was doing the 'right thing' by being home for a few years, David probably loved her and enjoyed having her at home, but Mrs Stewart is beginning to 'resent' her situation, her child, and her working husband. In this context, Ellen says staying home would be a 'negative trade off' unless there were child care problems making David extremely unhappy. In her assessment, David – like every child – might want his mother home, but does not seem that unhappy. Mrs Stewart can help David deal with the change in circumstances by bringing him to see where she works and explaining the benefits of her income.

Ellen's responses are scored primarily at Level 3 because she elaborates on the particular family, encourages mother–child communication, and advocates ongoing attention to their well-being. Interestingly, Mrs Stewart is the more elaborated figure; comments about meeting needs are scored at the somewhat lower 3(2) Level, because Ellen does not focus on David's particular conflicts and needs

IV Thematic Apperception Test

Story I, Card I

A little boy started playing the violin either because he wanted to or was encouraged by his parents. He is ambivalent and tells his parents he wants to stop playing. They encourage him to continue and try to get him involved with other children so he can 'enjoy the making of music together.' It 'doesn't work,' he 'gives it up.' As an adult, he's 'very sad that he did.'

Clinical assessment

Import: when you are too ambivalent about a task, encouragement doesn't help. Abandoning a task because of ambivalence is regretted later.

Conflicts: conflict about making a commitment to a difficult task.

Internal representations: child seen as serious, mature; parents seen as understanding, thoughtful.

Quality of relations: child is able to talk openly to parents, suggesting closeness and a good degree of communication.

Story II, Card 2

A father loves the land and has committed his life to it; his wife is first seen as insecure and then as a hard worker who feels good about her life. Their daughter loves her family and the land, is 'wrestling' with the 'pain' of leaving, but is being 'pulled by the world of ideas.' She brings a 'solid foundation' to whatever she does. She may return to a farming community but as a teacher, journalist, or activist for farm causes.

Clinical assessment

Import: physical separation from one's parents does not mean losing them; one takes a sense of values and belonging and can negotiate the process of separation.

Conflicts: conflicts about separation are evident, particularly the problem of how to remain close to one's roots but be one's own person. There are feelings of loss, but the parents are internalized and a solution is reached.

Internal representations: girl seen as conflicted, sad, insecure, loving, solid; parents seen as understanding, hard-working, strong, comfortable in their lives and contributions, proud of their daughter.

Quality of relations: there is closeness, understanding, empathy. There is the ability to see others' perspectives despite differences and sadness over separation.

Story III, Card 5

An orderly, neat mother finds her adolescent daughter sitting with a girlfriend. They are talking 'intimately,' their arms are around each other's shoulders. Mother is 'distraught' that her daughter may have 'perverted sexual tendencies,' forbids her to see the other girl, and is too 'embarrassed' to speak with her daughter. Daughter feels 'confused' and 'angry,' builds a life 'more independent of the family' and looks to the other girl for 'even more support.'

Clinical assessment

Import: when applied to adolescence, parental rigidity, lack of understanding, and punishment can only serve to enhance the behavior they attempted to extinguish.

Conflicts: there are concerns about sexuality, perhaps guilt over unconscious homosexual feelings. There are also conflicts about separation; the mother cannot distinguish her own feelings of shame from her daughter's feelings about her behavior.

Internal representations: mother seen as rigid, punitive, ashamed, sexually repressed; daughter seen as caring, victimized.

Quality of relations: there is capacity for intimacy and emotional closeness. But concerns about sexuality can mar relationships and result in anger, lack of communication, and alienation.

Story IV, Card 7GF

A mother feels that there are fundamental, religious values about roles for women and is reading her daughter the bible without looking for signs that her daughter might have other ideas. Daughter is dreaming about what she would rather be doing and has some 'ambivalent feelings' about her doll. She 'accedes' to her mother's wishes about what 'little girls should be' and 'follows much the same life' as her mother. Mother is pleased.

Clinical assessment

Import: a mother is pleased about her daughter if she succeeds in molding her in her own image.

Conflicts: conflicts about separation are seen in the mother's inability to see her daughter as a different person. The conflict remains largely unconscious as the girl – aside from a brief fantasy – grows up to be a mirror image of her mother. There are also superego conflicts about right and wrong and the role of religion in prescribing the correct behavior.

Internal representations: mother seen as rigid, narcissistic, driven, religious, austere; daughter seen as ambivalent but passive and compliant.

Overall clinical impression

As represented by these stories, this subject is concerned primarily with conflicts about separation–individuation. Her characters are concerned with growing up to be the 'same' or different from their parents. The subject has insight about these conflicts and is likely to be capable of coping with them without resorting to 'acting out' behavior. As she places a great deal of attention on the mother's role, it is possible that the subject experiences her separation conflicts with regard to her children, displacing issues with her own parents onto her children.

There are also indications of a punitive superego, particularly guilt over unconscious homosexual feelings.

From her stories, it appears that the subject has a great deal of capacity for intimacy and empathy, particularly with other women. Yet, conflicts over sexual impulses may bring much ambivalence and conflict into these relationships.

The ability to reflect and the strong superego suggest no serious impulsive tendencies. But specific conflicts can result in interpersonal impulsivity.

Within-subject comparison of measures

The issue of being the same as or different from others is crucial for Ellen in many circumstances. In the first and second TAT stories, the Newberger dilemma, and throughout the interviews Ellen speaks of the possibility of working toward intergenerational bonds based on both similarity and difference. These issues of connection are expressed most clearly in relation to women.

The case study suggests that relationships with men are presented as extremely meaningful, but without the problematized issue of same versus different. Instead, their differences are appealing. Scores on the Assessment of Qualitative and Structural Dimensions of Object Representations indicate that Ellen presents her husband and her father in particularly positive light. The case study suggests that Ellen looks to Neil and Don for the phallic qualities she lacks just as she looked to her father for the construction of meaningful values. Interestingly, however, these kinds of relationships with men are not depicted in the TAT analysis.

Relationships with women are the focus of the TAT stories and the Gilligan dilemma. The women in the last two TAT stories are presented in negative light, as constraining mothers whose overly moralistic values ruin relationships with their daughters. While the adolescent daughter seeks a life elsewhere, the younger daughter accedes and becomes like her mother. Interestingly, while the Children's Center director described in the Gilligan dilemma is advocating freedom rather than constraint for Neil, Ellen experiences her as moralistic, constraining, and ignoring Ellen's values. Ellen feels pushed to question her high valuation of sharing and mutuality.

While Ellen tries to present her mother in social context and as a person rather than as a constraining figure, she feels that her mother's limits on conversation and play have caused her serious damage. Ellen continues to feel that she herself is too nice. It is interesting that she looks to her husband and her son to repair this damage; they are 'other' in the sense of their shared maleness. There is little sense of the child as 'other' in terms of childishness, although Ellen does enjoy shared play.

Interestingly, although Ellen is a feminist who speaks of bonds with other women, except for her mother and the Children's Center director, women are absent from this interview. The issue of homosexual feelings toward women raised by the TAT analysis suggests Ellen may find bonds with other women appealing but dangerous, indicating a reason why relationships with women may require so much work and are difficult to maintain and develop.

It is particularly interesting to consider how Ellen is affected by her child's maleness. While her feminist stance allows Ellen to take a position in the world as a strong, competent, caring person, this liberating position also represents a wished for, to be worked for, self. Male-associated qualities of independence and assertiveness are necessary for Ellen to be authentic, rather than nice. It is her male child who provides the possibility of a greater sense of self-definition.

INDIVIDUAL PROFILE: KATHRYN

Case summary

Kathryn is a thirty-three-year-old real estate attorney and partner in a prestigious law firm. Her father worked in a similar profession and now is retired. Her mother has always been a full time homemaker. Kathryn has two adopted older brothers. She met her husband 'David' at college fifteen years ago, they went to the same law school and married ten years ago. Kathryn does not volunteer information about conception and birth but refers to the fetus as 'this person wandering around inside of me.' She returned to work full time when her son 'Lucas' was three months old and goes to her office after he has had breakfast. David is on an early morning work schedule and returns home in the late afternoon to cook dinner and take care of Lucas. At the time of the interviews, the family had hired a nanny and continued to employ a former teacher from a prestigious school as a babysitter; she also runs a two-mornings-a-week program for toddlers that Lucas attends.

Lucas was twenty-four months at the time of the first interview, twenty-nine months at the time of the second.

I met Kathryn at her home late one evening after a long workday. Although Kathryn was napping before my arrival, she immediately focused on our conversation and on making me feel comfortable. Kathryn seemed to take great pleasure in talking. Her speech was measured, perhaps because she is accustomed to having her words transcribed and treated as important. She also struck me as impish, sitting in a large chair in child-like, scrunched up fashion, and seeming at times to be playful during the interview. Except at the end of the second interview when she discusses problems with her mother, Kathryn speaks in superlatives and is not given to in-depth analyses of a psychological sort. Negative experiences and feelings are largely unmentioned. Yet, there is a complexity and weightiness to Kathryn's considerations.

Object relations

MOTHER Kathryn speaks of an early and positive relationship with her mother whom she introduces as a 'genius with small children,' 'empathic,' 'spontaneous,' and able to 'enjoy things at their level.' Bespeaking her admiration, Kathryn says, 'I would like to be like her. I think to a large extent I am.'

Kathryn later speaks of outgrowing and moving away from the mother she now characterizes as over-involved and unable to deal with her daughter's independence. Kathryn continues to associate her mother with regression and sees her as a disappointingly irresponsible, 'babbling' woman who 'lives her emotional life on the surface,' is unable to understand her daughter, and demands an emotional responsiveness that does not suit Kathryn's character or her age. This mother is described as 'insecure' and preoccupied with 'rejection.' Only once does Kathryn admit an emotional similarity between herself and these more negative aspects of her mother: 'I probably take after her more than she knows because when uh I, I, from time to time, I blow up at David and let off a little steam.'

FATHER Kathryn's father is presented in idealized fashion. He is described as 'calm,' 'patient,' 'good at guiding and teaching people of all ages' and more suited than her mother to ongoing identification. Perhaps in order to become as close to him as possible, Kathryn has chosen a career path like his. 'He understands on a day to day basis what I do. I can talk to him about what I do. He always says, he has interesting things to say about it.'

Despite numerous comments about their 'close relationship,' Kathryn also experiences her father as a 'remote,' 'reserved' man who kept 'a very, a low profile' in the midst of mother–daughter struggles. Kathryn speaks of struggling to find the right balance, being more 'responsive' without being a 'gusher' like her mother.

GOOD MOTHER Kathryn's description of the good mother focuses on the Mother's 'God-like' power to be 'responsible for the outcome of each

161

encounter.' This is 'emotionally demanding' and depends on 'planning and thinking' and 'anticipating the child's needs.'

> I think being an adult with a, a little demanding person there demanding a lot, in every different direction, asking for different things at different times. I think that's the most difficult thing [about being a parent]. (And you can't be the same way?) No, right, no, no, you can't be. It's, there's only one person who can act that way. The other person can't act that way, the other person has to be, you know, the God-like figure. That's, it's, otherwise it just doesn't work. You can't both be the children. And you can't even take turns, at least so far [laughs]. The way you can with another adult.

The good mother has to be a 'responsible' adult, planning, anticipating needs in order to avert problems. If the Mother is not emotionally available to the child, she is in danger of 'cutting the child off.' She may cease acting like an adult, become childishly needy, and drawn into confrontation. The child helps maintain the Mother's position by seeing Her as 'in between being a person, an individual and part of the universe, maybe the floor of the universe or something.'

The bad mother, in a sense, loses this position. She screams instead of controlling her anger and is 'emotionally distant' and 'preoccupied with herself.'

HUSBAND Kathryn speaks of her husband as her 'best friend.' Although he is more gregarious and physical, she emphasizes their shared careers and hobbies and their ability to talk and 'hang around together.' David is presented as a nurturant father but not as either needing or giving Kathryn emotional support. There is no discussion of romance or sexuality.

Lucas is a 'shared project' that has given the couple a 'purpose' and increased Kathryn's respect for David. He is portrayed as a 'wonderful' father, 'affectionate,' 'attentive,' 'spontaneous,' 'devoted.' He is also spoken of as a buddy to his child rather than as a parental, law-establishing figure.

> They're almost like buddies. It's very funny. I'll call up and I'll say 'I'm on my way home' and 'Lucas what are you doing?' He'll say, 'We're cooking chicken' [laugh]. And they are, they're cooking chicken. Lucas gets up on the chair and helps cook dinner. They have a lot of fun.

Kathryn indicates both the importance of her relationship with David and the transformation involved in having a child when she suggests that she now looks to her marriage less for 'personal fulfillment.' 'I don't, you know, I don't have to get every bit of joy out of, you know out of my relationship with David. I can get some of it someplace else.'

SON Lucas is immediately presented as the product of both parents, both in terms of sociability and intellect. He is consistently talked about in superlatives and the presentation resembles Miller's (1983/1981) portrayal of parental narcissism and the dilemma of the gifted child. Lucas 'amazes' Kathryn 'everyday in every way one can imagine and can't imagine.'He is described as 'sweet,' 'engaging,' 'loving,' 'just about the most charming person I ever met.' His intellectual and linguistic abilities are especially striking, his concentration and problem solving ability 'staggering.' Amazed at everything the child knows, Kathryn never credits the influence of the former nursery school teacher/babysitter.

Kathryn's sense of the child incorporates a sense of Lucas' power and allows him considerable mastery and playful spontaneity. Yet it avoids his aggressivity and leaves his ordinariness unmentioned. Kathryn praises Lucas' 'intrepid' and 'intractable' qualities. He is presented as 'big', 'always busy,' and as a powerful and direct 'initiator' and 'leader.' 'Even as an infant he guided us, to get us to perform however he wants.' Kathryn avoids confrontation and gives Lucas the chance to say 'No.' She takes great pleasure in his 'negotiating' and communication skills.

Kathryn says she is 'trying to help [Lucas] be himself rather than our ideas about him or ideas about ourselves.' Speech mystifies the generational distinction. Children 'sound, you know, more and more like we sound. And, yes, their behavior [pause] does conform more and more to what adults do. But there are enormous gaps,' especially in relation to anger:

> But once they get angry they, they can't really control their emotions until the storm passes. And then they're like little. I mean they holler and they carry on. It's really quite amazing and over *nothing* you know, usually until you figure out he's tired or he's hungry or whatever. But I mean they are, they're, they're no civilized adults. They don't abide by our standards.

Relationality

Kathryn is very responsive and interested in connection, although her involvements seem limited by her need for good relationships with wonderful others. Except for a few references to professional relationships, she speaks only of family members. There is no discussion of or interest in relationships with women. While Kathryn's early, cheerful relationship with her 'genius' mother may form a model for later relationships, it seems easier for Kathryn to admire and relate to men.

The relationship with David is consistently presented as based on shared interests and mutual respect. While David is presented as more gregarious and physical, there is no sense that this relationship relies on or benefits from any differences between husband and wife. In contrast, relationships at work involve a clear division of labor. Interestingly, it is only in this context that Kathryn speaks of taking care of other adults.

Kathryn feels deeply engaged with Lucas and struggles not to 'cut him off' or expect adult behavior. Yet, she can be described as captivated by his wondrous image. She likes it when he negotiates or 'play acts his feelings' through children's stories. In both cases, demands are mediated by cultural forms and are more appealing and less threatening than the 'close to the surface,' 'just talk' of her mother.

Kathryn seems most comfortable in situations in which people are the same or in which differences are clearly defined and lead to interdepend-ence. Separation is a problem, perhaps because her own independence involved a dramatic loss of the wondrous mother. In my estimation, Kathryn would like to achieve a situation of true differentiation, of being the same as and different from others – especially her own mother – but difference leads to lack of recognition and severe cutting off of relationships. Needi-ness poses a similar problem. Kathryn's presentation suggests that she finds her own needs dangerous and capable of ending the relationship with Lucas. She strives to be other-directed or, as in the relationship with David, to be satisfied without giving or getting anything.

Traditionality

Kathryn is thoroughly uninterested in questions about her relationship to traditional women. Instead, she focuses on the present and speaks of the 'enormous,' 'staggering' possibility that she sees as completely replacing earlier practices. Asked if she has a different sense of being a woman now that she has a child, Kathryn says that she 'understands a lot of the emotions that uh motivate women. Mothers. Which I didn't have much of an under-standing or an interest in before.' She speaks of a universal and 'unrelenting' concern for the child. Uncertain about whether men share this concern, she finally describes shared concerns expressed differently: men are 'less realistic and more romantic' but also more concerned about economic matters.

Despite the lack of attention to motherhood as institution, Kathryn sees motherhood as an individual experience, as the most 'exciting' and 'satis-fying' thing she's ever done. She does not set firm boundaries between fathers and mothers, between the public and private realms. She uses the same planning skills at home as at work; she negotiates and makes contracts with Lucas just as she negotiates at work. In addition, she sees Lucas as having his 'own business' of daily activities.

In contrast, Kathryn does struggle to make a distinction between adults and children. She deeply wants to follow Lucas' lead rather than to make him follow adult standards and does not want to act like a needy child. Kathryn and Lucas engage in word play, act out stories, and sing a great deal.

Kathryn does not speak of a sexual relationship with her husband or of a holding, physical relationship with Lucas as a baby. In the first interview, Kathryn speaks of Lucas as an affectionate child and how they would dance and would also hug and kiss in the middle of playing. These comments drop out in the second interview and this may be an indication of Kathryn's difficulty with what may feel like an actively sexualized relationship with him.

Kathryn's emphasis on cheerful relationships suggests an extreme need to manage anger and aggression. She seems to use negotiation and contracts to keep connected to others without the disruption of anger or unfair/uncontrollable demand. The extent of her anger is clear when Kathryn speaks of 'letting off steam' at David. This metaphor suggests a view of anger as hot air that dissipates when it is ignored by David. In another instance, however, she speaks of how the child who continues to receive intense and demanding attention from its mother will turn into a 'battleship.' Here, the child can blow up in considerably more destructive fashion.

Reference measures

I Object relations: Assessment of Qualitative and Structural Dimensions of Object Representations (AQSDOR)

	Mother	Father	Husband	Son
Factor I – Nurturance				
Nurturant	5	4*	5	5
Positive ideal	3	5	6	7
Benevolent	5	6	6	7
Cold–Warm	6	3	5	5
Degree of constructive involvement	3	6	6	5
Affectionate	4	4	4	6
Weak–Strong	2	7	6	7
Successful	4	4	4	7
Factor II – Striving				
Judgmental	4	4	4	4
Ambitious	4	4	4	4
Punitive	4	4	4	4
Intellectual	4	6	6	7
Degree of ambivalence**	3	2	1	1
Successful	4	4	4	7
Weak–Strong	2	7	6	7
Conceptual level***	9	5	5	7

* 4 = uncodable, inadequate material
** Three-point scale
*** Scored on scale of 1, 3, 5, 7, 9

Scoring indicates that Kathryn presents her mother with great ambivalence and at the highest conceptual level, in terms of an integrated picture of her feelings and behaviors. She is less ambivalent about her father but presents him at a lower conceptual level, in terms of behaviors rather than feelings. Although she is unambivalent about her husband, he is similarly presented in terms of behaviors. Kathryn is unambivalent about Lucas and presents him at a somewhat higher conceptual level, in terms of his feelings.

Kathryn presents Lucas in particularly positive terms. Notably, he is an extremely admired, intellectual, strong, fairly affectionate figure who is happy with himself. He is extremely benevolent, despite the fact that he is only somewhat nurturant, warm, or able to respond to her constructively. Kathryn also presents David as a positive figure who is more able to respond to Kathryn constructively but is less admirable, benevolent, affectionate, strong, or intellectual than Lucas. Kathryn presents her father as a benevolent, intellectual, strong man who has been able to respond constructively, although he is lacking in warmth and affection. In contrast to these male figures, Kathryn presents her mother as warmer but as a somewhat negative ideal, as a weak, irrational woman who can no longer respond to Kathryn constructively.

Interestingly, Kathryn's presentations omit discussion of judgment, ambition, or punitiveness. It is as if these people do not push her or themselves or have any standards that must be reckoned with.

II Relationality: Attanucci coding of Gilligan dilemma

Types of self-description	Number of responses by level			
	I	II	III	IV
Self in relation to colleagues and clients	0	0	0	2(?)
Self in relation to clients	0	2	0	0

Kathryn speaks of a work-related, 'structural' dilemma. Her job is to render services to clients. She must make sure they feel taken care of at the same time as she considers how hard she can 'press' herself and people who work for her. Because Kathryn speaks of the terms of all concerned, her response seems to be at Level IV. The coding IV(?) was developed to indicate that Kathryn is less clear about her own position – except as mediator of the terms of others – and that additional probing might have elicited this material.

Toward the end of her response, Kathryn focuses more clearly on the terms of the clients (Level II). She must make them feel as though 'they are the only client.' Whether she has done the right thing is defined by the client's reaction.

III Traditionality: Newberger dilemma

Issue	Final score
Resolving conflict	3
Meeting needs	3
	3: Global level

Kathryn's response to the dilemma focuses on communication between mother and child, on 'mediation' that allows both mother and child to have their needs met. Her comments are scored at Level 3 because of her emphasis on communication and treatment of mother and child as distinct persons. Kathryn stresses that the mother should help her child adjust by gradually returning to work. Based on her own experience, Kathryn asserts that Mrs Stewart should 'speak up;' colleagues and supervisors can be surprisingly 'understanding and completely accommodating about things related to small children.' If the child continues to be upset, Mrs Stewart should consider how her son feels about his babysitter and whether other things are making him feel 'pressured or uncared for.'

Kathryn's presentation becomes more complex and scored at Level 4 when she considers that the child may be suffering from 'confusion.' Kathryn describes how her own child, when playing Dumbo with his babysitter, called the sitter by the name reserved for Kathryn, which 'caused him great pain and unhappiness.' In Kathryn's estimation, this confusion is shared by mother and child: 'They have their own lives, separate lives. And, and yet their lives together are very important and ought to be important.' Kathryn's solution to the dilemma involves 'mediation,' although the child's adjustment takes some priority and the mother's needs can be easily met.

IV Thematic Apperception Test

Story I, Card 1

A boy has heard an admired person play the violin. He wants to play, is a bit frightened to touch the violin because he might break it, and asks his parents for lessons.

Clinical assessment

Import: we like to try to be like someone we admire.

Internal representations: child seen as admiring, ambitious.

Quality of relations: cannot be inferred, though the ability to admire others is evident.

Story II, Card 2

A woman who left the farm to be a scholar is daydreaming about the world she's 'separated herself from.' She's 'not remembering anything in particular' but is 'wistful' and 'lonely' and 'uncertain' but then decides she made the right decision. Subject cannot decide if the other woman is character's 'image of herself or image of her mother' but that woman is daydreaming she's pregnant and is content. Man enjoys working and is a 'fantasy, generalized male figure' of the 'earthy, more physical' type.

Clinical assessment

Import: one can decide to be happy despite doubts.

Conflicts: conflicts about separation are evident not only in the story's content but also in uncertainty about whether figure in background is character's image of herself or her mother.

Internal representations: women seen as dreamy, uncertain, happy, content; men seen as physical, content.

Quality of relations: there's a sense of alienation and detachment. Characters are in their own fantasy worlds and the main character is not 'remembering anything in particular' even though the card contains people. No indications of empathy or closeness.

Story III, Card 5

A woman hears a crash and opens the door to find a lamp broken. Child and dog are 'pretending they weren't there when it happened.' Child doesn't want woman to be angry, doesn't know how to appease her, and hopes it will pass. Woman is 'annoyed but not angry' and 'amused' at the pretending. 'Nothing happens. Except they clean it up.'

Clinical assessment

Import: when something goes wrong, it's not a big deal.

Conflicts: conflicts over feelings of anger. Unresolved feelings of guilt. The subject adds a dog to the situation, presumably to diffuse the child's responsibility. Still the issue is unresolved and the child and dog have to pretend they weren't there.

Internal representations: woman seen as annoyed, amused, distant; child seen as guilt-ridden, unable to take responsibility, impulsive (like a dog).

Quality of relations: there is a lack of relatedness. The woman is an authority figure, not a mother. She is only annoyed and amused but the child is fearful. Child is equated with a dog, and there is a lack of warmth or closeness in the relationship.

Story IV, Card 7GF

A girl and a woman – who may be the girl's mother – are waiting for some event. Girl is thinking about being a mother and 'enjoying the sensation of holding a small object.' Mother is 'snatching a moment for herself' and absorbed in reading. Characters are 'peaceful and calm,' enjoy being 'physically close,' 'but they're each doing separate things and um are content with that.' When they go to the 'event,' they talk about what they were doing by themselves.

Clinical assessment

Import: a mother and a daughter can be together and separate at the same time.

Conflicts: conflicts about separation are seen in the subject's description of separateness and togetherness. It seems that they can enjoy physical closeness only if they do 'separate things.' They can talk about their 'separate things' only when they go to their other thing. This suggests a fear of intimacy with the mother. Conflicts about motherhood are seen in subject's difficulty in deciding if the woman is a mother and in the daughter's holding doll as if it were a small 'object' instead of a baby.

Internal representations: mother seen as calm, content, aware, self-involved; daughter seen as calm, dreamy.

Quality of relations: the relationship involves closeness and communication. Mother and daughter can be physically close and are able to share their separate experiences. They are content with each other.

Overall clinical impression

This subject appears to have conflicts about separation. Her stories depict characters who struggle to negotiate their separateness from their families. There is a capacity for closeness but also a sense of alienation, with characters often in their own fantasy worlds.

She may also struggle with feelings of anger which she experiences as threatening. She copes with such feelings by denying them and by idealizing others. Her difficulties in naming authority figures as parents suggest either feelings of having been abandoned or intense, unconscious rage toward parental figures.

169

There are also indications of unresolved feelings of guilt, also defended against by denial. There are no indications of impulsivity.

Within-subject comparison of measures

Scores on the Assessment of Qualitative and Structural Dimensions of Object Representations support the case study analysis and reflect the importance of strength, intellect, and the presence of admirable figures to Kathryn. Interestingly, although the case study suggests that Kathryn sees and demands wonderfulness from her son, qualities of judgment and ambition are otherwise unmentioned. The scoring also suggests that Kathryn presents nurturance, affection, and warmth as less important.

Interestingly, Kathryn's responses to the Newberger and Gilligan dilemmas demonstrate her ability to think in terms of the needs of others. It is striking that Kathryn presents a dilemma that has nothing to do with motherhood and that, in the dilemma she describes, she is the responsive, caring mediator. Because her own terms and those of her assistants drop out of the presentation, there is no ongoing conflict. Kathryn moves from authentic connection to an exclusion of the concerns of herself and her staff. In a somewhat similar way, in the Newberger dilemma, the mother focuses on the problems of the hypothetical child in rather elaborate fashion. Her concerns are easily taken care of by benevolent colleagues.

These dilemmas support the case study in indicating Kathryn's responsiveness to others and her interest in negotiating rather than focusing on troubling difficulties. The TAT analysis, however, emphasizes difficulties in relationships which do not emerge clearly in either of these dilemmas. Characters are inadequately connected to others, have a capacity for closeness but are often involved in their own fantasy worlds. Instead of struggling to be closer, characters are presented as content but also as grappling with how to negotiate separateness.

This analysis does not provide evidence of the narcissistic dependence on others so central to the case analysis. It is interesting to consider whether cards depicting mothers and sons or men and women might have evoked this material. Instead, the cards seem to have evoked material about Kathryn and her own mother and reflected her desire to be separate as well as connected. The clinical assessment focuses on issues concerning anger, also central to the case analysis. However, that assessment suggests that Kathryn may idealize others in order to deny her frustration with them. Indications of difficulties with motherhood in her stories suggest that the idealization of Lucas may be prompted by some difficulties in being his mother and that her father and husband also have to be protected from unconscious rage. In this light, Kathryn's presentation of her mother is particularly interesting in that she moves from idealization to devaluation. It is not clear to what extent Kathryn feels responsible for diminishing her mother's 'genius' or feels abandoned by the mother who can no longer understand her. In either case there is a diminishing of shared wonderfulness that is not fully compensated for by her father. In attempting to be a 'genius' with her own child and to be like her father, Kathryn seems to be trying to have it both ways and to protect herself from losing her connection to her own child. In this context, her image of motherhood can be understood as defining the position of powerful, God-like mediator.

COMPARISON OF SUBGROUPINGS

In order to move beyond individual cases, the next stage of the analysis involves comparing and contrasting subjects within subgroupings. Two points of comparison are used. The first concerns similarities and differences between mothers of boys and mothers of girls. The second concerns similarities and differences among Children's Center and non-Children's Center populations, performed primarily to ascertain whether the twelve mothers could be treated as one population in the cross-case analysis.

The method used in both comparisons is similar. To build directly on the detail of the individual cases and yet provide a basis for comparison, the names of themes identified in the individual profiles were standardized. Since different subjects often used the same language when describing their experience, this shared language became the basis of the standardized labelling of themes. Subjects were then categorized by subgroupings according to the presence and absence of these themes. Tables were constructed to categorize subjects in terms of their presentations of: mother, father, good mother, husband, and child. In addition, tables were constructed to reflect relationality and traditionality characteristics.

Table 3.3 Subjects categorized by characteristics attributed to own mothers

Characteristics of own mothers	Children's Center	Non-Center	Boys	Girls
Adequately connected/ responsive	Sharon	Kathryn Susan	Kathryn	Sharon Susan
Suffocating/ unresponsive		Anna Harriet Kathryn Myra	Harriet Kathryn	Anna Myra
Not connected enough/ unresponsive	Ellen Karen Lauren Linda	Denise Julia	Denise Ellen Julia Karen	Lauren Linda

Characteristics of own mothers	Children's Center	Non-Center	Boys	Girls
Dependent on subject		Denise Harriet Kathryn Myra Susan	Denise Harriet Kathryn	Myra Susan
Demanding	Karen Lauren Linda	Denise Kathryn Myra	Denise Karen Kathryn	Lauren Linda Myra
Judgmental	Linda	Denise Myra	Denise	Linda Myra
Judgments resistible		Julia		Julia
Invested in propriety, impulse control, niceness	Ellen Lauren Linda	Denise Julia Myra	Denise Ellen Julia	Lauren Linda Myra
Accepting	Sharon	Anna Julia Susan	Julia	Anna Sharon Susan
Characterized by pleasure		Kathryn Susan	Kathryn	Susan
Task-oriented, accomplished	Ellen Karen Linda	Denise	Denise Ellen Karen	Linda
Inadequate at tasks		Myra		Myra
Wise	Sharon	Julia Kathryn	Julia Kathryn	Sharon
Powerful	Linda	Harriet Julia	Harriet Julia	Linda
Fearful	Sharon	Denise Julia Kathryn Myra Susan	Denise Julia Kathryn	Myra Sharon Susan

Table 3.4 Subjects categorized by characteristics attributed to own fathers

Characteristics of own fathers	Children's Center	Non-Center	Boys	Girls
Loving	Linda	Denise Harriet Julia	Denise Harriet Julia Linda	

172

Characteristics of own fathers	Children's Center	Non-Center	Boys	Girls
Understanding	Ellen Karen Lauren	Julia Kathryn Myra	Ellen Julia Karen Kathryn	Lauren Myra
Inadequate nurturer	Sharon			Sharon
Connected	Lauren Linda	Julia	Julia	Lauren Linda
Similar to subject	Lauren	Harriet Julia Kathryn	Harriet Julia Kathryn	Lauren
Undependable	Sharon	Denise Kathryn Myra	Denise Kathryn	Myra Sharon
Adequate in world	Karen Lauren	Kathryn	Karen Kathryn	Lauren
Inadequate in world/ powerless, fearful		Denise Julia Myra	Denise Julia	Myra
Wise	Ellen Karen Lauren	Kathryn	Ellen Karen Kathryn	Lauren
Enjoyed children	Karen Linda	Denise Harriet Susan	Denise Harriet Karen	Linda Susan
Invested in propriety, control		Anna Denise	Denise	Anna

Table 3.5 Subjects categorized by characteristics attributed to good mother

Characteristics of good mother	Children's Center	Non-Center	Boys	Girls
Own mother	Sharon	Anna Susan		Anna Sharon Susan
Selfless	Lauren	Anna Kathryn	Kathryn	Anna Lauren
Responds to child without own needs affecting response	Karen Linda Sharon	Harriet Susan Denise	Karen Harriet Denise	Linda Sharon Susan
Attends to own needs	Karen	Denise Myra	Denise Karen	Myra
Child takes cares of her		Julia	Julia	

Characteristics of good mother	Children's Center	Non-Center	Boys	Girls
Available	Ellen Karen Lauren Sharon	Harriet Kathryn Susan	Ellen Harriet Karen Kathryn	Lauren Sharon Susan
Accepting	Ellen Linda	Denise	Denise Ellen	Linda
Listening	Ellen Sharon	Susan	Ellen	Sharon Susan
Tolerant of unavoidable	Lauren Sharon	Denise	Denise	Lauren Sharon
Enjoys child	Linda	Denise	Denise	Linda
Powerful	Lauren	Kathryn Myra	Kathryn	Lauren Myra
Teaches	Lauren			Lauren

Table 3.6 Subjects categorized by characteristics attributed to husbands

Characteristics of husband	Children's Center	Non-Center	Boys	Girls
Similar to wife	Lauren	Denise Harriet Kathryn Susan	Denise Harriet Kathryn	Lauren Susan
Different from wife	Karen Linda Sharon	Julia	Karen Julia	Linda Sharon
Same and different	Ellen	Anna Julia	Ellen Julia	Anna
Supportive of wife	Ellen Lauren Linda Sharon	Harriet Susan	Ellen Harriet	Lauren Sharon Linda Susan
Involved parent	Ellen Karen Linda	Kathryn Susan	Ellen Karen Kathryn	Linda Susan
Less relational than wife	Sharon	Anna Julia Denise	Julia Denise	Anna Sharon
Romantic	Lauren	Denise	Denise	Lauren
Powerful	Ellen Karen Linda	Denise Julia	Ellen Karen Denise Julia	Linda

Characteristics of husband	Children's Center	Non-Center	Boys	Girls
Needy		Anna Denise Julia Myra	Denise Julia	Anna Myra
More playful/ physical	Karen Lauren Linda Sharon	Kathryn Myra	Karen Kathryn	Lauren Linda Myra Sharon
Bright	Ellen Karen Linda Sharon	Denise Kathryn Myra	Ellen Denise Karen Kathryn	Linda Myra Sharon

Table 3.7 Subjects categorized by characteristics attributed to children

Characteristics of Child	Children's Center	Non-Center	Boys	Girls
Similar to subject	Karen	Susan	Karen	Susan
Like subject and husband	Linda	Kathryn Julia	Kathryn Julia	Linda
More similar to husband	Ellen Lauren	Myra	Ellen	Myra Lauren
More similar to subject		Denise Harriet	Denise Harriet	
Different		Anna		Anna
Similar to subject's mother	Linda Sharon	Julia Myra Susan	Julia	Linda Myra Sharon Susan
New object capable of transforming subject	Ellen Lauren Linda Karen	Denise Julia Kathryn Myra	Denise Ellen Julia Kathryn Karen	Lauren Linda Myra
Loving	Karen Sharon	Denise Harriet Julia Kathryn Susan	Denise Karen Harriet Julia Kathryn	Sharon Susan
Bright	Lauren Linda Sharon	Denise Harriet Julia Kathryn	Denise Harriet Julia Kathryn	Lauren Linda Sharon

Characteristics of Child	Children's Center	Non-Center	Boys	Girls
Nurturant	Karen Lauren	Julia Susan	Karen Julia	Lauren Susan
Accepting	Ellen Linda	Denise Julia	Denise Ellen Julia	Linda
Positive power	Ellen Lauren Sharon	Anna Denise Julia Kathryn	Denise Ellen Julia Kathryn	Anna Lauren Sharon
Bothersome when frustrated	Karen	Harriet	Harriet Karen	
Negative power, aggressively demanding	Lauren Linda	Myra		Lauren Linda Myra
Fearful	Sharon	Anna Harriet	Harriet	Anna Sharon
Can be overly separate		Anna Denise Julia	Denise Julia	Anna
Female-to-female bond	Lauren Sharon	Anna Susan		Lauren Sharon Anne Susan
Female-to-female difficulty	Linda	Myra		Linda Myra

Table 3.8 Subjects categorized by relationality characteristics

Relationality characteristic	Children's Center	Non-Center	Boys	Girls
Capacity for empathy, real closeness	Ellen Karen Linda	Denise Julia Kathryn	Denise Ellen Julia Karen Kathryn	Linda
Lack of real closeness	Sharon	Susan		Sharon Susan
Alienated, detached, lonely	Lauren	Anna Denise Harriet Kathryn	Anna Denise Harriet Kathryn	Lauren

176

Relationality characteristic	Children's Center	Non-Center	Boys	Girls
Close to similar others	Lauren Sharon	Anna Denise Harriet Kathryn Susan	Denise Harriet Kathryn Lauren	Anna Sharon Susan
Bond with women	Ellen Sharon	Susan	Ellen	Sharon Susan
More comfortable with men	Ellen Linda	Denise Kathryn	Denise Ellen Kathryn	Linda
Likes symbiotic closeness		Anna Harriet Julia	Harriet Julia	Anna
Likes conflict-free relationships	Karen(ch) Linda Sharon	Anna Harriet Kathryn Susan	Harriet Karen Kathryn	Anna Linda Sharon Susan
Conflicts good for relationships	Ellen Karen(ad)	Julia	Ellen Julia Karen	
Values mutuality	Ellen Lauren Sharon		Ellen	Lauren Sharon
Sharing not caring	Linda	Kathryn	Kathryn	Linda
Nurturant to adults	Susan	Denise Julia Sharon	Denise Julia	Sharon Susan
Nurturant at work	Ellen Linda	Kathryn	Ellen Kathryn	Linda
Confident when giving	Sharon	Anna Julia Susan	Julia	Anna Sharon Susan
Not confident when giving	Ellen(ch) Karen	Denise Harriet Myra	Denise Ellen Harriet Karen	Myra
Depleted by child; needs to get away	Ellen Lauren Linda	Myra	Ellen	Myra Lauren Linda
Own needs dangerous	Linda	Kathryn Myra Susan	Kathryn	Linda Myra Susan
Needs to care for self		Julia	Julia	

Relationality characteristic	Children's Center	Non-Center	Boys	Girls
Looks to adults for care	Lauren	Anna Harriet Myra	Harriet	Anna Lauren Myra
Looks to child for care	Karen Lauren	Julia Susan	Julia Karen	Lauren Susan
Tries to be selfless	Karen Sharon	Susan	Karen	Sharon Susan
Relationships as power struggles	Lauren	Anna Harriet Myra	Harriet	Anna Lauren Myra
Uses physical separation as protection	Lauren Linda	Anna Harriet Julia(ad) Myra	Harriet Julia	Anna Lauren Linda Myra
Differences between people appealing	Ellen Karen Linda Sharon	Julia Kathryn Myra	Ellen Julia Karen Kathryn	Linda Myra Sharon
Differences problematic		Harriet Susan	Harriet	Susan
Strangers dangerous	Lauren Sharon	Anna Susan		Anna Lauren Sharon Susan
Separation a loss	Karen Sharon	Denise Julia Susan	Denise Karen Julia	Sharon Susan
Fears break in connection	Ellen Linda	Julia Kathryn Myra Susan	Ellen Julia Kathryn	Linda Myra Susan
Wants true differentiation	Ellen Sharon	Julia Kathryn	Ellen Julia Kathryn	Sharon
Values independence	Ellen Lauren Linda Sharon	Kathryn	Ellen Kathryn	Lauren Linda Sharon

Note: (ch) = in relation to children
(ad) = in relation to adults

INDIVIDUAL PROFILES OF SUBJECTS

Table 3.9 Subjects categorized by traditionality characteristics

Traditionality characteristic	Children's Center	Non-Center	Boys	Girls
Feels affiliation with women of different generations	Ellen Sharon	Myra Susan	Ellen	Myra Sharon Susan
Feels conflict among women of the same generation	Sharon	Anna Denise Susan	Denise	Anna Sharon Susan
Admires traditional women		Anna Denise Harriet Myra	Denise Harriet	Anna Myra
Separates from traditional women	Ellen Karen Lauren Linda	Julia Kathryn	Ellen Julia Karen Kathryn	Lauren Linda
Motherhood diminishes self		Harriet Julia	Harriet Julia	
Comfortable combining work and parenthood	Ellen Linda Sharon	Kathryn Susan	Ellen Kathryn	Linda Sharon Susan
Children lose without mothers home	Karen Lauren	Anna Harriet	Harriet Karen	Anna Lauren
Public/private distinction	Lauren Sharon	Anna Denise Harriet Susan	Denise Harriet	Anna Lauren Sharon Susan
Diminished public/private distinction	Linda	Kathryn Myra	Kathryn	Myra Linda
Male/female distinction	Ellen Karen Sharon	Anna Denise Myra	Denise Ellen Karen	Anna Myra Sharon
Diminished male/female distinction	Lauren Linda	Harriet Julia Kathryn Susan	Harriet Julia Kathryn	Lauren Linda Susan
Adult/child distinction	Ellen Karen	Kathryn Myra Susan	Ellen Karen Kathryn	Myra Susan
Diminished adult/child distinction	Lauren Linda	Anna Denise Harriet Julia	Denise Harriet Julia	Anna Lauren Linda
Heterosexuality prominent	Lauren	Denise Myra	Denise	Lauren Myra

179

Traditionality characteristic	Children's Center	Non-Center	Boys	Girls
Heterosexuality downplayed	Ellen Karen	Anna Harriet Kathryn Susan	Ellen Harriet Karen Kathryn	Anna Susan
Denial of anger and aggression		Denise Kathryn Susan	Denise Kathryn	Susan
Suppression of anger and aggression	Ellen Karen Lauren Linda Sharon	Anna Myra	Ellen Karen	Anna Lauren Linda Myra Sharon
Contact through aggression	Linda	Anna Harriet	Harriet	Anna Linda
Playful	Lauren Linda	Kathryn Susan	Kathryn	Lauren Linda Susan
Not playful	Sharon	Anna Myra		Anna Myra Sharon
Calm player	Karen	Denise Harriet Julia	Denise Harriet Julia Karen	
Authoritarian	Lauren	Myra		Lauren Myra
Anti-authoritarian but must be in control		Anna Harriet	Harriet	Anna
Wants child to be good without being authoritarian	Ellen Karen Sharon	Denise Julia Kathryn Susan	Denise Ellen Julia Karen Kathryn	Sharon Susan

Comparison of mothers of boys and mothers of girls

Mothers of boys

Mothers of boys more often report that they:

1 see their own mothers as unresponsive and task-oriented and their fathers as loving, understanding, wise, and similar to themselves;
2 see their children as loving and accepting;
3 are more comfortable with men, have a capacity for empathy and

closeness, see conflicts as good for relationships, value true differentiation, and lack confidence in their ability to give;

4 separate themselves from traditional women, feel that motherhood takes away from themselves, downplay heterosexuality, feel they are calm players, and want their children to be good without being authoritarian.

Mothers of girls

Mothers of girls more often report that they:

1 see their own mothers as accepting and as their image of a good mother;
2 see their husbands as supportive of them and as more playful and physical;
3 see their daughters as similar to their mothers and as having negative power;
4 feel depleted by their children, find their own needs dangerous, look to other adults for care, find unfamiliar people dangerous, and see relationships as power struggles;
5 have a sense of intergenerational affiliation with women and experience conflict with women in their own generation, make a public/private distinction, suppress anger, speak of themselves as authoritarian, feel a sense of mastery and play, or feel unplayful.

Comments

Differences between mothers of boys and girls are salient and suggestive. They will be considered further in chapter 4, Cross-Case Analysis.

Comparison of Children's Center and non-Children's Center populations

Similarities

Subjects in Children's Center and non-Children's Center populations are similar in the way in which they:

1 present their own mothers as connected, wise, powerful, demanding, judgmental, and invested in propriety;
2 present their fathers as understanding, connected, and adequate vis-à-vis the world, and as enjoying their children;
3 use similar characteristics to describe the good mother;
4 present their husbands as bright, romantic, powerful, and as involved parents;

5 present their children as bright, nurturant, and accepting, and in terms of negative power and bothersomeness;

6 have a capacity for empathy and real closeness, like conflict-free relationships, feel more comfortable with men, find differences between people appealing, see separation and unfamiliar people as problematic, lack confidence in their ability to give, and look to children for care;

7 feel an intergenerational affiliation with women, are comfortable with their work/parenthood arrangements, make male/female distinctions, feel a sense of mastery and playfulness, and want children to be good without they themselves having to act as authoritarian parents.

Differences

Subjects in these populations differ as follows:

1 Children's Center mothers more often see their own mothers as unresponsive and as task-oriented and accomplished. Only the non-Center population tends to see their mothers as suffocating or dependent on them and more of them see their mothers as accepting or fearful.

2 Children's Center mothers tend to speak of their fathers as wise. No Children's Center mother sees her father as controlling or inadequate while non-Center subjects tend to see their fathers as controlling and inadequate but also as loving and similar to them.

3 Children's Center mothers more often present their husbands as different, as more playful than themselves, and as supportive. Non-Center subjects more often see their husbands as similar to themselves and as needy.

4 Children's Center subjects do not speak of their children as loving. Non-Center subjects describe their children as extremely loving and either as very similar to themselves or as prone to being overly separate.

5 Children's Center mothers more often speak of feeling depleted by their children and they also value independence. Non-Center mothers more often speak of feeling close to similar others, they like symbiotic closeness, feel lonely, feel nurturant to adults, but also look to other adults for care, and find their own needs dangerous. They see relationships as power struggles more often and are fearful of breaks in connection.

6 Children's Center mothers more often separate themselves from traditional women and suppress anger and aggression. Only non-Children's Center mothers admire traditional women and deny feelings of anger. They also express more feelings of intergenerational conflict among women, feel that motherhood takes away from the self, make a public/private distinction, diminish heterosexuality and adult/child distinctions, and are more often calm players.

Comments

Children's Center and non-Children's Center mothers share many characteristics and can be treated as one population for the cross-case analysis. However, differences between these populations are interesting and suggest a psychological relationship between families and schools or other child care institutions. Such a relationship may be particularly apparent in the case of an institution like the Children's Center that can select families out of a pool of self-selected applicants. The present study was not designed to consider the link between families and institutions. In fact, the study was designed not to evaluate parents' feelings about the Children's Center either before or early on in their children's year at the Center. Because of lack of data, the relationship between families and child care institutions will not be explored further in this study. This topic should be the basis of interesting and important future research.

4

CROSS-CASE ANALYSIS

The cross-case analysis builds on the case presentations and charts and looks at material across individual subjects. Within this study, object relations material provides a detailed starting point for analysis, both in terms of the cases themselves and in terms of the considerable body of theory on the psychology of women. In particular, I will be focusing attention on how the cases relate to Chodorow's detailed presentation, but will also be considering the cases in relation to other theoretical perspectives.

Although the grouping of subjects into a typology was not the goal of this study, three constellations of subjects do emerge from the object relations analysis. Particular relationality and traditionality stances and testing profiles are associated with each. The relationality and traditionality perspectives will be discussed after, and in the context of, the three constellations.

OBJECT RELATIONS

Mother

Most of the women who participated in this study present their mothers negatively; they do not want to be like their mothers and have had to struggle to accept intergenerational similarities. In a sense, this is not a surprising finding; these women live markedly different lives from their mothers. In another sense, however, these subjects' negative presentations of their mothers and positive views of their fathers and husbands are surprising and contrast with what I have been calling the dominant model in the American psychology of women

Susan and Sharon are the only two subjects who speak of being adequately mothered and who present their own mothers as the nurturant, caring, responsive women Chodorow and others describe. Both subjects speak of their mothers as available, as understanding listeners and as participants in their activities, even though their ability to respond to their

184

daughters has been limited by their own fearfulness and, in Susan's less idealized presentation, by her mother's neediness.

Three subjects (Anna, Harriet, and Myra) present their mothers as suffocating and unresponsive to their needs. Because Chodorow and other theorists speak at length about maternal over-involvement, it is striking that only three of the twelve subjects present their mothers in quite these terms. Anna and Harriet fit Chodorow's presentation particularly well; they present their mothers as caring and nurturant but also indicate a blurring of boundaries between the needs of their mothers and themselves. In some contrast, Myra emphasizes her mother's intrusive, judgmental, and demanding qualities.

Seven subjects speak of feeling unmothered. Five (Karen, Ellen, Linda, Denise, and Julia) describe their mothers as unresponsive and as demanding, task-oriented, and overly invested in propriety. Two subjects (Lauren and Kathryn) speak of the loss of the good mother. Lauren's dead mother was replaced by a demanding, unresponsive woman. Kathryn's mother changed from 'genius' to demanding woman.

Subjects' experiences of maternal demand and unresponsiveness are antithetical to the picture of female nurturance and intimate mother–daughter connection central to current American work in the psychology of women. Their descriptions of maternal demand may be specific to this subject population and are consistent with the literature (e.g. Hoffman, 1972) indicating that achievement-motivated women tend to describe their mothers as demanding.

Notably, the subjects in this research speak of a wish for but lack of intimate connection with their mothers. Subjects speak of mothers who were superficial (Karen), were 'brick walls' unable to listen (Linda) or encourage 'intimate conversation' (Ellen), who were concerned only with their own interests (Julia), and who were unable to appreciate their daughters (Denise and Karen). The sense of a lack of intimacy relates to Chodorow's point that mothers depend on and misread their daughters. However, these subjects use a language of control and pressure unacknowledged in the notion of the mother as overly dependent but nurturant; they express feelings of anger, frustration, and loss rather than the blurring of boundaries Chodorow describes. There is, to use Benjamin's term, a 'battle of recognition' and a sense that these mothers recognized and accepted only parts of their daughters and defined a boundary between goodness and bad feelings (Benjamin 1980, 1988).

Alice Miller's (1983/1981) discussion of parental narcissism and the dilemma it poses for the sensitive child is directly related to these findings. Miller suggests that some children are particularly sensitive to their parents' feelings and are aware that their parents have contempt for parts of them. These parts are usually associated with rage, aggression, enjoyment of the body, and feelings of mess and dirtiness. Children introject this contempt and split off bad parts of themselves. They then may be responded to as good but, because of the split-off but ever-present bad parts, have fragile self-esteem, lack a sense of being loved for who they are, and need relationships to be cheerful rather than to be based on authentic feelings.

Wolfenstein (1955) and Harris (1987) place this response to impulsivity in historical perspective and suggest that an increasing attention to children as having predictable and cognitively-based patterns of behavior may contribute to parents' inability to acknowledge their children's disruptive characteristics. There is work suggesting that mothers are likely to respond more negatively to their daughters' impulsivity than to that of their sons and that women, then, are more likely to have to struggle with issues of control and goodness. Oliner (1984), following Chasseguet-Smirgel (1964, 1976), argues that during the anal phase the girl is restricted in her attempts to express aggression by the mother conflicted about aggressive impulses. To be free of what she experiences as her mother's intrusiveness, the daughter identifies with her mother's control and masters her own bodily products and impulses instead of mastering external objects. This impulse control inhibits the girl's ability to master the outside world and her ability to express the aggression necessary to 'hold on' and make satisfying connections to others. As a mother, she may be attracted to her children's disruptiveness but experience them as unacceptable until they conform to social standards.

In the light of these theories, it is striking that six of the twelve subjects (Linda, Ellen, Lauren, Denise, Myra, and Julia) speak directly of their mothers as invested in propriety (Linda, Ellen, Lauren, and Denise), impulse control (Myra, Julia, and Denise), or niceness (Ellen and Denise). Further research is needed to consider the extent to which certain characteristics of these subjects' two-year-old children make issues of demand and impulse control so prominent by studying mothers of different aged children. However, the fact that women associate the demand for propriety with their mothers rather than with males figures is important. While other groups of women may represent their mothers differently, the mother in the isolated nuclear family is *the* caretaker involved in daily regulatory activities and supervision of the children. She is likely to be associated with issues of control (Ruddick, 1980, 1989; Dinnerstein, 1976).

Notably, except for Kathryn and Susan, these subjects do not associate their mothers with play and present them instead as oriented to order, to house-cleaning, and to inhibiting rather than enjoying their daughters' play and messiness. This relation between impulse control and cleaning is supported by large sample analyses of maternal values carried out in the 1960s (Loevinger et al., 1962; Loevinger and Ernhart, 1969). The difficulty of seeing mothers as playful is central to Susan Suleiman's (in press) analysis of representations of mothers by the avant-garde.

There is another sense in which these research subjects see their mothers as constricted. Six of the subjects (Sharon, Denise, Susan, Kathryn, Julia, Sharon) speak of their mothers as fearful, either of not getting the approval of others (Sharon, Denise, Susan, Kathryn), of the outside world (Myra, Denise), or of lack of physical well-being (Julia, Sharon). These mothers seem to have presented their daughters with the idea that 'outside' certain bounds lay a lack of safety rather than adventure or support. Subjects seem to have learned that they have to be generally good and careful to avoid difficult circumstances.

While in Chodorow's framework needy mothers are to some extent satisfied by their children, these research subjects tend to speak of their mothers as unsatisfied and, except for Kathryn and Susan, do not speak directly of their mothers' pleasure. Despite the 'fun morality' Wolfenstein (1955) identified, these women do not associate their mothers with pleasure. Certainly, the absence of pleasure can be understood in terms of the difficulty of mothering in the isolated nuclear family (Bader and Philipson, 1980; Kitzinger, 1978; Minturn and Lambert, 1964; Weiss, 1978) and the mother's need for other meaningful activity. However, instead of considering their mothers' lives, these subjects associate the absence of pleasure with their own lack and their mothers' demands. They accept the position of being their mothers' caretakers. The inability to satisfy their mothers contributes to feelings of being the 'bad seed' (Denise), to humiliation (Myra), and to concerns about their own ability to establish a pleasurable mother–child relationship.

At the same time, these subjects are now mothers themselves and need care and help with their own children. Conflict between the grandmother who is uninterested in or unavailable to help with child care and the needs of her grown daughter may create particular strains among female family members (Cohler, 1984; Cohler and Grunebaum, 1981) and may contribute to subjects' presentations of their mothers as unresponsive. Questions of when and how subjects' mothers and fathers interacted with their grandchildren and the ways in which they supported their daughters in the transition to parenthood are important to further research.

Father

It is striking that most of these subjects (all but Anna, Sharon, and Susan) represent their fathers in considerably more positive terms than their mothers. In contrast to the image of female nurturance contained in much of the theory, these women describe their fathers as *the* dependable, warm, accepting, and compassionate figures in their lives. Certainly, it is possible that the nurturant qualities of these fathers have been enhanced by aging (Gutmann, 1975) and were less apparent earlier. However, in contrast to a feeling of disappointment with their mothers, the subjects treat indications of their fathers' warmth and involvement with grandchildren as central to their positive view of these men as fathers. Within the interviews, subjects present their fathers as supporting growth, a characteristic which Chodorow presents as having a 'masculine' association, but also in terms of the 'female'-associated characteristics of warmth and understanding. The nature of this presentation indicates both a positive evaluation of 'female' qualities and a lack of clear distinction between parents in terms of gender-associated characteristics.

The idea of a lack of clear male–female distinction is supported by the fact that four subjects speak of being similar to their fathers and that two of these four also feel similar to their mothers. While theories like Chodorow's suggest that the *conscious* sense of different male and female roles and characteristics is matched by *unconscious* distinctions between men and women, these subjects suggest that gender distinctions are a murkier matter. This idea is supported by Klein's work on the child's fantasy of the fused parental couple as well as by uses of Lacanian theory to understand gender (Rose, 1982; Broughton, 1983).

At the same time that gender distinctions are not fully clear, subjects *are* affected by female mothering. They do not expect the same availability from their fathers and, unintentionally, indicate their fathers' remoteness and inability to compensate for or ameliorate mother–daughter difficulties. This is not surprising given that these working fathers were less involved in family activities. What is striking is that these women are so sympathetic to their fathers and present them as so responsive. In psychological terms, it seems that the father's position as good, available object is contradicted by his absence. With his position as good object in question, he must be protected from aggression and supported by understanding, a point made by Chasseguet-Smirgel (1964).

Interestingly, while mothers are depicted primarily outside a social context, the father's place in the outside, difficult world is incorporated into the sympathetic representation of him. In this context, it is meaningful that Myra and Denise present their fathers as somewhat depressed and Ellen and Julia also see their fathers as lacking in 'male' characteristics of power and ability to negotiate the outside world. Only Kathryn and Lauren, the two women who speak of the loss of the good mother, idealize their fathers' success and, it seems, their capacity to endure. Additional research is needed to examine the relationship between the meaning made of social status and position as a parental figure.

Good mother

Chodorow's model assumes that women's representations of their own mothers reflect their mothers' nurturant qualities and constitute *the* internal sense of the maternal that they subsequently reproduce. This sense of isomorphism – maternal object = experienced maternal qualities = characteristics reproduced in the next generation and needed to perform maternal role – distinguishes Chodorow's object relations theory from some others and has attracted criticism of Chodorow's work. In particular, attention has been called to Chodorow's lack of concern with issues of representation and meaning (Garner *et al.*, 1985), her use of role psychology (Rose, 1982), and her overemphasis on reproduction and socialization at the expense of attention to resistance and creation (Kaplan and Broughton, in press). The presence of a distinction between representations of the good mother and the subject's representation of her own mother in ten of the twelve cases is an important finding and introduces issues of desire, resistance, and cultural meaning into current models of female object relations.

Given the negative presentations of their own mothers, subjects' images of motherhood can be understood in terms of the mother–child relationship of their desire. In most cases, the language subjects use to describe the good mother is directly opposed to the complaints they lodge against their own mothers. Thus, Myra speaks of the Mother as adequate when her own mother is described as inadequate, Linda speaks of the Mother as accepting while her own mother is unaccepting, and Harriet says the Mother should not be overbearing while her own mother is described as overbearing.

At the same time that subjects are moved by their unique experience, they appropriate cultural meanings and share an image of motherhood. In this way, they are participants in what Murphy (1971) calls a 'collective fantasy.' Overall, these modern women do not subscribe to the traditional notion of the all-giving, ever-present, selfless Mother but also do not question many assumptions of traditional social arrangements. Instead of seeing the Mother as ever-present, seven of the subjects emphasize the Mother's psychological availability and ability to be on-call. Instead of the Mother being all-giving, they speak of Her as effective and capable of being used by the child when needed. Instead of seeing motherhood as a necessarily full time job, subjects with full and part time employment suggest that a good mother could work outside the home and still be used by her child.

The availability subjects describe is very much what many of these women felt they did not get from their own mothers: responsiveness to needs defined by the child. Comments about the Mother as accepting, listening, tolerant of unavoidable messiness and problems inherent in childhood seem to provide further elaboration of this notion of availability and suggest the importance of the mother accepting the child for who s/he is.

Interestingly, only three subjects (Lauren, Anna, and Kathryn) emphasize the Mother's selflessness. Six subjects indicate that even good mothers cannot be fully satisfied by motherhood and have needs that go beyond the parent–child relationship, an idea consistent with the more modern notion

189

of Mother as person (Rapoport *et al.*, 1980). However, within this research group, subjects are particularly aware that the Mother's needs can problematize the relationship. They do not move to Gilligan's (1982) post-conventional position and consider how the Mother might include herself in the equation of care. Nor do they follow Benjamin (1987, 1988, in press) and assert that the Mother's subjectivity is important for the child's development. Julia seems to begin to make this point but focuses on her own need to be taken care of by her child. Myra is the only subject who names and explores the Mother's needs and seeks satisfaction with the help of other people and institutions.

In the other cases, while the Mother has needs, she must take care of them herself. She gets no clearly stated support from institutions, family members, or friends. Further, there is no sense in these presentations that the Mother's situation is shared by or responded to by other women. While this is not surprising given the preponderance of isolated nuclear families in the American middle class, it is striking that these women introduce this unfortunate isolation into their images of motherhood. It is here that subjects' desires for connection and well-being can be seen as 'named', as defined and channeled by our particularly privatized culture.

In this context, it is interesting that the images of motherhood these subjects present are dyadic in eleven of the twelve cases. Myra is the exception here. While she values multiple mothering, she speaks of the importance of the child going to live with his father – in another dyad – while the Mother takes care of her own needs. This is hardly an ideal vision of shared parenting or of the Mother herself involved in a network of care. Instead, despite subjects' presentations of fathers and husbands as understanding and supportive, the Mother is located squarely within the traditional, dyadic relationship.

Interestingly, as these subjects speak of the mother–child relationship, their position is not always clear and often seems to shift from the vantage point of the still unsatisfied child looking for the good mother to the vantage point of the mother herself. The complexity of location indicates that women do not simply move to the maternal place in the relational triangle in the way that Chodorow suggests. Instead, the intensity of the mother–child relationship suggests what, in Lacanian terminology, is its shifting, unfixed, 'imaginary' quality. With positions in flux, attention must be paid to the blurring of boundaries between mother and child and the ensuing aggressive struggle for location and recognition (Lemaire, 1977; Urwin, 1984).

It is notable that only two subjects speak of the Mother as enjoying her child. Theorists like Ann Kaplan (1983 and in press) and Julia Kristeva (1980a, 1980b, 1981a) emphasize that the mother's pleasure is central to her questioning of a culture that leaves maternal pleasure, sexuality, and satisfaction unspoken. Although the subjects' mothers seem so lacking in pleasure and playfulness, these women do not develop images of motherhood to counter that particular lack. In the process, they avoid the issue of the Mother using her child for her own, perhaps incestuous, satisfaction, but also do not fully reckon with the Mother's subjectivity. She is not associated with desire and agency.

Husband

Much feminist work focuses on men's separateness and difficulty with relationships and contrasts this to women's rich web of connections. The subjects in this study present a somewhat different picture – of marital closeness and male–female similarity. This may reflect a 1980s, upper middle class, urban phenomenon in which isolated families are the unit of achievement and the arena for expression of a consumption mentality.[1] The emphasis on sameness as based on role similarity has been found in studies of dual career marriages (Hertz, 1986).

The object relations analysis adds to a consideration of the marital relationship. The close connections to husbands these women describe are consistent with their positive presentations of their fathers and indications of difficulties with their mothers. While the demands and disruptions involved in the recent move to parenthood may contribute to a romanticizing of the marriage, it is striking that these subjects tend to speak of relationships with their husbands as so satisfying.

Instead of being presented as the needy and unresponsive males described by Chodorow and others, six of these subjects (Ellen, Lauren, Linda, Sharon, Harriet, and Susan) describe their husbands as nurturant and supportive and five (Ellen, Karen, Linda, Kathryn, and Susan) describe their husbands as very involved parents. Interestingly, except for Karen who diminishes the importance of her husband's considerable child care involvement, their husbands' active fatherhood contributes to subjects' presentations of them as good partners. Instead of waging war when husbands are not full partners in child care, these women see shared parenting as having a positive effect on the marriage, substantiating the husband's goodness, and encouraging a form of togetherness that contrasts with the unity based in difference that Schneider (1968) found in his earlier cultural account of American kinship.

At the same time as subjects value togetherness, they also characterize the mother–child relationship as distinct and emotionally stronger than the father's relationship with the child. Except for Linda, subjects feel they are more realistic about and more responsive to the needs of their children, even as they admire the easier, more playful and less intense father–child connection.

Four subjects (Anna, Myra, Denise, and Julia) do speak of their husbands as needy rather than supportive. Denise and Julia speak of their husbands as displaced by their children. Anna sees her husband as burdened by his financial responsibilities and upset that she does not help by working. Myra presents a somewhat different picture. She sees her husband as giving over to being a child, and she feels threatened by the intensity of his love for his daughter. Myra's presentation is supported by Ehrensaft's (1985) proposal that many men find it safer to connect with their daughters than with what they see as considerably more threatening adult women.

The other subjects do not speak of their husbands as needing their care. These privileged men are not presented as burdened, lacking in ability to make a place in the world, or as needing to be nurtured at the end of the day. They are invested in contact with their families but, except for Anna's husband, are needy for psychological reasons; like their wives they had difficult backgrounds and need support.

Overall, there is no clear sense from these interviews that subjects see their husbands as fully different from themselves and they do not seem invested in making a clear male–female distinction. Besides seeing their husbands as supportive, five subjects (Lauren, Denise, Harriet, Kathryn, and Susan) see their husbands as like themselves and three others see their husbands as different but similar to themselves in basic ways (Ellen, Anna, and Julia). At the same time, subjects do describe their husbands in terms of what may be seen as male characteristics suited to career achievement. Seven (Ellen, Karen, Linda, Sharon, Denise, Kathryn, and Myra) see their husbands as bright and five (Ellen, Karen, Linda, Denise, and Julia) speak of their husbands as pleasingly powerful figures. Only Denise presents her husband's power in a negative, rigid way.

Child

The women in this study share something of a view of the child. In general, both mothers of boys and of girls tend to see their children as bright (Denise, Harriet, Julia, Kathryn, Lauren, Linda, and Sharon), as wonderfully powerful (Anna, Denise, Ellen, Julia, Kathryn, Lauren, and Sharon), and as new objects capable of having some positive, transformative effect on them (Denise, Ellen, Julia, Kathryn, Lauren, Linda, and Myra). The child's good-ness (Denise), optimism (Myra), awesome power and ability (Ellen and Kathryn), and capacity to be loving (Julia, Karen, and Denise) and accepting (Lauren, and Linda) are especially striking here.

While most of the mothers interviewed for this study see their children as other than themselves, they do not see the children's aggressive, sensual, inchoate characteristics as the focus of their appeal. The valuing of power, love, and intelligence may relate to particular characteristics of this research sample of influential, highly educated, upper middle class professionals. Subjects' presentations suggest a more civilized and grown-up – rather than child-like – other. The sense of the child as bright is relevant here. Although the attribution of intelligence does not necessarily imply a view of the child as rational, these mothers speak of their children's cognitive ability rather than of child-like creativity, an observation consistent with the claims of Harris (1987) and Wolfenstein (1955).

In four cases, the child is not seen as having what I describe as transformative potential. In these instances, the child is presented as reinforcing and supporting existing maternal qualities, as similar to the subject (Harriet, Sharon, and Susan) or in some sense sharing in the subject's power (Anna). It is striking that three of these children are girls and that these are the four cases that fit Chodorow's analysis. Although Chodorow has been criticized elsewhere (Kaplan and Broughton, in press) for her lack of attention to the possibility of psychological change through parenthood, these four 'Chodorow subjects' do not speak of an experience of change.

In contrast, all five women who felt unmothered and the two women who felt the loss of the good mother see their children as distinct objects offering them something new. In particular, they look to their children to help them get beyond their own self-doubts, to feel good, loved, accepted, and powerful. Denise and Myra are particularly striking because each speaks of fears of reproducing her problematic self and of how the presence of the child as a good object has contributed to her self-esteem.

These cases suggest that parenthood can be experienced as a source of adult development. While a carefully designed longitudinal study is needed to explore this point more fully, these subjects suggest that the mother's experience of her child and of herself changes in the process of parenting. As both Benedek (1959, 1970a, 1970b) and Klein (1964/1937) caution, this valuable effect of parenting is derived when the child is seen as a real and distinct object. Parents from both groups – those looking to their children for change and those looking to them for reinforcement – may include parents unable to respond to their 'real' children.

While Benedek and Klein do not pay consistent attention to issues posed by the child's sex, this research supports feminist theory and underscores the importance of gender. Within the present population, mothers are more likely to see their daughters as like themselves and to see their sons as new objects.

The current findings also suggest that the child's sex may have broader impact on the mother and relate to the presentation of other objects. Women tend to see their sons as able, powerful, aggressive, loving, and accepting. As Chodorow indicates, their presentations suggest a sense of a male other who is charming or sensuous. Interestingly, within this research sample, it is mothers of sons who most often present their own mothers as demanding. It is worth exploring whether the presence of boy children who are perceived as powerful and aggressive reactivates a sense of maternal control. These subjects present their fathers more positively, as understanding, wise, and similar to themselves. Perhaps influenced by their sons' maleness, these mothers tend to present themselves as comfortable with men, to downplay their sexual relationships with their husbands, and to look for both similarities and differences in others.

It is important that all six mothers of sons present their sons' demands as reasonable and do not seem to expect ongoing consideration and care from them. For the most part, these mothers tend to see their sons' power as wonderful; they do not want to engage in confrontation or the setting of limits. Such an acceptance of the male child's sometimes aggressive demands can be seen to contribute to the perpetuation of gender differences in impulsivity and mastery.

Consistent with Chodorow's theory, the mother's relationship with her daughter resembles her relationship with her own mother. However, while Chodorow emphasizes the intense dependency on the daughter as need satisfier, these subjects suggest other possibilities. In Myra's, Lauren's, and Linda's cases, the daughter, like her own mother, is filled with powerful, intrusive, and damaging needs. These subjects sometimes feel that their daughters have a horrific power, that they are being sucked dry or obliterated by their daughters and feel they must get away to survive. At no time do the mothers of sons speak of the same desperate need for separation because of their children's horrific demands.

In contrast to the other mothers of daughters, Sharon and Susan emphasize the benevolent connection to their daughters. They are the only two subjects to speak very positively of their own mothers. These two subjects describe their daughters as loving and do not find their daughters' demands to be dangerous or problematic. Sharon does not seem to look to her daughter for care but appears to get the support she needs from her own mother. Susan feels burdened by her own mother's neediness and does look to her daughter for care. Anna also speaks of her daughter as caring and does not find her demands intrusive. However in this case, the daughter's need to differentiate is threatening.

Interestingly, the mothers of girls more often speak of an intergenerational affiliation with women and also speak of unfamiliar people as dangerous. This suggests that having a daughter may relate to an investment in similarity rather than difference. While the mothers of sons speak more comfortably of difference, they are concerned about breaks in connection and are more often concerned that their children are, or will become, overly separate.

THE THREE CONSTELLATIONS OF SUBJECTS

Group I – 'Good relations mothers'

Two women, Sharon and Susan, seem to be relational women and fit Chodorow's and Gilligan's models remarkably well. Both speak of themselves as closely connected to others, speak positively of their own mothers, and see them as caring, connected, good although fearful mothers. Both see their fathers as secondary figures although they differ considerably in terms of closeness to their fathers and husbands. Notably, both of these women have daughters, see their daughters as like themselves, feel close to them, and appreciate their assertiveness. Neither feels her daughter is demanding or depleting. Neither sees her daughter as a new object with transformative potential.

Both Susan and Sharon feel close to familiar others, see strangers as dangerous, and feel vulnerable rather than close to outsiders. Both present themselves as strong, confident women and want their relationships to be conflict-free and safe.

While Susan and Sharon feel that they are not traditional women of the 1950s because they have interests in working, they feel a sense of progress and connection with what they depict as a female tradition. They want to mother like their own mothers and feel supported by their mothers and other women from different generations. At the same time, they experience conflicts among women from their own generation. Both of these women have a sense of a public–private distinction and see home as the place for a particular kind of warmth and intimacy. However, neither speaks of an actively sexual relationship with her husband. Both want their daughters to be good without having to be authoritarian and they have problems with their own anger.

These women differ considerably in terms of whether they make a distinction between men and women and with respect to playfulness and comfort with career decisons.

Interestingly, despite their presentation of themselves as connected women, neither of these women scored as 'authentically connected' in terms of the Attanucci coding of the Gilligan dilemma. Instead of demonstrating engagement between self and other, both women try to present themselves as selfless and instrumental to their daughters' needs. However, both describe dilemmas in which their own needs might be seen to figure: Susan speaks of her daughter getting sick the night of her anniversary celebration, Sharon of whether her daughter goes to camp in her final weeks of pregnancy. Gilligan's (1982) analysis of the relationships of conventional, Level 2 women is directly relevant. Consistent with Gilligan's discussion, Sharon and Susan are not direct about their own needs and couch their wishes in terms of responsiveness to others.

An even more striking basis for the interpretation of interpersonal difficulty is provided by the clinical assessment of the TAT material, which suggests that these two women lack real interpersonal engagement. They tend to see characters superficially, as unconnected to each other or as self-absorbed. They present relationships as nice and warm but without conversation or empathy. Susan and Sharon seemed to see the cards as a somewhat threatening environment and responded in what the clinician saw as a guarded and constricted fashion. However, the lack of engagement between characters is an extraordinary finding and one that suggests the extent to which reliance on conflict-free relationships can impoverish relationships.

Group II – 'Powerful connections mothers'

The women in this group all have suffocating mothers. While Chodorow does not consistently distinguish between having a responsive or a suffocating mother, this research suggests the importance of making such a distinction. Anna, Harriet, and Myra fit in Group II although Myra is a special case because she also sees her mother as judgmental.

All three of these women look to other adults for care and deal with power issues in relationships. Myra speaks openly of battles. Anna and Harriet have extensive needs for control but are ambivalent about setting limits and making demands. Both speak of the value of expressing anger, have difficulty with their own rage, and find aggressive physical contact valuable although problematic. Anna and Harriet feel close to similar others and value a calm, 'family' feeling of togetherness. Myra speaks of a wish for this kind of relationship with her daughter. Interestingly, all three of these women find relief in separation and Anna and Harriet feel detached from many people.

The Attanucci coding of the Gilligan dilemma for each of these subjects shows a shifting of attention from the needs of the mother to the needs of the child. Each woman presents a situation in which she wants to set a limit but feels deeply uncomfortable that she has acted inappropriately – either because of the presence of divergent outside opinions (Myra and Anna) or because she has acted violently (Myra and Harriet).

The TAT analysis of stories produced by these three subjects further suggests the importance of issues of obedience–defiance to these women. They produce stories of demanding and unempathic mothers whose daughters feel rebellious; they comply but must suppress or displace considerable rage. These three subjects struggle to contain impulses but find impulse control and play difficult. Anna and Harriet speak of flattened relationships, produce stories with tired, bland women, and see themselves as stodgy and middle aged. Myra presents herself as histrionic and girlish. None of these women appears able to find a middle ground.

It is interesting that these three subjects admire traditional women. Chodorow is correct here in suggesting that women who feel that their mothers did not encourage them to move out into the world or to be masterful stay closer to tradition. Although Myra provides something of a special case, Anna and Harriet are probably the most traditional and least achievement-oriented women in this sample.

Group III – 'Engagement with conflict mothers'

The women in this group all present their mothers as unresponsive to their interests and tend to describe them as demanding, judgmental, task-oriented, and overly invested in propriety. Julia, Denise, and Linda fit in this group as do Myra, Kathryn, and Lauren, all special cases. These women all find relationships with other women problematic. The mothers of daughters in this group (Linda, Lauren, and Myra) all see their children as intrusive and disturbingly demanding. In addition, the mothers in this group tend to feel inadequate and sensitive to criticism and rejection.

Ellen and Karen present a somewhat different picture in that they represent their mothers as overly superficial. However, they too feel that their mothers were unresponsive and in some ways demanding. They themselves are unsure of their ability to give deeply and effectively.

Interestingly, the majority of women in this group are mothers of sons. All of these women speak of their fathers as more understanding, loving figures. They seem more comfortable in relationships with men and tend to find differences among people to be appealing rather than threatening. All see their children as new objects with transformative potential. These subjects value independence but feel separation is a loss and struggle to remain connected in difficult situations.

Interestingly, their responses to the Gilligan dilemma often focus on issues of affiliation with other women, especially other mothers. They feel insecure and alienated, may want to be connected to these others, and feel they must hold onto their own viewpoints and interests. In other cases, dilemmas revolve around child rearing; again, the issue is one of maintaining their own opinions while also being sensitive to the needs and interests of the child and the opinions of others, especially, it seems, female experts.

These women tend to separate themselves from traditional women, to see the good mother as one who takes care of herself as well as her child, to be invested in careers as well as parenthood, and to diminish the distinction between adults and children.

While they speak of difficulties in relationships and some want conflict-free relationships, women in this group are the only women in this study to suggest that conflicts are good for relationships.

Interestingly enough, the TAT analysis suggests that all women in this group, except for Myra, who is a special case in this and Group II, have some capacity for empathy and real closeness. Stories show an awareness of characters' inner lives and needs and also indicate attempts to negotiate conflicts over separation–individuation without becoming detached, rejected, or compromised.

The TAT analysis also suggests that relationships with men are often problematic or disappointing and that many of these subjects yearn for close relationships with women. In some cases, this intimacy with women is threatening because of conflicts over homosexuality. This issue of close female relationships involving, for some women, a conflict over a potentially sexual connection is discussed by Flax (1978) but not addressed by Chodorow, despite her emphasis on the fact that girls' earliest love relationships are with other women.

RELATIONALITY

Relationality is the key element of the American approach to the psychology of women. It distinguishes a uniquely female connectedness that contrasts with male individuality and separateness. Within the current research, being the mother of a two-year-old may highlight issues of nurturance, connection, and separation, both in relation to the child and in terms of other family members and broader reference groups like mothers and career women. This research suggests that women's experiences of relationships vary considerably depending on the particular other to whom they are relating. These women can be understood as articulating an 'internal working model' of relationships (Bowlby, 1969/1971; Main *et al.*, 1984; Marris, 1982). However, this internal sense is quite differentiated, and is affected by social meanings as well as personal experiences and desires.

Within the present research, an object relations framework has been used to explore this differentiation. Notably, particular object relations patterns are associated with particular relational stances.

1 *Group I – 'Good relations mothers.'* Women who emphasize the good quality of their relationships with their mothers and daughters tend to feel close to other women and nurturant and caring. However, within this sample of twelve women, good relationships may be achieved at the cost of a lack of real engagement.

2 *Group II – 'Powerful connections mothers.'* Women who speak of their mothers as smothering speak of struggles for control, often feel detached from others, look to other adults for care, have considerable rage, and find aggression to be a troubling source of connection.

3 *Group III – 'Engagement with conflict mothers.'* Women who find their mothers demanding and unresponsive to them may feel uncomfortable with their daughters and other women and turn to others, especially men, while struggling to be both connected to and separate from others. While they feel a lack of good relationships, they have a capacity for close relationships, acknowledge conflict within connection and devote considerable attention to dealing with both positive and negative feelings and to moving beyond problematic relationships.

Despite these differences between groups, all twelve women desire close relationships with others. Their notion of closeness can be compared with

198

Gilligan's sense that relationality involves both connectedness and care. Consistent with Gilligan's work, this sample suggests that closeness is defined by connectedness. However, within this population, 'close' does not necessarily imply a caring, nurturant relationship. Instead, it may be defined by what seems a more primitive, less differentiated feeling of togetherness rather than by distinguishing and responding to the particular needs and interests of other and/or self. This sense of togetherness relates to more generalized feelings of satisfaction in which no one person gives or receives. For these mothers of toddlers, such experiences may relate to a heightened sense of the now lost pleasure of contact with infants.

In a variety of ways, these subjects suggest that giving may be problematic. It is not just, as Gilligan (1982) has rightly suggested, that women struggle with how to deal with their own needs, but that some of these women are not confident of their ability to be giving. They are concerned that what they have to give their children will be inadequate and even damaging, or that it will have no impact and will not be acknowledged.

It is particularly important that so many of the women interviewed here speak of the value of conflict-free relationships. While Gilligan and her students (Attanucci, 1984; Willard, 1983) have emphasized the importance of 'authentic' relationships in which self and other are present, issues of power, aggression, sexuality, and rage have not yet been adequately explored in this literature. The current research suggests that it is not simply that women always see safety in relationships, but that they often try to make relationships safe from dangerous and bad feelings. Interestingly, the popularized notion of relationality leaves these same problematic feelings unspoken. While feminist theorists of relationality have tended to locate the opposite of female connectedness in male separateness, this research suggests that we must look more closely at the complexity of women's relationships – their movement away from as well as toward engagement with others. Gilligan's Preface to the 1990 anthology is an important step in this direction; it treats conflict and anger as inherent aspects of relationships.

TRADITIONALITY

Yolanda and Robert Murphy (1974) indicate the paradoxical relationship between women and tradition. As they suggest, women have often been considered 'stumbling blocks to progress, conservative elements in social change' (p.179). While the Murphys agree that the female domestic position has been insulated from the large scale social changes typically taking place outside of the family, they argue that this does not mean that women are 'resistant or indifferent' to change. Instead, they indicate that 'men are the true cultural conservatives . . . if men yearn for a stable past and cherish their traditions, it is because the traditions and the past belonged to them'

199

(*ibid.*, p.181). In contrast to men's emotional attachment to the past, women can be understood as having a 'manifest traditionalism and not any deep emotional adherence to tradition' (*ibid.*, p.180).

The association between women and change is highlighted by an examination of women's changing role in the political process (Klein, 1984). While Klein explores the relationship between what she calls the decline of motherhood and an increase in social change, other theorists associate motherhood itself with change. Oakley's (1980) research on average, first-time mothers in England indicates that subjects had a heightened sense of issues of discrimination against women after having children. Hirsch's recent work on motherhood and rememory and Elshtain's study of the mothers of the Plaza de Mayo (both in Bassin, Honey and Kaplan, in press) explore how motherhood can become a powerful source of historical understanding and political action. Other authors (Miller, 1976; Ruddick, 1980, 1989) see child rearing as *necessarily* involving responsiveness to change. As Jean Baker Miller (1976) puts it:

> Thus, in a very immediate and day-to-day way women *live* change. It is amazing, in view of this, that women have been portrayed as the traditionalists, the sex that upholds the past while men march on to 'progress.' Here is perhaps one of the major places we have fallen into a terrible twisting of reality, for if anything women are *closer* to change, real change. They have always been closest to direct involvement in the most important growth of all.
>
> (p.54)

In contrast to these images of women and change, Nancy Chodorow articulates a specifically female tradition of mothering, reproduced from one generation of women to another. *Mothers' images of motherhood* begins to explore women's relation to this female tradition and to explore women's sense of connection to other women. As the three constellations of subjects suggest, the women in this rather homogeneous sample vary considerably in terms of their depictions of and feelings about affiliation with a female tradition.

1 *Group I – 'Good relations mothers.'* Women who present their mothers and daughters positively affiliate themselves with other women and feel a gradual sense of progress and support that enables them to mother like their own mothers while also working outside the home.

2 *Group II – 'Powerful connections mothers.'* Women who present their own mothers as suffocating have been unable to move away from their mothers. They have identified sources of value in traditionality, affiliate themselves with the traditional woman, and admire her strength and capacity.

3 *Group III – 'Engagement with conflict mothers.'* Women who speak of

their mothers as demanding seem to have turned to men and the outside world for comfort. They tend to depict the traditional woman in negative terms, acknowledge conflict with and separate themselves from her, and associate convention with constricting propriety.

Interestingly, except for Harriet, all the research subjects emphasize that they are mothering at a time of change. Most contrast the 1950s with what they describe as a more modern, superwoman mentality and feel their lives are different from their mothers'. In contrast to Chodorow's notion of reproduction, most of these subjects are trying not to reproduce their mothers' lives. Despite their overarching sense of social change and need to make decisions about how to organize their lives as mothers, they associate the difficulties of mothering with conflicts among women. Only Sharon complained that she would like her husband to be more supportive. While Kathryn indicated that 'society' did not know how to see mothers any more and Denise argued that social values were distorted, most subjects engaged in no social critique. While they were pained by the idea that motherhood was devalued and felt 'damned' whether they decided to work or not, most focused on the devaluation and lack of support offered by other women.

Complaints about other women do suggest a desire for closer, more supportive ties with women. At the same time, however, these subjects indicate a lack of affiliation with women. The idea of women having difficulty bonding with other women is notably absent from the work of Chodorow and Gilligan; however, it is raised by Heilbrun (1979). Following Smith-Rosenberg (1975) Heilbrun suggests that the tradition of female connection and caring may have been made possible by the ongoing distinction between male and female domains. As these distinctions break down and male characteristics and activities continue to be more highly valued, women may not want to associate themselves with women or even view their activities as female.

Flax (1978) also considers difficulties in women's relationships with other women. She suggests that girl children typically do not get support for their nurturance and activity strivings from their own devalued mothers and continue to desire this support from other women. Instead of feelings of female connection, Flax suggests that women are now polarized, feel threatened and frustrated by each other's appropriation of either a nurturant (full time motherhood) or striving (career achievement) position. Connections among women are further complicated by unresolved wishes for physical closeness with other women and conflicts about homosexuality. These difficulties can be seen in conflicted and fragmented political movements as well as in interpersonal relationships.

The present research with women from one social location suggests the idea that it is as mothers that women see each other as particularly judgmental, intrusive, unresponsive, and dangerous. Although they are mothers themselves, their response is what Rich (1986/1976) calls matriphobic. Rich suggests that women who identify themselves as mothers are 'threatening and repellent' to women who do not and that mothers 'stand for the victim in ourselves, the unfree woman, the martyr' (p.236). The present research suggests that some of today's mothers may well see *other mothers* as threatening – as cruel and powerfully demanding.

Instead of questioning what has been called an institution of motherhood, these modern women most frequently question other mothers and resist affiliating themselves with women. They feel particular affiliation with their husbands and express confusion over whether their own dramatic experience as parents is a female experience or not. To the extent that they identify an institution of motherhood, they see that institution as transforming and as confused; it is not limiting. Their own, seemingly modern views of the good mother suggest that they do not feel inordinately constrained by the idea that they must be all-giving and ever-present. While motherhood is personally meaningful, it does not lead to social critique or the basis for connections outside the family.

5

CONCLUSION

The findings of this study suggest that small-scale, systematic qualitative research is of great value in exploring and building theory. Some of the most striking findings of this study concern the relationship between the twelve participants and dominant views in the American psychology of women. In particular, most of these women do not present themselves in terms of the kind of close connection to their mothers and other women that theory would lead us to expect. Instead, many subjects express discomfort and a lack of intimate connection with their often intrusive or unavailable mothers and more positive views of their fathers and husbands. They construct an alternative image of the good mother that is in direct opposition to their own mother. While, in each case, the subject's own mother has considerable primacy, even the twelve women in this rather homogeneous group present a variety of object relations configurations. This variety suggests that any single model of female object relations and concomitant vision of femaleness is simplistic.

This research does suggest that an object relations framework is meaningful and that combined attention to object relations, relationality, and traditionality can be extremely useful in understanding the thoughts and feelings of individual women and in considering similarities and differences among women. The three constellations I identified are worthy of considerable additional research. One of the most prominent findings of the analysis of constellations is that the two women who seemed most relational had problems with deep connection. They were overly invested in 'good' relationships at the expense of more authentic, but conflict-filled relationships. This investment in good relationships merits further study. Interestingly, it has a parallel in feminist literature which, it may be argued, also has not yet focused enough attention on conflicts within close and nurturant relationships.

To understand these research subjects, we must focus on their particularity and place them in social context. They were brought up at the height of the 'feminine mystique,' at a time when middle-class mothers were isolated, overburdened, and under-supported in nuclear families. While further study is needed to examine how representative the women I interviewed are of the larger population fitting the research criteria, these subjects are members of the very cohort *not* to reproduce their mothers' lives. Their desire to be different has been supported by large scale questioning of traditional values during their adolescence in the 1960s, by the feminist movement, the expanding economy, and substantial opportunities for women in the 1970s. Their affiliation with their husbands is supported by views of male–female similarity prominent in the early 1970s in the midst of efforts to argue for workplace equality. Their affiliation with their husbands is also supported by the fact that they and their spouses have shared similar educational and work experiences and that both husband and wife may treat their privileged household as a unit of achievement and consumption.

While the findings in this study of twelve women are hardly conclusive, these women's divergence from theories that generalize about femaleness is striking enough to raise questions about those theories. In the light of these research findings, feminist visions of female connectedness across the generations sound more like a statement of desire than a true reflection of women's experience. These findings do not discredit or disprove the vision. Instead, they begin to document its power and attraction. Although we can discount the image of female nurturance and connection as 'traditional,' its appeal may be located both in its opposition to male separateness and in women's attempts to *repair* breaks in connections.[1]

Interestingly, many of the women who theorize about and hold dear the notion of female connectedness come from basically the same generation as my subjects. Like myself, they may also be living in ways that are different from their own mothers, with love relationships that do not reflect the same role differentiation as was reflected in their families of origin or 1950s norms. These theorists may also experience polarization among women and conflict with at least some other groups – non-feminists, right to lifers, and advocates of 'woman's place is in the home' come to mind. Proponents of relationality may be trying to avow a connectedness that certainly has some truth and great appeal but is not fully reflected in women's lives or feelings. This celebration of female connection and the dignifying of the difference between women and men has tended to leave unspoken some difficulties in connection. In the process of emphasizing relationality, we have promoted a vision of 'good' relationships and of mother–child histories that do not speak the whole story. This is changing. For example, some recent feminist work (Harris, 1989; Heilbrun, 1988; Hirsch, 1989; Gilligan, 1990) focuses attention on anger as an element in relationships, and a recently published anthology focuses on conflicts among feminists and in feminist theory (Hirsch and Fox Keller, 1990).

The women I studied value good relationships but do not, for the most part, cherish relationality. Interestingly, in this sense, they do not seem feminist. Although they have friends, they do not experience or seek a network of caring and concern outside of their households. Instead, although dependent on spouses, housekeepers, and toddler programs, they are mothering in some isolation. They find other mothers to be potentially threatening – unhelpful or intrusive and judgmental, like their own mothers.

There are political implications to this stance. These privileged women are not focused on the lack of social supports for families. They see their decisions about working in personal terms. Although they are part of a privileged group of people who do not have to work for economic reasons, when this research was done in the mid-1980s, they did not consider that their career decisions were affected by problems in the structure of work, by the lack of services to help families meet work demands, and by the asymmetrical gender arrangements that made it likely that they, rather than their husbands, would have the primary child rearing responsibility. They are unlikely to identify themselves as parents or to join with other parents in arguing for increased services and against forms of discrimination and devaluation without some mediation from 'outside' experts. Their image of the Mother is modern enough to accommodate the Mother's needs and career interests but reinforces maternal isolation. She is to take care of herself as well as her child with no help from spouses, friends, or social institutions.

It would be difficult to know how to generalize from these twelve women to all mothers. We need further research to ascertain how representative they are of women from their particular circumstances, to consider the responses of other groups of women, and to study mothers over time. It is to be hoped that additional research will build on the findings of this exploratory study and the methodology used here can contribute to other explorations. It is also to be hoped that questions of mothers' own images of motherhood will be considered worthy of further attention.

APPENDIX: STANDARDIZED MEASURES AND GUIDE TO THE SECOND INTERVIEW

INTRODUCTORY STATEMENT

It's been a few months since your first interview. Do you have any thoughts or feelings about that interview? Have you found yourself thinking about anything raised by that interview?

GILLIGAN DILEMMA

Have you ever been in a situation where you weren't sure what was the right thing to do?

Could you describe the situation?
What were the conflicts for you?
What did you do?
Did you think it was the right thing to do?

NEWBERGER WORKING MOTHER DILEMMA

Mr and Mrs Stewart have a four-year-old daughter/son. Mr Stewart earns a good living, so that Mrs Stewart doesn't have to work, but with her daughter/son in nursery school, Mrs Stewart started feeling unhappy at home and wishing she could get out of the house. She decided to get a job, and after much looking, she found a wonderful job. She loves it and feels much happier. The problem is Susan/David comes home to a babysitter. The sitter is a kind woman who does nice things with Susan/David and whom the child seems to like, but s/he told her/his mother that it's not the same as coming home to your own mother. Susan/David says that it's not fair for other children to have their mothers home every day and not s/he. Mrs Stewart doesn't know what to do. She feels it isn't fair for her to have to give up her job when Susan/David has a kind, reliable babysitter, and she is much happier working than staying home. But she wants to be a good mother to Susan/David too.

206

Newberger interview questions

1 What do you think a good mother would do? Why?
2 Do you think Susan/David is being a good daughter/son by wanting her/his mother home every day? Why? Why not?
3 Do you think Susan/David sees her/his mother working differently from how Mrs Stewart sees herself working? How would you explain that?
4 Do you think Mrs Stewart might have mixed feelings about working? How would you explain that?
5 Do you think Susan/David might have mixed feelings about her/his mother working? How would you explain that?
6 What do you think is more important, that Susan/David have her/his mother there when s/he gets home from school, if that makes her/him happier or that her/his mother have a job if that makes the mother happier? What are your reasons for the way you feel?

THEMATIC APPERCEPTION TEST

Instructions to subject

This is a storytelling test. I have some pictures here that I am going to show you, and for each picture I want you to make up a story. Tell what has happened before and what is happening now. Say what the people are feeling and thinking and how it will come out. You can make up any kind of story you please. Do you understand? Well, then, here is the first picture. See how well you can do.

Instructions for interviewer

After subject tells initial story, take card out of sight. Select from the following to invite subject to fill in incomplete parts of the story:

What is happening?
What led up to it?
What will be the outcome?
What is —— (particular character) feeling and thinking?

INTERVIEW GUIDE

Transitional statement. I'd like to make this discussion as responsive to your interests as possible. Were there things discussed last time you'd like to talk more about? Things that didn't come up that you'd like to discuss?

Object relations

1 What is your child like now?
2 What about your child surprises you? Do you ever feel like asking 'Is this my child?'
3 What childish parts of yourself are brought out by your child? Grown up parts?
4 A lot of people don't really know what babies are like. If you wanted to clue them in, what would you say? How would you tell them about a child of (use child's approximate age)? Probe for competence, impulsivity.

Relationality

1 We've talked a lot about family relationships. Thinking about your relationships in general, what about them makes you happy? What about them makes you unhappy?

Traditionality

1 Do you have a different sense of what it is to be a woman now that you have a child?
2 How would you describe a traditional woman? How do you see yourself as like her? Different from her?
3 Do you think even today that there is one acceptable way to be a mother?
4 We talked last time about your ideas about motherhood. I would like to try and make that as tangible as possible. When you think of the embodiment of motherhood, what comes to your mind?

NOTES

1 THE CONCEPTUAL FRAMEWORK

1 An analysis of recent films (Kaplan, in press) suggests the difficulty of setting the Superwoman vision in motion. Ann Kaplan argues that modern films do not show women combining sex, work, and motherhood, and do not present the mother as subject.

2 I will be calling these women privileged because of their social position and race. (See for example, Patricia Hill Collins (in press), 'Shifting the center: Race, class, and feminist theorizing about motherhood' for the racial ethnic contrast to the position of these twelve research subjects.) However, although these women are privileged, they are also mothers. As mothers they have had to deal with a change in their position, with the lack of support for families, and with the devaluation/ambivalence directed to mothers. Theirs is not a simple or uniform status and this research is, in part, directed to exploring their relationship to the position of mother. (See Valerie Walkerdine's discussion (1981) of the complex position of the female schoolteacher, in a simultaneous position of power and devaluation, for a model approach to this kind of complexity).

3 The analysis of advice to women played a prominent role in feminist studies in the 1970s and helped women find their own perspective in opposition to that of the experts who had spoken for and about women. While I will be focusing on only a few of these studies, Ehrenriech and English (1978) provide probably the most thorough overview of experts' advice to women and a context for my discussion.

4 The ideas in this and the following two sections are also elaborated in a paper by the author and John Broughton, 'The mother herself: Reproduction and change in theories of women's development' (Kaplan and Broughton, in press). Chapter 2 of this book owes a great deal to that collaboration, to the feminist psychology study group at Teachers College, and to the many students I have taught and learned from in courses in the psychology of women.

5 Alice Walker's 'Beauty: When the other dancer is the self' provides a striking example of how the child's recognition can transform the mother. In this powerful autobiographical piece focusing on the impact of a childhood eye injury, Walker describes how her relation to her permanently maimed eye was changed by her daughter's response to that eye as wondrous rather than a sign of lack: 'Mommy, there's a world in your eye.'

2 RESEARCH FRAMEWORK AND METHOD

1 According to the scoring manual for the Loevinger Sentence Completion Test (Loevinger *et al.*, 1970), for example, middle class women most often saw the good mother as 'available to her children and husband at all times,' 'unselfish, self-sacrificing,' 'loving,' 'patient,' 'understanding,' 'dependable,' and 'caring.' She 'enjoys fully being a mother' and 'wants, keeps her family happy.'

2 Blatt *et al.* identify five conceptual levels: sensorimotor-preoperational, concrete-perceptual, external iconic, internal iconic, and conceptual representation. They use a nine-point scale allowing for gradations within some levels. Since these gradations were not clearly defined within the scoring manual available at that time, in the present research each of the five conceptual levels was assigned one score. The category *length of description* was suitable for timed written descriptions but was omitted in the present study.

4 CROSS-CASE ANALYSIS

1 At a presentation of my findings to the other members of the New York Institute for Humanities Seminar on Psychoanalysis and Sexual Difference in 1989, participants emphasized that the kind of marital closeness, ties to spouses, and lack of connection with other women described by these research subjects were particularly characteristic of this group of upwardly mobile New York City couples. This emphasis on the particularity of my research subjects is important to a consideration of these findings.

5 CONCLUSION

1 During my presentation of findings at the Seminar on Psychoanalysis and Sexual Difference, participants were particularly interested in this aspect of my analysis and emphasized the importance of questioning why relationality is of such appeal. The idea of relationality as reparation for separation from our own mothers has been a significant element of my thinking. Its importance was emphasized in group discussions and I am grateful for participants' interest in this point.

BIBLIOGRAPHY

Aber, L., Slade, A., Berger, B, Bresgl, I and Kaplan, M. Mahrer (1984) Parent development interview. Unpublished ms. Centre for Toddler Development, Barnard College, New York.

Adams, P. (1983). Mothering. *m/f*, 8, 41–52.

Adorno, T.W., Frenkel-Brunswick, E., Levinson, E., and Sanford, R.N. (1982/1950). *The authoritarian personality* (abridged edn). New York: W. W. Norton & Co.

Ariès, P. (1962). *Centuries of childhood: A social history of family life* (R. Baldick, trans.). New York: Random House. (Original work published 1960).

Attanucci, J. S. (1984). Mothers in their own terms: A developmental perspective on self and role. Unpublished doctoral dissertation, Harvard University, Cambridge, Mass.

—— (1988). In whose terms: A new perspective in self, role, and relationships. In C. Gilligan, J. V. Ward, J. McLean Taylor (eds), *Mapping the moral domain* (201–24). Cambridge, Mass.: Harvard University Press.

Bader, M. and Philipson, I. (1980). Narcissism and family structure: A socio-historical perspective. *Psychoanalysis and Contemporary Thought*, 3, (3), 299–328.

Bassin, D., Honey, M., and Mahrer Kaplan, M. (in press). *Representations of motherhood*. New Haven: Yale University Press.

Belenky, M., Clinchy, B., Goldberger, N., and Tarule, J. (1986). *Women's ways of knowing: The development of self, voice, and mind*. New York: Basic Books.

Benedek, T. (1959). Parenthood as a developmental phase. *Journal of the American Psychoanalytic Association*, 7, 389–417.

—— (1970a). Parenthood during the lifecycle. In E. Anthony and T. Benedek (eds), *Parenthood: Its psychology and psychopathology* (185–206). Boston: Little, Brown.

—— (1970b). The family as a psychologic field. In E. Anthony and T. Benedek (eds), *Parenthood: Its psychology and psychopathology* (109–36). Boston: Little, Brown.

Benjamin, J. (1978). Authority and the family revisited; Or, a world without fathers. *New German Critique*, 4, (3), 35–57.

—— (1980). The bonds of love: Rational violence and erotic domination. *Feminist Studies*, 1, 144–74.

—— (1987). The oedipal riddle. In J. M. Broughton (ed.), *Toward a critical developmental psychology* (211–44). New York: Plenum Press.

—— (1988). *The bonds of love: Psychoanalysis, feminism, and the problem of domination*. New York: Pantheon Books.

—— (in press). The omnipotent mother: A psychoanalytic study of fantasy and reality. In D. Bassin, M. Honey, and M. Mahrer Kaplan (eds), *Representations of motherhood*. New Haven: Yale University Press.

Bernard, J. (1974). *The future of motherhood*. New York: Dial Press.

Bernstein, B. (1975). *Class, codes and control, Volume 3: Towards a theory of educational transmission*. London: Routledge & Kegan Paul.

Bibring, G. (1959). Some considerations of the psychological processes in pregnancy. *Psychoanalytic Study of the Child*, 14, 113–21.

Bibring, G., Dwyer, T., Huntington, D.S., and Valenstein, A. (1961). A study of the psychological processes in pregnancy and of the earliest mother–child relationship. *Psychoanalytic Study of the Child*, 16, 9–72.

Blatt, S.J., Chevron, E.S., Quinlan, D.M., and Wein, S. (1981). The assessment of qualitative and structural dimensions of object representations. Unpublished manuscript, Yale University, New Haven.

Boulton, M.G. (1983). *On being a mother: A study of women with pre-school children*. London: Tavistock.

Bowlby, J. (1969/1971). *Attachment and loss, Volume I: Attachment*. London, Penguin Books.

Broughton, J.M. (1983). Women's rationality and men's virtues. *Social Research*, 50, (3), 597–642.

—— (1986). The historical constitution of modern selfhood. In K. Larsen (ed.), *Dialectics and ideology in psychology*. Norwood, N.J. : Ablex Press.

Chasseguet-Smirgel, J. (1964). Feminine guilt and the oedipus complex. In J. Chasseguet-Smirgel (ed.), *Feminine sexuality* (94–134). Ann Arbor: University of Michigan Press.

—— (1976). Freud and female sexuality: The consideration of some blind spots in the exploration of the 'Dark Continent.' *International Journal of Psychoanalysis*, 57, 275–86.

—— (in press). The difficulty of being a mother and being a psychoanalyst, of speaking about the mother: Two impossible professions. In D. Bassin, M. Honey, and M. Mahrer Kaplan (eds), *Representations of motherhood*. New Haven: Yale University Press.

Chodorow, N. (1971). Being and doing: A cross-cultural examination of the socialization of males and females. In V. Gornick (ed.), *Women in sexist society: Studies in power and powerlessness* (183–97). New York: Basic Books.

—— (1974). Family structure and feminine personality. In M.Z. Rosaldo and L. Lamphere (eds), *Women, culture, and society* (43–66). Stanford: Stanford University Press.

—— (1978). *The reproduction of mothering: Psychoanalysis and the sociology of gender*. Berkeley: University of California Press.

—— (1979). Feminism and difference: Gender, relation, and difference in psychoanalytic perspective. *Socialist Review*, 46, 51–69.

—— (1981). On the reproduction of mothering: A methodological debate. Reply by N. Chodorow. *Signs*, 6, (3), 500–14.

—— (1989). *Feminism and psychoanalytic theory*. New Haven: Yale University Press.

Chodorow, N. and Contratto, S. (1982). The fantasy of the perfect mother. In B. Thorne and M. Yalom (eds), *Rethinking the family: Some feminist questions* (54–75). New York: Longman Press.

Cohler, B. (1984). Parenthood, psychopathology and child care. In R. Cohen, B. Cohler, and S. Weissman (eds), *Parenthood: A psychodynamic perspective* (119–47). New York: Guilford Press.

Cohler, B. and Grunebaum, H. (1981). *Mothers, grandmothers, and daughters: Personality and childcare in three generation families*. New York: Wiley.

Coleman, R.W., Kris, E., and Provence, S. (1953). Study of variations in early parental attitudes. *Psychoanalytic Study of the Child*, 8, 20–47.

Comer, L. (1974). *Wedlocked women*. Leeds: Feminist Books.

Corbett, K. (1989). Interpreting male homosexual development. Unpublished doctoral dissertation, Columbia University, New York.

de Beauvoir, S. (1952). *The second sex* (H.M. Parshley, trans.). New York: Alfred A. Knopf. (Original work published 1949.)

de Mause, L. (1974). *The history of childhood*. New York: The Psychohistory Press.

Degler, C. (1980). *At odds: Women and the family in America from the revolution to the present*. New York: Oxford University Press.

Deutsch, H. (1944 and 1945). *Psychology of women, vols I and II*. New York: Grune & Stratton.

Dinnerstein, D. (1976). *The mermaid and the minotaur: sexual arrangements and human malaise*. New York: Harper & Row.

Ehrenreich, B. (1989). *Fear of falling: The inner life of the middle class*. New York: Pantheon Books.

Ehrenreich, B. and English, D. (1978). *For her own good: 150 years of the experts' advice to women*. New York: Anchor Press/Doubleday.

Ehrensaft, D. (1985). Dual parenting and the duel of intimacy. In G. Handel (ed.), *The psychosocial interior of the family* (323–38). New York: Aldine Press.

Elshtain, J. Bethke (in press). Antigone's daughters: The mothers of the dissappeared. In D. Bassin, M. Honey, and M. Mahrer Kaplan (eds), *Representations of motherhood*. New Haven: Yale University Press.

Fairbairn, W.R. (1952). *An object relations theory of personality*. New York: Basic Books.

Flax, J. (1978). The conflict between nurturance and autonomy in mother–daughter relationships and within feminism. *Feminist Studies*, 4, (2), 171–91.

Frenkel-Brunswick, E. (1982/1950). The interviews as an approach to the prejudiced personality. In T.W. Adorno, E. Frenkel-Brunswick, D. Levinson, and R.N. Sanford, (eds) *The authoritarian personality* (abridged edn) (221–55). New York: W.W. Norton Inc.

Friedan, B. (1963). *The feminine mystique*. New York: W.W. Norton & Co.

—— (1981). *The second stage*. New York: Summit Books.

Garner, S. N., Kahane, C., and Sprengnether, M. (1985). Introduction. In S.N. Garner, C. Kahane, and M. Sprengnether (eds), *The (m)other tongue: Essays in feminist psychoanalytic interpretation* (15–29). Ithaca: Cornell University Press.

Gilligan, C. (1982). *In a different voice: Psychological theory and women's development*. Cambridge, Mass.: Harvard University Press.

—— The willing suspension of disbelief: Conflicts of female adolescence. Unpublished manuscript.

—— (1986). Exit-voice dilemmas in adolescent development. In A. Foxley, M.S. McPherson, and G. O'Donnell (eds), *Development, democracy, and the art of trespassing: Essays in honor of Albert O. Hirschman* (283–300). Indiana: University of Notre Dame Press.

—— (1988). Remapping the moral domain: New images of self in relationship. In C. Gilligan, J.V. Ward, and J. McLean Taylor (eds). *Mapping the moral domain*. Cambridge, Mass.: Harvard University Press.

Gilligan, C. and Belenky, M.F. (1980). A naturalistic study of abortion decisions. In R. Selman and R. Yando (eds), *Clinical developmental psychology*. New Directions for Child Development, 7. San Francisco: Jossey-Bass.

Gilligan, C., Langdale, S., Lyons, N., and Murphy, J.M. (1982). The contribution of women's thought to developmental theory: The elimination of sex bias in moral development research and education. Final report submitted to National Institute of Education. Massachusetts; Harvard University Press.

Gilligan, C. (1990). Preface. In C. Gilligan, N.P. Lyons and T.J. Hanmer (eds), *Making connections: the relational worlds of adolescent girls at Emma Willard School* (6–29). Cambridge, Mass.: Harvard University Press.

Glaser, B. and Strauss, A. (1967). *The discovery of grounded theory: Strategies for qualitative research*. Chicago: Aldine Press.

Gordon, L. (1977). *Woman's body, woman's right: A social history of birth control in America*. New York: Penguin.

Gould, R. (1978). *Transformations: Growth and change in adult life*. New York: Simon & Schuster.

Greenberg, J. and Mitchell, S. (1983). *Object relations in psychoanalytic theory*. Cambridge, Mass.: Harvard University Press.

Greenspan, S. and Lourie, R.S. (1981). Developmental structuralist approach to the classification of adaptive and pathologic personality organizations: Infancy and early childhood. *The American Journal of Psychiatry*, 138, (6), 725–35.

Gutmann, D. (1975). Parenthood: A comparative key to the life-cycle. In N. Datan and L. Ginsberg (eds), *Life-span developmental psychology: Normative crises*. New York: Academic Press.

Harris, A. (1987). The rationalization of infancy. In J.M. Broughton (ed.), *Toward a critical developmental psychology* (31–59). New York: Plenum Press.

—— (1989). Bringing Artemis to life: A plea for militance and aggression in feminist peace politics. In A. Harris and Y. King (eds), *Rocking the ship of state*, 93–114. Boulder: Westview Press.

Heilbrun, C.G. (1979). *Reinventing womanhood*. New York: W.W. Norton and Co.

—— (1988). *Writing a woman's life*. New York: W.W. Norton & Co.

Henry, W. (1951). The thematic apperception technique in the study of group and cultural problems. In H. Anderson and G. Anderson (eds). *Projective techniques and other devices for understanding the dynamics of human behavior* (230–78). Englewood Cliffs, N. J. : Prentice-Hall, Inc.

Hertz, R. (1886). *More equal than others: Women and men in dual career marriages*. Berkeley: University of California Press.

Hill Collins, P. (in press). Shifting the center: Race, class, and feminist theorizing about motherhood. In D. Bassin, M. Honey, and M. Mahrer Kaplan (eds), *Representations of motherhood*. New Haven: Yale University Press.

Hirsch, M. (1986). Feminist discourse/Maternal discourse: 'Cruel enough to stop the blood.' Paper presented at Representations of Motherhood Lecture Series, Institute for Research on Women, Rutgers University.

—— (1989). *The mother/daughter plot: Narrative, psychoanalysis, feminism*. Bloomington: Indiana University Press.

—— (in press). Maternity and rememory. In D. Bassin, M. Honey and M. Mahrer Kaplan (eds), Representations of motherhood. New Haven: Yale University Press.

Hirsch, M. and Fox Keller, E. (1990). *Conflicts in feminism*. New York and London: Routledge.

Hoffman, L.W. (1972). Early childhood experiences and women's achievement motives. *Journal of Social Issues*, 28, 129–56.

Hunt, D. (1970). *Parents and children in history: The psychology of family life*. New York: Basic Books.

Jacoby, R. (1975). *Social amnesia*. Boston: Beacon Press.

Jameson, F. (1977). Imaginary and symbolic in Lacan: Marxism, psychoanalytic criticism, and the problem of the subject. *Yale French Studies*, 55, 56, 338–95.

Kaplan, E.A. (1983). *Women and film: Both sides of the camera*. New York: Methuen Press.

—— (in press). Sex, work and motherhood: maternal subjectivity in recent visual culture. In D. Bassin, M. Honey, and M. Mahrer Kaplan (eds), *Representations of motherhood*. New Haven: Yale University Press.

Kaplan, M. Mahrer (1987). Female object relations: A study of four cases. Unpublished manuscript.

Kaplan, M. Mahrer and Broughton, J. (in press). The mother herself: Reproduction and change in theories of women's development. *The Psychoanalytic Review*.

Keniston, K. (1960). *The uncommitted: Alienated youth in American society*. New York: Harcourt, Brace, & World.

Kitzinger, S. (1978). *Women as mothers*. New York: Random House.

Klein, E. (1984). *Gender politics*. Cambridge, Mass.: Harvard University Press.

Klein, M. (1964/1937). Love, guilt and reparation. In M. Klein and J. Riviere, *Love, hate and reparation*. New York: W.W. Norton & Co.

Kohlberg, L. (1969). Stage and sequence: The cognitive-developmental approach to socialization. In D.A. Goslin (ed.), *Handbook of socialization theory and research* (347–480). Chicago: Rand McNally.

Kohlberg, L. and Kramer, R. (1969). Continuities and discontinuities in child and adult moral development. *Human Development*, 12, 93–120.

Kovel, J. (1974). Erik Erikson's psychohistory. *Social Policy*, (March, April), 60–4.

—— (1981). *The age of desire: Case histories of a radical psychoanalyst*. New York: Random House.

Kristeva, J. (1980a). Motherhood according to Bellini. In *Desire in language: A semiotic approach to literature and art* (237–70). (T. Gora, A. Jardine, and L. Roudiez, trans.). New York: Columbia University Press. (Original work published 1975.)

—— (1980b). Place names. In *Desire in language: A semiotic approach to literature and art* (271–94). (T. Gora, A. Jardin, and L. Roudiez, trans.). New York: Columbia University Press. (Original work published 1976.)

—— (1981a). The maternal body (C. Pajaczkowski, trans.). *m/f*, 5, 6, 158–63. (Original work published 1977.)

—— (1981b). Women's time (A. Jardine and H. Blake, trans.). *Signs*, 7, (1), 13–36. (Original work published 1979.)

Lasch, C. (1976). Planned obsolescence: Review of Sheehy's 'Passages.' *New York Review of Books*, 28, 7.

—— (1979). *The culture of narcissism: American life in an age of diminishing expectations*. New York: Warner Books.

Leifer, M. (1980). *Psychological effects of motherhood: A study of first pregnancy*. New York: Praeger.

Lemaire, A. (1977). *Jacques Lacan*. London: Routledge & Kegan Paul.

Levinson, D.J. (1978). *Seasons of a man's life*. New York: Alfred A. Knopf.

Loevinger, J. and Ernhart, C. (1969). Authoritarian family ideology: A measure, its correlates, and its robustness. *Multivariate Behavior Research Monograph*, 69, (1).

Loevinger, J., Sweet, B., Ossorio, A., and La Perriere, K. (1962). Measuring personality patterns of women. *Genetic Psychology Monographs*, 65, 53–136.

Loevinger, J., Wessler, R., and Redmore, C. (1970). *Measuring ego development, Volume II: Construction of a sentence completion test*. San Francisco: Jossey-Bass, Inc.

Maccoby, E.E. and Martin, J.A. (1983). Socialization in the context of the family: Parent–child interaction. In P.H. Mussen (ed.), *Carmichael's handbook of child psychology, Volume 4* (4th edn). (1–101). New York: J. Wiley & Sons.

Mahler, M. (1968). *On human symbiosis and the vicissitudes of individuation, Volume I: Infantile psychosis*. New York: International Universities Press.

Mahler, M., Pine, F., and Bergman, A. (1970). The mother's reaction to her toddler's drive for individuation. In E.J. Anthony and T. Benedek (eds), *Parenthood: Its psychology and psychopathology* (257–74). Boston: Little, Brown.

—— (1975). *The psychological birth of the human infant*. New York: Basic Books.

Main, M. and Goldwyn, R. (1984). Predicting rejection of her infant from mother's representation of her own experience: Implications for the abused – abusing intergenerational cycle. *International Journal of Child Abuse and Neglect*.

Main, M., Kaplan, N., and Cassidy, J. (1984). Security in infancy, childhood, and adulthood: A move to the level of representation. *Monographs of the Society for Research in Child Development* (Serial no. 209), 50, 1–2, 66–104.

Marris, P. (1982). Attachment and society. In C.M. Parkes and J. Stevenson-Hinde (eds), *The place of attachment in human behavior* (185–201). New York: Basic Books.

Miles, M. B. and Huberman, A. M. (1984). *Qualitative data analysis: Sourcebook of new methods*. Newbury Park, California: Sage Publications.

Miller, A. (1981/3) *The drama of the gifted child*. New York: Basic Books. (First published in German, 1979. First published in English in 1981 as *Prisoners of childhood*, New York: Basic Books.)

Miller, J.B. (1976). *Toward a new psychology of women*. Boston: Beacon Press.

Minturn, L. and Lambert, W. (1964). *Mothers of six cultures: Antecedents of child rearing*. New York: John Wiley.

Mitchell, J. (1974). *Psychoanalysis and feminism*. New York: Pantheon Press.

Mitscherlich, A. (1963). *Society without the father: A contribution to social psychology*. New York: Schocken Books, 1970.

Murphy, R. (1971). *The dialectics of social life: Alarms and excursions in anthropological theory*. New York: Basic Books.

Murphy, Y. and Murphy, R. (1974). *Women of the forest*. New York: Columbia University Press.

Newberger, C. (1977). Parental conceptions of children and child rearing: A structural developmental analysis. Doctoral dissertation, Harvard University, Cambridge, Mass.

Oakley, A. (1980). *Women confined: Towards a sociology of childbirth*. Oxford: Martin Robertson.

Oliner, M. (1984). The anal phase. In D. Mendell (ed.), *Early female development* (25–60). New York: S.P. Medical and Scientific Books.

Piotrkowski, C.S. (1978). *Work and the family system*. New York: The Free Press.

Pipp, S., Shaver, P., Jennings, S., Lamborn, S., and Fischer, K. (1985). Adolescents' theories about the development of their relationships with their parents. *Journal of Personality and Social Psychology*, 48, (4), 991–1001.

Plaza, M. (1982). The mother/the same: Hatred of the mother in psychoanalysis. *Feminist Issues*, 2, (1), 75–99.

Rapoport, R. and Rapoport, R. (1976). *Dual-career families re-examined: New integrations of work and family*. New York: Harper Colophon.

Rapoport, R., Rapoport, R., and Strelitz, Z. (1980). *Fathers, mothers, and society: Perspectives on parenting*. New York: Vintage Books.

Rich, A. (1986/1976). *Of woman born*. New York: W.W. Norton & Co. Inc.

Rich, S. (1990). Daughters' views of their relationships with their mothers. In C.

Gilligan, N.P. Lyons, and T.J. Hanmer (eds), *Making connections: the relational worlds of adolescent girls at Emma Willard School* (258–73). Cambridge, Mass: Harvard University Press.

Riley, D. (1983). *War in the nursery*. London: Virago Press.

Rose, J. (1982). Introduction II. In J. Mitchell and J. Rose (eds), *Feminine sexuality: Jacques Lacan and the Ecole Freudienne*. New York: W.W. Norton & Co.

Rossi, A.S. (1968). Transition to parenthood. *Journal of Marriage and the Family*, 30, 26–39.

—— (1980). Life-span theories and women's lives. *Signs*, 6 (1), 4–32.

Ruddick, S. (1980). Maternal thinking. *Feminist Studies*, 6, (3), 343–67.

—— (1989). *Maternal thinking: Toward a politics of peace*. New York: Ballantine Books.

Sander, L. (1962). Issues in early childhood mother–child interaction. *Journal of the American Academy of Child Psychiatry*, 1, 141–66.

Schneider, D.M. (1968). *American kinship: A cultural account*. Englewood Cliffs, N.J.: Prentice-Hall.

Shereshefsky, P., and Yarrow, L. (1973). *Psychological aspects of a first pregnancy and early postnatal adaptation*. New York: Raven Press.

Shorter, E. (1975). *The making of the modern family*. New York: Basic Books.

Simmel, G. (1950). In K. Wolff (ed. and trans.). *The sociology of Georg Simmel*. New York: The Free Press.

—— (1968), *The conflict in modern culture and other essays* (K.P. Etzkorn, trans.). New York: Teachers College Press.

Slade, A. and Aber, L.J. (1986). The internal experience of parenting toddlers: Toward an analysis of individual and developmental differences. Paper presented at the International Conference of Infant Studies, Los Angeles, Ca.

Smith-Rosenberg, C. (1975). The female world of love and ritual: Relations between women in nineteenth-century America. *Signs*, 1, 1–30.

Sroufe, L. A. (1979). The coherence of individual development. *American Psychologist*, 34, (10), 834–41.

Suleiman, S. (1990). *Subversive intent: Gender, politics and the avant-garde*. Cambridge, Mass.: Harvard University Press.

—— (in press). Mothers and the avant-garde: A case of mistaken identity? In D. Bassin, M. Honey, and M. Mahrer Kaplan (eds), *Representations of motherhood*. New Haven: Yale University Press.

Urist, J. (1980). Object relations. In R.H. Woody (ed.), *Encyclopedia of clinical assessment, Volume 2* (821–32). San Francisco: Jossey-Bass, Inc.

Urwin, C. (1984). Power relations and the emergence of language. In J. Henriques, W. Holloway, C. Urwin, C. Venn, and V. Walkerdine (eds), *Changing the subject: Psychology, social regulation, and subjectivity* (264–322). London: Methuen.

Vaillant, G. (1977). *Adaptation to life: How the best and the brightest came of age*. Boston: Little, Brown.

Walker, A. (1983). Beauty: When the other dancer is the self. In A. Walker (ed.), *In search of our mothers' gardens* (384–93). New York: Harcourt.

Walkerdine, V. (1981). Sex, power and pedagogy. *Screen Education*, 38, 14–21.

Weiss, N. Pottishman (1978). The mother–child dyad revisited: Perceptions of mothers and children in twentieth century child-rearing manuals. *Journal of Social Issues*, 34, (2), 29–45.

Weisskopf, S. (1980). Maternal sexuality and asexual motherhood. *Signs*, 5, 766–82.

White, R. (1952). *Lives in progress*. New York: Holt, Rinehart, & Winston.

Whiting, B. and Whiting, J. M. (1975). *Children of six cultures: A psycho-cultural analysis*. Cambridge, Mass.: Harvard University Press.

Whiting, J.M. and Child, I. (1953). *Child training and personality*. New Haven: Yale University Press.

Willard, A. (1983). The potential for growth in the experience of mothering. Unpublished thesis proposal, Harvard University, Cambridge, Mass.

—— (1988). Cultural scripts for mothering. In C. Gilligan, J. V. Ward, and J. McLean Taylor (eds), *Mapping the moral domain*, (225–43). Cambridge, Mass.: Harvard University Press.

Winnicott, D. (1973). *The child, the family, and the outside world*. Harmondsworth, England: Penquin.

Wolfenstein, M. (1955). Fun morality: An analysis of recent American child-training literature. In M. Mead and M. Wolfenstein (eds), *Contemporary cultures*. Chicago: University of Chicago Press.

Wood, N. (1983). Motherhood dossier: Introduction. *m/f*, 8, 17–21.

Zayas, L. (1988). Thematic features in the manifest dreams of expectant fathers. *Clinical Social Work Journal*, 16, 282–96.

INDEX